Henry Hazlitt

A Giant of Liberty

Henry Hazlitt

A Giant of Liberty

Introduction by Llewellyn H. Rockwell, Jr.
Bibliography Compiled by Jeffrey A. Tucker
Annotations by Murray N. Rothbard

Ludwig von Mises Institute
Auburn, Alabama 36849

Published by the Ludwig von Mises Institute, Auburn, Alabama 36849.

Printed in the United States of America

Library of Congress Catalog Card Number: 94-079699

ISBN: 0-945466-16-1

Cover photo courtesy of the Foundation for Economic Education.

Contents

The Ludwig von Mises Institute gratefully acknowledges the generosity of Mr. Henry Hazlitt, whose bequest made the publication of this book possible.

Introduction

I f you want to know where American conservatives learned economics, take a look at *Economics in One Lesson* by Henry Hazlitt. A brilliant and pithy work first published in 1946, at a time of rampant statism at home and abroad, it taught millions the bad consequences of putting government in charge of economic life. College students all across America and the world still use it and learn from it. It may be the most popular economics text every written.

Mr. Hazlitt—journalist, literary critic, economist, philosopher—was one of the most brilliant public intellectuals of our century. He was born on November 28, 1894, and died on July 8, 1993, at the age of 98. In his final years, he often expressed surprise that *Economics in One Lesson* had become his most enduring contribution. He wrote it to expose the popular fallacies of its day. He did not know that those fallacies would be government policy for the duration of the century.

This chapter is based on information provided in an October 17, 1987, speech by Henry Hazlitt at the Ludwig von Mises Institute's dinner in his honor, reprinted in *The Free Market* (Auburn, Ala.: Ludwig von Mises Institute, December, 1987); "The Art of Thinking" and "Reflections at 70" by Henry Hazlitt, "A Man for Many Seasons" by Bettina Bien Greaves, and "Indefatigable Leader" by Ludwig von Mises from *The Wisdom of Henry Hazlitt* (Irvington-on-Hudson, N. Y.: Foundation for Economic Education, 1993); and an interview with Hazlitt in *Reason* (December 1984).

Hazlitt also wanted to be remembered for his other contributions. This lifetime bibliography includes a novel, a trialogue on literary criticism, two large treatises on economics and moral philosophy, several edited volumes, some sixteen other books, and countless chapters in books, articles, commentaries, reviews—more than 6,000 entries in all—and even so, our compilation cannot include everything. He once estimated that he had written 10 million words and that his collected works would run to 150 volumes.

Hazlitt was not trained as an economist, although few scholars are as familiar with the relevant literature. He was inspired initially by the writings of Philip Wicksteed, a disciple of the English economist William Jevons, and later by the works of Herbert Spencer. Yet he was familiar with the work of every important thinker in nearly every field. At an early age, he embarked on private study to compensate for what he lacked in formal education but ended in knowing more than most learned men of any age; and he certainly was more principled than most.

Hazlitt was also the most important public intellectual within the Austrian tradition of Ludwig von Mises, F. A. Hayek, and Murray N. Rothbard, all of whom he credited as primary sources in economics. He wrote in every important public forum of his day, most prominently *The Nation*, *The Wall Street Journal*, *The New York Times* (frequently headlining the powerful book review section), *The American Mercury*, *Century*, *The Freeman*, *National Review*, *Newsweek*, and many more. His every article is unfailingly poignant, provocative, and learned. At various points in his career, he was among the most influential literary critics, editorialists, and financial writers in the country, as a biography of his life and influence would easily demonstrate. For example, Hazlitt's review of Ludwig von Mises's first book to be translated into English made *Socialism* an instant classic in this country. A review of F. A. Hayek's *Road to Serfdom* led *Reader's Digest* to publish a condensed version that catapulted Hayek to fame.

Henry Stuart Hazlitt was born in Philadelphia, son of Stuart Clark Hazlitt and Bertha Zaunder Hazlitt. Stuart died at the age of 28, when Henry was a baby. When Henry was six, his mother enrolled him in Girard College, a home for "fatherless white boys" set up by a local philanthropist. His mother remarried and they moved to Brooklyn when Henry was nine, where he attended public schools. His earliest ambition was to become a psychologist "like William James," but his family's financial situation forced him to give up that idea. After a year-and-a-half of night school at City College, he had to look for a way of earning money.

Late in life, he told the story of his job search to an interviewer, not passing up the opportunity to explain something about labor economics:

> I had no skills whatever. So I would get a job, and I would last two or three days and be fired. It never surprised me or upset me, because I read the *Times* early in the morning, went through the ads, and I'd practically have a job that day. This shows what happens when you have a free market. There was no such thing as a minimum wage at that time. There was no such thing as relief, except maybe there were places where you could get a soup handout for something, but there was no systematic welfare. You had a free market. And so I usually found myself at a job the next day, and I'd get fired about three or four days after

that. . . . I didn't have the skills. But each time I kept learning something, and finally I was getting about $3 or $4 a week.

"At some point I decided that I wanted to be a newspaperman," he explains, "because it was the only way I could see to get into writing." At the age of 20, when he finally got a job at the *Wall Street Journal* as a stenographer, he had already finished his first book, *Thinking as a Science*, which was published by E. P. Dutton in 1915, reprinted one year later, and reissued again in 1969 with a new introduction.

His first book, as with everything he ever wrote, made a strong argument and made it well. "I don't think it's worthwhile," he told an interviewer late in life, "if you haven't made up your mind, to write a piece saying, 'Well, on one hand, but on the other hand.' " It's the kind of old fashioned attitude that made Hazlitt's work stand out.

Whatever Hazlitt wrote, it was always in virile and unsurpassed English. He adhered to the rule he set out for himself: "Aim first at the essential qualities—coherence, clarity, precision, simplicity, and brevity. Euphony and rhythm are of course also desirable, but they are like the final rubbing on a fine piece of furniture—finishing touches justified only if the piece has been soundly made."

In 1916, he left the *Wall Street Journal* to write editorials for the *New York Evening Post* and later the *New York Evening Mail*. While at the *Mail* in 1922, his second book appeared. Also published by Dutton, *The Way to Will Power* was a defense of individual initiative against the deterministic claims of Freudian psychoanalysis. By the late 1920s, Hazlitt's reputation as a writer and thinker had grown, thanks also to his reviews and essays in the *New York Sun*, which appeared weekly from October 1926 to September 1929.

In these years, he met the British philosopher Bertrand Russell, widely considered (probably incorrectly) as the most brilliant man alive. Russell so admired the young journalist's talent that Russell and his publisher W. W. Norton asked Hazlitt to write the philosopher's official biography. Hazlitt spent much of 1928 and 1929 interviewing Russell in New York, until one day, agreeing with Hazlitt, Russell announced: "You know, I have had a very interesting life. I think I'd like to do my own biography."

In the meantime, fortunately, the editors of *The Nation* had noticed his work and hired him as literary editor. "*The Nation* was pretty much a leftist magazine then, as it has always remained," he explained to an interviewer. "One of the reasons they took me on was that they wanted me not only to write and handle the book reviews but to be able to write editorials on economic subjects." And his work there was extraordinary. He wrote on contemporary literature as a springboard to his own rich observations on philosophy, culture, history, economics, and politics. And while there, he penned an early refutation of literary deconstructionism, *The Anatomy of Criticism* (1933).

Throughout his life, Hazlitt became more and more opposed to government intervention in the economy, and time and again he refused to give in to pressure from publishers and editors to change his views. He chose principle and integrity over fame and fortune, and as a consequence, he was squeezed out of a series of prestigious jobs. The first such occurrence was when the New

Deal brought state planning to national economic life. Hazlitt used his literary fame and post at *The Nation* to attack Roosevelt's regimentation. After some internal debate, and a series of public debates between Hazlitt and prominent socialist Louis Fischer, the magazine shifted to a pro–New-Deal position. Hazlitt's adherence to principle led to his ouster.

In the early thirties, the literary set also turned against H. L. Mencken, founding editor of *American Mercury*, because of his opposition to the New Deal. When Mencken decided to turn the journal over to a new editor, he named Hazlitt, calling him the "only competent critic of the arts that I have heard of who was at the same time a competent economist, of practical and well as theoretical training." And, Mencken added, "he is one of the few economists in human history who could really write." True to his indefatigable spirit, his first article, "The Fallacies of the N.R.A.," was an implicit attack on the entire American left, including *The Nation*. Hazlitt was editor for nearly two years until he decided to go back into newspaper work.

In those days, even the *New York Times* was not so left-wing as it is today, and the paper hired Hazlitt to write unsigned editorials and signed review essays, which he did from 1934 to 1946. This bibliography reveals for the first time which editorials are his. Appearing almost daily, they covered an extraordinarily wide range: the dangers of economic controls, the evils of wartime price controls, the glories of Chesterton, the fallacies of Keynesian economics, the futility of foreign aid, the importance of a free market in securities, the stupidity of socialism and inflation, the ill-effects of unionization.

While at the *Times*, he did whatever he could to hold back the tide of statism. Whatever steps were taken away from price controls and unionization after the war could be due in part to his influence. His lengthy review essays on the covers of *New York Times Book Review* demonstrate a brilliant grasp of contemporary literature, economics, and politics.

During this time, he also met the emigré economist Ludwig von Mises, whose work Hazlitt had admired. Hazlitt and Mises became fast friends, and Mises thrilled to Hazlitt's editorial blasts against government planning and often consulted Hazlitt on editorial matters and contemporary politics. It is said that Hazlitt even prepared, at Mises's request, a version of *Human Action* as a journalist would have written it. Mises thanked him, but rejected most of the changes.

As with his previous positions, Hazlitt eventually came under pressure from the publisher to compromise himself. Hazlitt had taken on Keynes's plans to reconstruct the monetary system after the war, and predicted world-wide inflation in the decades ahead. The *Times*, however, was moving to the Left and so wanted to endorse the Bretton Woods agreement, including the World Bank and International Monetary Fund.

"Now, Henry," Times publisher Arthur Sulzberger said to him, "when 43 governments sign an agreement, I don't see how *The Times* can any longer combat this."

"All right," Hazlitt said, "but in that case I can't write anything further about Bretton Woods. It is an inflationist scheme that will end badly and I can't support it." Hazlitt was not fired, but at one point, management threatened to put a disclaimer under his editorials. Soon after, he was squeezed out, but landed a job with *Newsweek* magazine, and became one of the most influential financial writers in the country. His weekly "Business Tides" column was enduringly popular.

While at *Newsweek*, Hazlitt wrote *Economics in One Lesson*, which has sold nearly one million copies and is available in at least ten languages. Hazlitt argued that government intervention focuses on the consequences that are seen and ignores those that are not. The latter include wealth not created and even destroyed by regulation, inflation, and taxation. In 1947, he wrote *Will Dollars Save the World?*, a book attacking the Marshall Plan, which he saw as an international welfare scheme. The subsequent history of U.S. foreign aid shows just how right he was.

In 1950, Hazlitt became editor, along with John Chamberlain, of the fortnightly magazine *The Freeman*, published by the Foundation for Economic Education; some of his best articles published there were later collected into *The Wisdom of Henry Hazlitt*. Also as a prophet, Hazlitt wrote *The Great Idea* (reprinted a year later as *Time Will Run Back*), a novel showing how a country can move from socialism to market economics at a time when most people thought socialism was the unstoppable wave of the future. Gorbachev should have read it.

In 1959, Hazlitt came out with *The Failure of the 'New Economics'*," an extraordinary line-by-line refutation of John Maynard Keynes's *General Theory*. And though it was panned by the American academic journals at the time, it enlivened a growing movement favoring free markets over state planning and continues to be an essential resource. A year later, Hazlitt collected a series of scholarly attacks on Keynes as *The Critics of Keynesian Economics*, which is still in print today.

In the mid-sixties, Hazlitt turned his attention to the ethical basis of capitalism. Thus his book *The Foundations of Morality*, which Hazlitt has said is his proudest achievement, is the final product of a lifetime of thinking about philosophy. Also notable was his book *Man vs. the Welfare State* which demonstrated that welfare promotes what it pretends to discourage. This was 20 years before Charles Murray's *Losing Ground* showed that Hazlitt was right. Parts of these books also appeared in *National Review*. His last published scholarly article appeared in the first volume of the *Review of Austrian Economics* (1987), the journal published by the Ludwig von Mises Institute. He served as Distinguished Advisor to the Institute, and at his death, named the Ludwig von Mises Institute as a principal heir.

On November 28, 1964 a group of friends gathered on the occasion of Hazlitt's 70th birthday. It was only weeks after Lyndon Baines Johnson had been elected, and these freedom lovers were saddened at the state of the world, but at the same time looked forward to the fight ahead. Ludwig von Mises rose to the podium to pay tribute to his "distinguished friend." "In this age of the great struggle in favor of freedom and the social system in which men can live as free men, you are our leader. You have indefatigably fought against the step-by-step advance of the powers anxious to destroy everything that human civilization has created over a long period of centuries. . . . You are the economic conscience of our country and of our nation."

"Every friend of freedom may today, in this post-election month, be rather pessimistic about the future. But let us not forget that there is rising a new generation of defenders of freedom." If we succeed, Mises said, "this will be to a great extent your merit, the fruit of the work that you have done in the first 70 years of your life."

Hazlitt then rose to the podium to reflect on his life, and in so doing painted a very dark picture of the state of human liberty. Yet "none of us is yet on the torture rack; we are not yet in jail; we're getting various harassments and annoyances, but what we mainly risk is merely our popularity, the danger that we will be called nasty names."

So long as this is true, he said, "We have a duty to speak even more clearly and courageously, to work hard, and to keep fighting this battle while the strength is still in us. . . . Even those of us who have reached and passed our 70th birthdays cannot afford to rest on our oars and spend the rest of our lives dozing in the Florida sun. The times call for courage. The times call for hard work. But if the demands are high, it is because the stakes are even higher. They are nothing less than the future of human liberty, which means the future of civilization."

This great voice of Henry Hazlitt, "the economic conscience of our country and our nation," is now stilled. But he will not be forgotten. In a time dominated by prevaricators and planners, and a nation threatened once again by statism, Hazlitt's written legacy, herein chronicled, will continue to inspire writers and scholars.

We need more economists like Henry Hazlitt, who are willing to write in defense of free enterprise, and to do so in plain English; and to adhere to principle, whether analyzing history, theory, or present policy, regardless of the personal cost or the names they will be called. And if we win, as Mises said, we can thank Henry Hazlitt.

Llewellyn H. Rockwell, Jr.

Notes From the Compiler

This bibliography of Mr. Hazlitt's work is, unfortunately, not complete. First, many of his articles, especially those written for *Newsweek*, were widely reprinted. Some of these reprints are noted in the bibliography, depending on the circulation and significance of the forum. But as a rule, the bibliography confines itself to listing only the first appearance of articles or reviews. For example, Hazlitt's columns for the Los Angeles Times Syndicate (1966–69) were sold to hundreds of newspapers and magazines on a weekly basis all over the world. They are listed here only by their original source. Second, no attempt has been made to include *all* of the hundreds of foreign-language editions of Mr. Hazlitt's books and articles. *Economics in One Lesson*, e.g., was translated into at least ten languages. Third, the bibliography omits Mr. Hazlitt's unsigned editorials and articles for the *New York Evening Post* (1916–18), the monthly financial letter of the Mechanics & Metals National Bank (1919–20), the *New York Evening Mail* (1921–23), the *New York Herald* (1923–24), and the *New York Sun* (1924–25). Mr. Hazlitt's personal papers did not contain these articles; and even though the newspapers are available, it is impossible to identify which unsigned editorials were Mr. Hazlitt's. I have my suspicions, based on style and content, but to attribute these articles to Mr. Hazlitt would have been too speculative. Adding them would have undoubtedly added another thousand or so items, and their absence explains the gaps in articles between 1917 and 1926.

The main purpose of this extensive bibliography is to generate an appreciation for the range of Mr. Hazlitt's interests, his extraordinary productivity, and his immense contribution to many of this century's debates on politics, economics, culture, and literature. The bibliography's primary contribution is to identify nearly three thousand unsigned articles or editorials as Mr. Hazlitt's own, thereby providing a foundation for future scholarly research.

This project involved cooperative efforts from a number of individuals and institutions. A special thank you to the staff, and especially Ms. Kathleen Manwaring, of the George Arents Research Library at Syracuse University; the staff has been diligent in keeping Mr. Hazlitt's papers in top condition and were extremely helpful during my stay there. Thanks also to Brian Kreischer, then a student at Syracuse, for his help in handling and cataloging Mr. Hazlitt's scrapbooks and files at Arents. Thanks to the staff of the Foundation for Economic Education in Irvington-on-Hudson, New York, which graciously permitted me access to the part of Mr. Hazlitt's personal library and papers which is stored there. Thanks also to members of the staff of the Library of Congress for their help in finding otherwise inaccessible pamphlets and cataloging foreign language editions of Mr. Hazlitt's books. Finally, a special thanks to Llewellyn H. Rockwell, Jr., for his suggestions and guidance.

Jeffrey A. Tucker

Books

1915 *Thinking as a Science*, New York: E.P. Dutton. Reissued 1916; with epilogue, Los Angeles: Nash Publishing, 1969.

Hazlitt's first book, written at the age of twenty-one. Discussion and comments on the art of thinking and of the allocation of time between thinking and reading. Hazlitt's twenty-five page epilogue in the second edition, written over a half-century later, updates the text and indicates his change of mind on thinking vis-à-vis reading, now heavily emphasizing the importance of reading thoroughly before attempting to think things through on one's own in any particular field.

1922 *The Way to Will Power*, New York: E. P. Dutton.

Lucid and entertaining book on psychology, applying common sense to discussions of will, self-confidence, and desires. Applies economic concepts of value-scales, and choice among values or desires. Valuable early critique of psychoanalysis.

1932 *A Practical Program for America* (ed.), New York: Harcourt and Brace. Reprinted, Freeport, N.Y.: Books for Libraries, 1967.

A collection of essays, originally published in *The Nation*, gathered and edited by Hazlitt, then a *Nation* editor. Published in the midst of the Great Depression,

Annotations written by Murray N. Rothbard.

the essays are a series of suggestions on how to remedy the depression.

The essays are a mixed bag, ranging from H. Parker Willis's critique of inflationary banking to pleas for government planning from Walton Hamilton and Morris L. Cooke. Hazlitt's own chapter is a hard-hitting critique of international tariffs and war debts and reparations and a plea for a drastic reduction in tariffs and cancellation of debts in order to free the increasingly complex and interrelated world market from crippling restrictions and controls.

1933   *The Anatomy of Criticism*, New York: Simon & Schuster.

A discussion of the problems of esthetics and literary criticism in the engaging form of a trialogue among critics of varying schools of thought. Defending the function of criticism, Hazlitt attempts to reconcile the clash between objective and subjective esthetics by postulating a "social mind" that evaluates artistic productions. The explicit analogy is between economic value as decided on the market and esthetic value decided by social influence weighted by the reputations of the critics.

1933   *Instead of Dictatorship*, New York: The John Day Company.

A brief, early version of Hazlitt's proposal for constitutional reform, in which the legislature would consist of thirteen people elected at large, by proportional representation, across the country. The legislature would, in turn, choose a Premier.

1942   *A New Constitution Now*, New York: McGraw. 2nd edition, New Rochelle, N.Y.: Arlington House, 1974.

Deeply troubled by the aggrandizement of presidential power under the U.S. Constitution, Henry Hazlitt proposes, as a far better check on that power, the transformation of the United States into a European-style parliamentary government. In his second edition, Hazlitt points out that a Watergate affair under parliamentary government would have avoided a constitutional crisis and led to a far more speedy and painless removal of the chief executive. Hazlitt leaves unsolved, however, the problem of how to check tyranny by parliament. As he later recognized, he doesn't explain how it came to pass that European nations were even further down the road to socialism than the U.S.

1945   *Freedom in America: The Freeman* with Virgil Jordon, Los Angeles: Pamphleteers.

1945   *The Full Employment Bill: An Analysis*, American Enterprise Association.

1946   *Economics in One Lesson*, New York, London: Harper and Brothers. Also 2nd, 3rd, 4th editions, 1946; New York: MacFadden, 1946; New York: Pocketbooks, 1948, 1952. Revised edition, New York: Manor Books, 1962, 1974. Reprinted, New Rochelle, N.Y.: Arlington House, 1979.

La ciencia de la economa en una sola leccion, Valenica, Fundacio Ignacio Villalonga, 1958, Biblioteca de estudios economicos. *La Economia en una leccion* (3rd ed.), Union Editorial, 1979. *L'Économie Politique une lecon,* trans. Gaetan Pirou, 1949–50. *Über Wirtschaft und Misswirtschaft* (Lektion und Beispiele); Aus d. Amerikan Un Rhiel: Wolfgang, 1983.

A runaway best-seller, a scintillating primer on economics based on Bastiat's insight that interventionism focuses on what is directly seen (e.g., employment needed to repair a broken window) but fails to take into account unseen but important consequences (e.g., the investment that would have been made if the owner did not have to repair the window). The best introduction to free-market economics ever written.

1947   *Will Dollars Save the World?* New York: D. Appleton Century Company; reprinted, Irvington-on-Hudson, N.Y.: Foundation for Economic Education, and Appleton.

A prophetic and illuminating critique of the Marshall Plan and other schemes for U.S. foreign aid. In later years, as the foreign aid program became institutionalized and sanctified, Hazlitt's critique was forgotten, even among free-market economists.

1948   Forum: *Do Current Events Indicate Greater Government Regulation, Nationalization, or Socialization?*, Proceedings from a Conference Sponsored by The Economic and Business Foundation, December, 1948, New Wilmington, Pennsylvania.

1950   *The Illusions of Point Four*, Irvington-on-Hudson, N.Y.: Foundation for Economic Education.

A brief pamphlet, applying the analysis of *Will Dollars Save the World?* to aid to the Third World.

1951   *The Great Idea*, New York: Appleton, 1951. Reprinted as *Time Will Run Back*, London: Ernest Benn Ltd., 1952. Reprinted, New Rochelle, N.Y.: Arlington House, 1966; Lanham, Maryland: University Press of America, 1986.

An act of creative imagination, the only novel ever written that exemplifies and explains the Misesian doctrine of the impossibility of calculation under socialism. Hazlitt starts with a benign but ignorant young man who inherits the role of dictator of a world communist system and who, trying to relieve the economic mess, finds his way, step by logical step, back to a purely free-market economy, a free society, and a gold standard. Remarkably prophetic of similarly logical paths taken by Communist countries in recent years. Many gems, including a chapter illustrating and expounding the fallacies of the attempt of mathematical socialists to "play at" simulated markets under a socialist system.

1956   *The Free Man's Library*, Princeton, N.J.: D. Van Nostrand.

An annotated bibliography of libertarian and free-market books, arranged alphabetically and based on a then three-decade old libertarian bibliography published in London by the economist W. H. Hutt.

1959   *The Failure of the 'New Economics': An Analysis of the Keynesian Fallacies*, Princeton, N.J.: D. Van Nostrand. Reprinted New Rochelle, N.Y.: Arlington House, 1973; Lanham, Maryland: University Press of America, 1983. *Los Errores de la Nueva Ciencia, economica*, Ru.z de Cenzano, J. Agular S.A., 1961., *Das Fiasko de Keynes'schen Wirtschaftslehre: Eine Analyse ihrer Fehlschlusse* (Aus d. Amerikan. Dt. Über.: Bertre) Bockli. a. mi. Knapp, 1960.

Hazlitt's *magnum opus*. A comprehensive, point-by-point Misesian refutation of Keynes's *General Theory*. A devastating, lucidly written critique that would have demolished Keynesianism had the book been widely read and heeded by the economics profession.

1960 *The Critics of Keynesian Economics* (ed.), Princeton, N.J.: D. Van Nostrand. Reprinted with new bibliography and preface, New Rochelle, N.Y.: Arlington House, 1977; Lanham, Maryland: University Press of America, 1983.

A companion volume to the *The Failure*, collecting the major critiques of Keynesian economics published before 1960. Particularly important are the contributions of Viner, Modigliani, Anderson, Burns, Rueff, and Mises. W. H. Hutt's "Significiance of Price Flexibility" is particularly devastating.

1960 *What You Should Know About Inflation*, Princeton, N.J.: D. Van Nostrand, 2nd edition, 1965; reprinted, New York: Funk & Wagnalls, 1968; Conservative Book Club Omnibus, Volume 2.

Based on his popular column in *Newsweek*, a series of lucid and trenchant critiques of inflation from a Misesian viewpoint. Shows that inflation is always an increase in the supply of money, which results in price inflation visible to the public. Important critique of policies of "moderate" or "controlled" inflation, of "cost-push" inflation, and of the idea that inflation of the money supply is legitimate if limited to the increase in the production of goods. A call for a return to the gold standard, and a recognition that, even at that early date, the dollar

was artificially overvalued and gold undervalued at
the then-fixed rate of $35 ounce.

1964   *The Foundations of Morality*, Princeton, N. J.: D. Van Nostrand, 2nd ed. Los Angeles: Nash, 1972. Reprinted, Lanham, Maryland: University Press of America, 1988.

Hazlitt's major philosophical work, in which he
attempts to ground a policy of private property and
free markets in an ethic of classical utilitarianism.

1969   *Man vs. The Welfare State*, New Rochelle, N.Y.: Arlington
House. Reprinted Mitchell Press (Canada), 1971;   Lanham, Maryland: University Press of America, 1983.

A critique of various aspects of the welfare state,
including government deficits, dollar debasement,
price controls, agricultural policy, foreign aid, and
various forms of government relief. There is an
admiring chapter on Spencer's classic *Man vs. the
State*, on which the title of this book is based.
Includes a brilliant critique of Milton Friedman's
proposed negative income tax, logically demon-
strating its destructive consequences.

1973   *The Conquest of Poverty*, Los Angeles: Nash Publishing; also
New Rochelle, N.Y.: Arlington House, 1973. Re-
printed Lanham, Maryland: University Press of America,
1986.

Essays on poverty, including a critique of the definition of poverty; a discussion of Malthus and the
population question; treatment of the historical
consequences of poor relief; a critique of social
insurance, unemployment insurance, and welfare

expenditures; discussion of the destructive consequences of unions and minimum wage laws; criticism of foreign aid. Includes a warning of the
consequences of an egalitarian appeasement of envy
in making poverty worse. The only long-run cure
for poverty, Hazlitt explains, is private saving and
investment.

1974 *To Stop Inflation, Return to Gold*, Greenwich, Conn.: Committee for Monetary Research and Education.

1978 *The Inflation Crisis and How to Resolve It*, New Rochelle, N.Y.:
Arlington House. Reprinted, Lanham, Maryland: Univer-
sity Press of America, 1983.

1984 *From Bretton Woods to World Inflation*, Chicago: Regnery
Gateway.

A collection of prophetic *New York Times* editorials
written at the time of the Bretton Woods conference, criticizing the new world monetary system,
and forecasting its eventual inflationary collapse.

1984 *The Wisdom of the Stoics: Selections from Seneca, Epictetus, and
Marcus Aurelius*, Lanham, Maryland: University Press of
America.

A collection of writings and aphorisms by Stoic
philosophers which Hazlitt found particularly important for living the good and virtuous life.

1993 *The Wisdom of Henry Hazlitt*, Irvington-on-Hudson, N.Y.:
Foundation for Economic Education.

Chapters in Books, Introductions, and Short Monographs

"The Man Mencken, by Isaac Goldberg," in *Current Reviews*, Lewis Worthington Smith (ed.), New York: Henry Holt, 1926.

"Humanism and Value," in *The Critique of Humanism*, Clinton Hartley Grattan (ed.), New York: Brewer and Warren, 1930; and Freeport N.Y.: Books for Libraries Press, 1968.

"Emerson," in *American Writers on American Literature*, John Albert Macy (ed.), Westport, Conn.: Greenwood Press, 1931.

"Introduction," to *Maggie and Other Stories by Stephen Crane*, New York: Alfred A. Knopf, 1931.

"World Action for World Recovery," in *A Practical Program for America*, Henry Hazlitt (ed.), Freeport, N.Y.: Books for Libraries Press, 1932.

"In Praise of Escape," in *American Spectator Yearbook*, George Nathan et al. (eds.), New York: Frederick A. Stokes, McClenden, 1933.

"The World of Babbitt's Son: 1942," in *Essay Annual, 1933,* Erich Walter (ed.), New York: Scott Foresman, 1933.

"Our Greatest Authors (How Great Are They?)," *Essays and Addresses Toward A Liberal Education*, A. C. Baird, (ed.), Boston: Ginn and Company, 1934; and S. S. Morgan and W. H. Thomas (eds.), *Opinions and Attitudes in the Twentieth Century*, New York: T. Nelson and Sons, 1934.

"Literature as Propaganda," in *The Practice of Book Selection*, Louis Round Wilson (ed.), Chicago: University of Chicago Press, 1940.

"Nietzsche: Beyond Good and Evil," by Dorothy Thompson, Henry Hazlitt, and Mark Van Doren in *New Invitation to Learning*, Mark Van Doren, Mark (ed.), New York: Random House, 1942.

"The Bretton Woods Agreements and Freedom of Trade," in *Money and the Law*, New York: Proceedings of the Institute on Money and the Law, 1945.

"Implications of State Guarantee of Employment," an Address Before the Academy of Political Science. New York: Columbia University Academy of Political Science, 1945.

"Whose Corporations Are They?" in *The Controller's Interest in Public Relations*, New York: The Controllers Institute of America, 1946.

"How Can America Rescue the World?" Irvington-on-Hudson, N.Y.: Foundation for Economic Education, 1947. Ninety copies printed, marked, "Issued as Confidential Copy"

"Irresponsible Government," excerpt from *A New Constitution Now* in *Basic Issues of American Democracy*, H. M. Bishop and S. Hendel (eds.), New York: Appleton, 1948.

"Who is a Dark Horse?" in *Plain Talk: An Anthology*, Isaac Don Levine (ed.), New Rochelle, N.Y.: Arlington House, 1976. Original June 1948.

"Economics of the President's Economists" (with Solomon Fabricant, et al.), in *Studies in Business Economics*, no. 20, National Industrial Conference Board, 1949.

"Introduction," to *Economics and the Public Welfare*, Benjamin M. Anderson, Princeton, N.J.: D. Van Nostrand, 1949.

"Capitalism and Our Economic Goals," in *The National Economy in Time of Crisis: Its Meaning to Lawyers and Their Clients*, The New Jersey State Bar Association, 1951.

"Profits and Freedom," reprint of Address Before the National Machine Tool Builders' Association, White Sulphur Springs, W. Va., 1952.

"Ends and Means," in *Preface to Literature*, E. C. Wagenknecht (ed.), New York: Henry Holt, 1954.

Life and Death of the Welfare State, La Jolla, Calif.: La Jolla Rancho Press, 1954.

"Literature vs. Opinion," in *The Writer and His Craft*, Roy S. Cowden (ed.), Ann Arbor: University of Michigan, 1954.

"The Ethics of Capitalism," New York: Educational Division of the National Association of Manufacturers, 1965; (from *Foundations of Morality*, 1964).

"Government Planning vs. Economic Growth," Zürich: International Freedom Academy, 196-. (Date appears this way.)

Income Without Work. Can We Guarantee It? Arlington, Va.: Crestwood Books, 1969.

"The ABC of Inflation," Lansing, Mich.: Constitutional Alliance, 1969 (Excerpt from *What You Should Know About Inflation*, 1960).

"Socialism is the Wave of the Future"; "Wars Bring Jobs and Prosperity"; "Rent Control Protects Tenants"; "Industrialization Assures Progress in Undeveloped Countries"; in *The Clichés of Socialism*, Irvington-on-Hudson, N.Y.: Foundation for Economic Education, 1970.

"Economics in One Lesson," in *Did You Ever See a Dream Walking?* William F. Buckley (ed.), Indianapolis & New York: Bobbs Merrill, 1970. (Short version of the book.)

"The Future of Capitalism," in *Toward Liberty*, vol 2., Menlo Park, Calif.: Institute for Humane Studies, 1971.

The Strike: For and Against, Harold H. Hart (ed.), New York: Hart Publishing Company, 1971.

"The Fallacy of Foreign Aid," in *The Libertarian Alternative*, Tibor R. Machan (ed.), Chicago: Nelson-Hall, 1974.

"To Restore Monetary Order," in *Gold is Money*, Hans F. Sennholz, Westport, Conn.: Greenwood Press, 1975.

"Introduction," to *Beyond Failure: How to Cure a Neurotic Society*, Frank G. Goble, Ottawa, Ill.: Caroline House Books, 1977.

"Unemployment and Inflation," in *Inflation and Unemployment*, G. Carl Wiegand (ed.), Old Greenwich, Conn.: Devin Adair, 1980.

Articles and Editorials

1918

"Old-time Government Control," *The Nation*, January 24, 1918.

"Repudiation," *The Nation*, February 21, 1918.

"Our Economic War Machine," *The Nation*, April 11, 1918.

"Written on the Back of Puffs," *The New Republic*, April 13, 1918.

"War-time Markets," *The Nation*, April 25, 1918.

"Before and After a War Loan," *The Nation*, May 11, 1918.

1920

"On Profiteer Hunting," *Review* (New York), May 1, 1920.

1926

"Program For the Wets," *Independent*, April 24, 1926.

"How High Is Up?" *New York Sun*, October 2, 1926.

"Some Impressions of the New *Britannica*," *New York Sun*, October 9, 1926.

"The 'Real' Washington," *New York Sun*, October 16, 1926.

"Saint Darwin, A 'Psychograph' of the Great Evolutionist," *New York Sun*, October 23, 1926.

"Incurable Democracy" (on H. L. Mencken), *New York Sun*, October 30, 1926.

"Prose in America," *New York Sun*, November 6, 1926.

"Galahad's Reputation," *New York Sun*, November 13, 1926.

"Thinking About Thinking," *New York Sun*, November 20, 1926.

"A Story Teller's Childhood," *New York Sun*, November 27, 1926.

"Shouts Without," *New York Sun*, December 4, 1926.

"What is an Education?" *New York Sun*, December 18, 1926.

"This Golden Age of Science," *New York Sun*, December 24, 1926.

"Only the Best, You Know," *New York Sun*, December 31, 1926.

1927

"A Kiss for Communism" (on John Maynard Keynes), *New York Sun*, January 8, 1927.

"The Subtle Santayana," *New York Sun*, January 15, 1927.

"The Humanizing of Science," *New York Sun*, January 29, 1927.

"Genius When Young," *New York Sun*, February 5, 1927.

"Main Street and Wall Street," *New York Sun*, February 12, 1927.

"Insults Across the Sea," *New York Sun*, February 19, 1927.

"Radicalism in Fiction" (on Garet Garrett), *New York Sun*, February 26, 1927.

"Babbittry in the Pulpit" (on Sinclair Lewis), *New York Sun*, March 12, 1927.

"Modern Girls and Such," *New York Sun*, March 19, 1927.

"Spinoza Redivivus," *New York Sun*, April 16, 1927.

"The Will to Believe," *New York Sun*, April 23, 1927.

"The Book Column," *New York Sun*, May 3, 1927.

"Diderot and Voltaire, Fresh Adventures in the Age of Reason," *New York Sun*, May 14, 1927.

"Mr. Wells Scrapes the Bin," *New York Sun*, July 30, 1927.

"Music for the Soul," *New York Sun*, August 6, 1927.

"Acres of Canvas, the Seamy Side of a Circus," *New York Sun*, August 13, 1927.

"The Art of Reviewing," *New York Sun*, August 20, 1927.

"The Newest Morality," *New York Sun*, August 27, 1927.

"Portraits and Politics," *New York Sun*, September 23, 1927.

"One Who Read Philosophy" (on Will Durant), *New York Sun*, October 8, 1927.

"Our Elegant Insides," *New York Sun*, October 15, 1927

"Haldane Looks Ahead," *New York Sun*, October 29, 1927.

"Bertrand Russell's Universe," *New York Sun*, November 5, 1927.

"No Rib, No Apple," *New York Sun*, November 19, 1927.

"The Poets on Parade," *The Sun*, November 26, 1927.

"Boomlay, Boomlay, Boom!" (on H. L. Mencken), *New York Sun*, December 3, 1927.

"Glorifying New Yorkers," *New York Sun*, December 10, 1927.

"Physics and Metaphysics," *New York Sun*, December 17, 1927.

"America in Science," *New York Sun*, December 29, 1927.

1928

"The Tarkington Girl: What a Modern Prom-Trotter Thinks About," *New York Sun*, January 7, 1928.

"The Reviewing Stand," *New York Sun*, January 7, 1928.

"Henry Adams," *New York Sun*, January 14, 1928.

"Winces of the Galled," *New York Sun*, January 21, 1928.

"Life Among the Essences," *New York Sun*, February 4, 1928.

"The Book Column," *New York Sun*, February 8, 1928.

"Aldous, Chip off Thomas," *New York Sun*, February 11, 1928.

"An Andalusian Story," *New York Sun*, February 18, 1928.

"Polonius Plus: Agreeable Platitudes and Sound Criticism," *New York Sun*, February 25, 1928.

"This Art of Criticism," *New York Sun*, March 10, 1928.

"Irreverent Portraits," *New York Sun*, March 17, 1928.

"Monarchs of Philosophy," *New York Sun*, March 24, 1928.

"The 'Tyranny' of Science," *New York Sun*, March 31, 1928.

"Babbitt's Friend Schmaltz," April 7, 1928.

"The King of Good Company: Dr. Johnson and His Friends," *New York Sun*, April 21, 1928.

"Julien Green, A Student of Solitary Souls," *New York Sun*, April 28, 1928.

"A Critic of Critics" (on Emile Faguet), *New York Sun*, May 12, 1928.

"Why Gentlemen Prefer Them," *New York Sun*, May 19, 1928.

"The Literary Scientist," *New York Sun*, May 26, 1928.

"The Unrepentant Socialist," *New York Sun*, June 9, 1928.

"Candidates and Such," *New York Sun*, June 16, 1928.

"Dorothy Fires," *New York Sun*, June 23, 1928.

"American Criticism," *New York Sun*, June 23, 1928.

"An Italian's Portraits," *New York Sun*, August 18, 1928.

"The Fifteen 'Finest'," *New York Sun*, September 1, 1928.

"Wells Writes a Bible, and Demands That the Universe Improve," *New York Sun*, September 8, 1928.

"A Serene Revolutionist" (on Bertrand Russell), *New York Sun*, September 15, 1928.

"The American Abroad," *New York Sun*, September 22, 1928.

"The Incomparable One" (on Max Beerbohm), *New York Sun*, September 29, 1928.

"The American Omen" (on Garet Garrett), *New York Sun*, October 6, 1928.

"Fugue by Huxley," *New York Sun*, October 13, 1928.

"Freud on Religion," *New York Sun*, October 20, 1928.

"The Truth About India," *New York Sun*, October 27, 1928.

"Mankind's Destiny," *New York Sun*, November 3, 1928.

"The Meaning of Spenglerism," *New York Sun*, November 10, 1928.

"Erskine vs. Homer," *New York Sun*, November 17, 1928.

"Macbeth," *New York Sun*, November 20, 1928.

"No Necessity At All," *New York Sun*, November 24, 1928.

"And Now Elizabeth," *New York Sun*, December 1, 1928.

"A Chest of Pearls," *New York Sun*, December 8, 1928.

"The Prospects of Literature and Other Gloomy Predictions," *New York Sun*, December 15, 1928.

"The Art of Thinking," *New York Sun*, December 22, 1928.

"Bang's 'Houseboat'," *New York Sun*, December 26, 1928.

"Paul Elmer More," *New York Sun*, December 29, 1928.

1929

"The Boswell Discovery," *New York Sun*, January 5, 1929.

"Deep Harlem," *New York Sun*, January 8, 1929.

"This World of Shadows," *New York Sun*, January 12, 1929.

"Repertory Plays," *New York Sun*, January 15, 1929.

"If the Artists Ruled," *New York Sun*, January 19, 1929.

"Not So Hot," *New York Sun*, January 22, 1929.

"Low Views of the Great," *New York Sun*, January 26, 1929.

"In Those Days" (on Harvey Ferguson), *New York Sun*, February 2, 1929.

"Tell, What is Beauty?" *New York Sun*, February 9, 1929.

"A South American Aurelius" (on J. E. Rodo), *New York Sun*, February 23, 1929.

"Beyond Human Knowledge," *New York Sun*, February 25, 1929.

"Through a Heavy Beard," *New York Sun*, March 2, 1929.

"Herman Melville," *New York Sun*, March 9, 1929.

"The Town's Woman," *New York Sun*, March 12, 1929.

"Babbitt Abroad" (on Sinclair Lewis), *New York Sun*, March 16, 1929.

"Sons of New England," *New York Sun*, March 23, 1929.

"All This Sexcitement: Twenty-three Books on Morals and Marriage," *New York Sun*, March 30, 1929.

"Back To Judaism," *New York Sun*, April 29, 1929.

"Morals for Moderns" (on Walter Lippmann), *New York Sun*, May 4, 1929.

"The Unseen World," *New York Sun*, May 7, 1929.

"From Violets to Scotch," *New York Sun*, August 10, 1929.

"He Thought of Proust," *New York Sun*, August 17, 1929.

"The Newest Morality," *New York Sun*, August 27, 1929.

"A Philosopher's Notebooks," *New York Sun*, September 10, 1929.

"Take Hemingway" (on *A Farewell to Arms*), *New York Sun*, September 28, 1929.

"The First Night 'The Sea Gull' Was Shot," *New York Sun*, October 1929.

"The New *Britannica*," *New York Sun*, October 1929.

1930

"Consolation or Control?" (on John Dewey), *The Nation*, January 22, 1930.

"Cultural History," *The Nation*, January 29, 1930.

"The Pioneer Soul," *The Nation*, February 5, 1930.

"All Too Humanism," *The Nation*, February 12, 1930.

"Tradition and Experiment," *The Nation*, February 19, 1930.

"Mr. Wilder Turns to Terence," *The Nation*, February 26, 1930.

"Turn to the Left," *The Nation*, March 5, 1930.

"The Pretensions of Humanism," *The Nation*, March 5, 1930.

"Kaleidoscope," *The Nation*, March 12, 1930.

"The Gods Damned" (on H. L. Mencken), *The Nation*, March 19, 1930.

"An Apology for the Present," *The Nation*, April 2, 1930.

"Gide's First Novel," *The Nation*, April 2, 1930.

"The Analysis of Morals," *The Nation*, April 9, 1930.

"Who Reads the Classics Now?" *The Nation*, April 16, 1930.

"Last Testament," *The Nation*, April 30, 1930.

"A Great Trilogy," *The Nation*, May 7, 1930.

"Fake Culture for Real," *The Nation*, May 14, 1930.

"Artists in Exile," *The Nation*, May 28, 1930.

"This Petty Pace," *The Nation*, June 4, 1930.

"Economics of Dollar Books," *The Nation*, June 11, 1930.

"Liberty, Classic, and Romantic," *The Nation*, June 18, 1930.

"Drama, 'Lysistrata'," *The Nation*, June 25, 1930.

"The Metaphysicians Confess," *The Nation*, July 2, 1930.

"Style and Thought," *The Nation*, July 19, 1930.

"Heredity or Environment?" *The Nation*, August 13, 1930.

"Below the Babbittry," *The Nation*, August 20, 1930.

"The Classical Canons," *The Nation*, August 27, 1930.

"Americans Do Not Read," *The Nation*, September 3, 1930.

"Our Intellectual Rulers," *The Nation*, September 10, 1930.

"The Neurosis of Civilization" (on Sigmund Freud), *The Nation*, September 17, 1930.

"Misplaced Investment Trusts" (on J. T. Flynn), *The Nation*, September 24, 1930.

"Cult of Anonymity," *The Nation*, October 1, 1930.

"The Art of Being Happy," *The Nation*, October 8, 1930.

"An Exquisite Materialist" (on George Santayana), *The Nation*, October 15, 1930.

"Progress Without a Goal" (on John Dewey), October 22, 1930.

"The Soul of Swift," *The Nation*, October 29, 1930.

"Here's Mr. Foerster Again," *The Nation*, November 5, 1930.

"Charles Horton Cooley," *The Nation*, November 12, 1930.

"Einstein," *The Nation*, November 19, 1930.

"Communist Criticism," *The Nation*, November 26, 1930.

"Modern Architecture," *The Nation*, December 10, 1930.

"Standards (Loud Cheers)," *The Nation*, December 17, 1930.

"Rainer Maria Rilke," *The Nation*, December 17, 1930.

"William Hazlitt," *The Nation*, December 31, 1930.

"Prohibition: A Plan"; "Legislative Versus General Opinion"; "Public Support"; "The Machinery of Amendment"; "Counting the Vote"; "Wanted: Critics of Architecture"; "The Commercial Incubus"; "Blood Sacrifice, Modern Style"; "Mei Lan-Fang . . ."; "Glorifying a Mechanical Limitation"; "William Howard Taft"; in "Quarterly Comment," *Century*, Spring, 1930.

"Civilized Warfare"; "Legal Illegalities"; "The World Court"; "Knowledge is Power"; "In Dispraise of Noise"; "A Nation of Noise Makers"; "Our Inadjustable Ears"; "Fashions in Phrases"; "In Defense of Expatriates"; "Wet and Dry Savings"; in "Quarterly Comment," *Century*, Winter, 1930.

1931

"Dollar Books: An Autopsy," *The Nation*, January 7, 1931.

"Laski on Liberty," *The Nation*, January 28, 1931.

"Debate," *The Nation*, February 4, 1931.

"Our Obsolete Constitution," *The Nation*, February 4, 1931.

"George Jean Nathan," *The Nation*, February 18, 1931.

"The Stream of Life," *The Nation*, February 25, 1931.

"Edmund Wilson," *The Nation*, March 4, 1931.

"Goethe and Dr. Johnson," *The Nation*, March 18, 1931.

"How Novels Get Bad Marx," *The Nation*, April 1, 1931.

"The Philosophy of Morris R. Cohen," *The Nation*, April 15, 1931.

"With a Preface," *The Nation*, April 22, 1931.

"Economics: The Lively Science," *The Nation*, May 6, 1931.

"In Dispraise of Fine Books," *The Nation*, May 20, 1931.

"Another Book About Himself," *The Nation*, June 3, 1931.

"Pictures from Plays," *The Nation*, September 30, 1931.

"Art and Social Change: The Eclectic Approach" (debate with V. F. Calverton), *The Modern*, Winter 1931.

"Rubber Money and Iron Debts," *The Nation*, December 23, 1931.

1932

"Shall We Cancel the War Debts?" *These Times*, January 1, 1932.

"Two Critics," *The Nation*, January 20, 1932.

"Emergency Currency," *The Nation*, January 27, 1932.

"What's Wrong With Utopia?" (on Huxley's *Brave New World*), *The Nation*, February 17, 1932.

"How High Is Up?" *Forum and Century*, February, 1932.

"A Philosophy for Carnivores," *The Nation*, February 24, 1932.

"Liberalism and Economics" (Keynes's *Essays in Persuasion*), *The Nation*, March 9, 1932.

"Panorama," *The Nation*, March 23, 1932.

"Shall We Devaluate the Dollar? Part I," *The Nation*, March 30, 1932.

"Shall We Devaluate the Dollar? Part II," *The Nation*, April 6, 1932.

"Emerson," *The Nation*, April 13, 1932.

"Gamaliel Bradford," *The Nation*, April 27, 1932.

"World of Babbitt's Son: 1942," *Scribner's Magazine*, May 1932.

"The Graces, the Graces!" *The Nation*, May 1, 1932.

"World Action for World Recovery," *The Nation*, June 8, 1932.

"Can America Plan?" (on George Soule), *The Nation*, June 15, 1932.

"Without Benefit of Congress," *Scribner's Magazine*, July 1932.

"Whither the American Writer?" *The Modern Quarterly*, Summer 1932. Answers to Questionaire on the Future of Literature.

"The Meaning of Individualism," *The Nation*, July 6, 1932.

"David Hume," *The Nation*, July 20, 1932.

"A Compact Encyclopedia," *The Nation*, August 24, 1932.

"Little Wonder House," *The Nation*, August 31, 1932.

"The Myth of Overproduction," *Current History*, September 1932.

"Bowdlerized Lawrence," *The Nation*, September 7, 1932.

"Voltaire," *The Nation*, September 14, 1932.

"Our Greatest Authors," *Forum and Century*, October 1932.

"The Mind of T. S. Eliot," *The Nation*, October 5, 1932.

"Literature and the Class War," *The Nation*, October 19, 1932.

"Family of Minds," *The Nation*, November 9, 1932.

"Prose in America," *The Nation*, November 16, 1932.

"Our Superstitious Education," *The Nation*, November 30, 1932.

"A Modern Diogenes," *The Nation*, December 7, 1932.

"On Translating Homer," *The Nation*, December 21, 1932.

1933

"No Taxes to Pay," *Scribner's Magazine*, January 1933.

"In Praise of Escape," *American Spectator*, January 1, 1933.

"Marxism or Tolstoyism?" *The Nation*, January 18, 1933.

"Scrambled Ergs; Examination of Technocracy," *The Nation*, February 1, 1933.

"Sinclair Lewis, Campaigner," *The Nation*, February 1, 1933.

"Is Inflation the Way Out?" *Common Sense*, February 16, 1933.

"Culture vs. 'Life'," *The Nation*, February 22, 1933.

"Bernard's Progress," *The Nation*, March 8, 1932.

"In Defense of Hoarding," *The Nation*, March 22, 1933.

"The Twilight of Capitalist Democracy" (on Harold J. Laski), *The Nation*, April 12, 1933.

"The King's English," *The Nation*, April 26, 1933.

"Dollar Adrift," *The Nation*, May 3, 1933.

"Crises Are Not 'So Simple'," *The Nation*, May 24, 1933.

"Inflation: How Much?" *The Nation*, May 31, 1933.

"Programs for the Jobless," *Scribner's Magazine*, June 1933.

"Law, Life, and Morals," *The Nation*, June 7, 1933.

"Mr. Keynes's Way Out" (on *The Means to Prosperity*), *The Nation*, July 5, 1933.

"Sir Arthur Plans Planning," *The Nation*, July 19, 1933.

"Can Currencies be Managed?" *The Nation*, July 26, 1933.

"They Stand Out From the Crowd," *Literary Digest*, October 28, 1933.

"The Fallacies of the N.R.A.," *American Mercury*, December, 1933.

1934

"Philosophers of the New Deal," *American Mercury*, January 1934.

"The Dollar: A Political Toy," *The Nation*, January 31, 1934.

"These Economic Experiments," *American Mercury*, February 1934.

"Babbitt as Hero," *American Mercury*, March 1934.

"Review of J. P. Warburg's *The Money Muddle*," *New York Times Book Review*, May 13, 1934. Replies to criticism May 24, 1934.

"Debts and Armaments," *New York Times*, June 4, 1934.

"Wages of Textile Workers," *New York Times*, June 6, 1934.

"The Stock Exchange Act," *New York Times*, June 7, 1934.

"Another NRA Retreat," *New York Times*, June 9, 1934.

"Exchange Restriction," *New York Times*, June 10, 1934.

"No Monetary Magic," *New York Times*, June 11, 1934.

"A Convalescing World," *New York Times*, June 12, 1934.

"Code Nightmares," *New York Times*, June 13, 1934.

"Payments in Kind," *New York Times*, June 14, 1934.

"The German Moratorium," *New York Times*, June 16, 1934.

"A Survey of the Present Currents of American Ideas" (on George Soule), *New York Times Book Review*, June 17, 1934.

"Wages Under Inflation," *New York Times*, June 17, 1934.

"Why Germany Defaults," *New York Times*, June 18, 1934.

"Records in Sport," *New York Times*, June 19, 1934.

"What Determines Wages" (on P. H. Douglas on Wages), *The Nation*, June 20, 1934

"'Self-Regulation'," *New York Times*, June 20, 1934.

"Debts and Threats," *New York Times*, June 23, 1934.

"Trade is Triangular," *New York Times*, June 26, 1934.

"Mr. Hopkins Looks Ahead," *New York Times*, June 27, 1934.

"Realism and the Debts," *New York Times*, June 29, 1934.

"Germany's Isolation," *New York Times*, June 30, 1934.

"Another NRA Retreat," *New York Times*, July 2, 1934.

"The Silver Program," *New York Times*, July 2, 1934.

"America's 'Overequipment'," *New York Times*, July 4, 1934.

"Labor Under the NRA," *New York Times*, July 4, 1934.

"Britain to be Paid," *New York Times*, July 6, 1934.

"Codes and Critics," *New York Times*, July 7, 1934.

"Unemployment Insurance," *New York Times*, July 8, 1934.

"Mr. Brailsford Looks Gloomily at the Democracies" (on *Property or Peace*), *New York Times Book Review*, July 1, 1934.

"The Return to Gold," *New York Times*, July 9, 1934.

"Economics and Ethics," *New York Times*, July 10, 1934.

"Thomas to the Rescue," *New York Times*, July 11, 1934.

"AAA vs. NRA," *New York Times*, July 12, 1934.

"No 'Painless' Reductions," *New York Times*, July 13, 1934.

"The New 'Basic Code'," *New York Times*, July 14, 1934.

"Durable Goods Industries," *New York Times*, July 16, 1934.

"The Railroad Dilemma," *New York Times*, July 17, 1934.

"England and Gold," *New York Times*, July 16, 1934.

"An Expensive Default," *New York Times*, July 20, 1934.

"Housing and Production," *New York Times*, July 21, 1934.

"Planning in Action," *New York Times*, July 22, 1934.

"The Inflationary Appetite," *New York Times*, July 23, 1934.

"Mr. Henderson's 'Tip'," *New York Times*, July 24, 1934.

"The Uses of Criticism," *New York Times*, July 25, 1934.

"Our International Accounts," *New York Times*, July 26, 1934.

"The Davis Cup," *New York Times*, July 25, 1934.

"Reassuring Business," *New York Times*, July 27, 1934.

"Managed Money," *New York Times*, July 29, 1934.

"More Manhattan Families," *New York Times*, July 30, 1934.

"Prolonged 'Emergency'," *New York Times*, July 31, 1934.

"America Loses Again," *New York Times*, August 1, 1934.

"A Mistaken Defense," *New York Times*, August 2, 1934.

"NRA in Transition," *New York Times*, August 3, 1934.

"Potential Credit," *New York Times*, August 4, 1934.

"Foot-Fault," *New York Times*, August 5, 1934.

"Our 'Surplus' Economy," *New York Times*, August 5, 1934.

"Employers and Jobs," *New York Times*, August 7, 1934.

"Foreign and Domestic Bonds," *New York Times*, August 8, 1934.

"Still Hope for Shorts," *New York Times*, August 8, 1934.

"What Labor Gets," *New York Times*, August 9, 1934.

"Cotton," *New York Times*, August 10, 1934.

"Silver Nationalized," *New York Times*, August 10, 1934.

"Prospects for Silver," *New York Times*, August 11, 1934.

"Dangers of 'Planning'," *New York Times*, August 12, 1934.

"Paper for Silver," *New York Times*, August 12, 1934.

"How Many Jobless?" *New York Times*, August 13, 1934.

"Missing an Opportunity," *New York Times*, August 14, 1934.

"Raymond Hood," *New York Times*, August 15, 1934.

"Silver Certificates," *New York Times*, August 19, 1934.

"Where 'Inflation' Begins," *New York Times*, August 20, 1934.

"An 'Economic Council'," *New York Times*, August 21, 1934.

"Buying Silver With Gold," *New York Times*, August 23, 1934.

"'Fair' Profits," *New York Times*, August 24, 1934.

"Mr. Flynn's Vigorous Attack Upon Security Speculation," *New York Times Book Review*, August 26, 1934.

"Suicidal Nationalism," *New York Times*, August 27, 1934.

"The Recovery Record," *New York Times*, August 28, 1934.

"Reconsidering NRA," *New York Times*, August 29, 1934.

"Schacht vs. Schacht," *New York Times*, September 1, 1934.

"Job Insurance," *New York Times*, September 3, 1934.

"Silver and China," *New York Times*, September 3, 1934.

"Of Their Own Choosing," *New York Times*, September 4, 1934.

"Where They Stand," *New York Times*, September 5, 1934.

"If They Can Get It," *New York Times*, September 7, 1934.

"Work and Population," *New York Times*, September 8, 1934.

"The Thirty-Hour Week," *New York Times*, September 9, 1934.

"An Introduction to the Sociology of Pareto" (by George C. Homans (et al.), *New York Times Book Review*, September 9, 1934.

"The Ungrateful Chinese," *New York Times*, September 19, 1934.

"Feminism and Semitism," *New York Times*, September 10, 1934.

"Our Cotton Abroad," *New York Times*, September 10, 1934.

"Prices and Consumers," *New York Times*, September 11, 1934.

"Critics in Yachts," *New York Times*, September 12, 1934.

"Protection for Tennis," *New York Times*, September 14, 1934.

"Bankers are People," *New York Times*, September 15, 1934.

"German Trade and Debts," *New York Times*, September 16, 1934.

"'Conditioning' the Child," *New York Times*, September 16, 1934.

"Poland's Minorities," *New York Times*, September 17, 1934.

"Reciprocal Trade," *New York Times*, September 18, 1934.

"Office by Lottery," *New York Times*, September 20, 1934.

"Trading in Tobacco," *New York Times*, September 21, 1934.

"Debt-Calling Laws," *New York Times*, September 21, 1934.

"A Basis for Settlement," *New York Times*, September 22, 1934.

"The Strike Settlement," *New York Times*, September 24, 1934.

"On Ludwig Vogelstein's Death," *New York Times*, September 24, 1934.

"Bertrand Russell's Men of Destiny" (on *Freedom Versus Organization*), *New York Times Book Review*, September 23, 1934.

"Barter Trade," *New York Times*, September 24, 1934.

"Business and Confidence," *New York Times*, September 25, 1934.

"For the Gold Basis," *New York Times*, September 29, 1934.

"China Protest," *New York Times*, October 1, 1934.

"Germany's Trade Control," *New York Times*, October 2, 1934.

"The Labor Program," *New York Times*, October 3, 1934.

"The Aims of National Planning" (on Henry Wallace's *New Frontiers*), *New York Times Book Review*, October 7, 1934.

"Making Jobs," *New York Times*, October 9, 1934.

"The Five-Day Week," *New York Times*, October 10, 1934.

"Death Duties," *New York Times*, October 13, 1934.

"Prices and Recovery," *New York Times*, October 13, 1934.

"Payment by Index," *New York Times*, October 14, 1934.

"Nazi Trade Policy," *New York Times*, October 15, 1934.

"On Not Producing," *New York Times*, October 17, 1934.

"A Plan to End Planning," *New York Times*, October 18, 1934.

"The NRA Tomorrow," *New York Times*, October 19, 1934.

"Retreat From Nationalism," *New York Times*, October 22, 1934.

"Contrary to Opinion, We Still Underproduce" (on Maurice Leven), *New York Times Book Review*, October 21, 1934.

"World Banking," *New York Times*, October 23, 1934.

"The Case for Production," *New York Times*, October 24, 1934.

"Pound and Dollar," *New York Times*, October 25, 1934.

"Why Inflation is Feared," *New York Times*, October 27, 1934.

"Gold and World Trade," *New York Times*, October 29, 1934.

"Russia's Planned Economy," *New York Times*, October 30, 1934.

"Technique of Repudiation," *New York Times*, October 31, 1934.

"Unemployment Insurance," *New York Times*, November 1, 1934.

"Comparative Recovery," *New York Times*, November 3, 1934.

"England Will be Paid," *New York Times*, November 3, 1934.

"A Militant Campaign Document by Secretary Ickes" (on *The New Democracy*), *New York Times Book Review*, November 4, 1934.

"Snowden on Gold," *New York Times*, November 5, 1934.

"A Common Interest," *New York Times*, November 6, 1934.

"Taxes in Kind," *New York Times*, November 8, 1934.

"Potential Credit," *New York Times*, November 9, 1934.

"Limiting Machine Hours," *New York Times*, November 10, 1934.

"Is Competition Dead?" *New York Times*, November 11, 1934.

"Voting on Cotton," *New York Times*, November 12, 1934.

"The Right to Move," *New York Times*, November 13, 1934.

"Not a Substitute," *New York Times*, November 14, 1934.

"Stock Exchange Acquiesces," *New York Times*, November 15, 1934.

"A Good Swiss Idea," *New York Times*, November 16, 1934.

"Coal Meets Competition," *New York Times*, November 18, 1934.

"Helping the 'Gold Bloc'," *New York Times*, November 21, 1934.

"An RFC Lesson," *New York Times*, November 22, 1934.

"Mr. Richberg's Program," *New York Times*, November 23, 1934.

"Recovery and Costs," *New York Times*, November 24, 1934.

"Removing Trade Barriers," *New York Times*, November 28, 1934.

"A Novelist Resigns," *New York Times*, November 27, 1934.

"Solo By Mr. Peek," *New York Times*, November 27, 1934.

"Our Export Balance," *New York Times*, November 28, 1934.

"Taxing the Gross," *New York Times*, November 30, 1934.

"The Gold Standard," *New York Times*, December 1, 1934.

"The New Books," *New York Times*, December 2, 1934.

"The Republican Problem," *New York Times*, December 4, 1934.

"Trade With Germany," *New York Times*, December 6, 1934.

"Newspaper Accuracy," *New York Times*, December 8, 1934.

"Stalin to Wells," *New York Times*, December 9, 1934.

"Non-Reporting Reports," *New York Times*, December 10, 1934.

"Income Paradoxes," *New York Times*, December 11, 1934.

"The President on Crime," *New York Times*, December 12, 1934.

"Wages and Work," *New York Times*, December 13, 1934.

"Strain in Belgium," *New York Times*, December 14, 1934.

"Unknown Croesuses," *New York Times*, December 15, 1934.

"Price-Fixing," *New York Times*, December 16, 1934.

"Perry Forgot Publius," *New York Times*, December 17, 1934.

"The Cult of Planning," *New York Times*, December 18, 1934.

"A Case of Nerves," *New York Times*, December 19, 1934.

"How to Live on 20,000 Words A Year," *New York Times*, December 22, 1934.

"The Vanishing Ear-Muff," *New York Times*, December 23, 1934.

"Taking Over A Railroad," *New York Times*, December 24, 1934.

"By What Authority?" *New York Times*, December 25, 1934.

"If Deficits Continue," *New York Times*, December 26, 1934.

"The Money Maze," *New York Times*, December 27, 1934.

"Stamping out 'Heresies'," *New York Times*, December 27, 1934.

"An Unsatisfactory Reply," *New York Times*, December 28, 1934.

"On Proceeding Legally," *New York Times*, December 31, 1934.

1935

"False Alarms," *New York Times*, January 4, 1935.

"Science in the New," *New York Times*, January 4, 1935.

"France Tries 'Credit'," *New York Times*, January 5, 1935.

"The Road to Recovery: Spending or Saving?" *New York Times*, January 6, 1935.

"A Final Test," *New York Times*, January 7, 1935.

"The Post Office 'Surplus'," *New York Times*, January 9, 1935.

"Pressure Planning," *New York Times*, January 10, 1935.

"Oil Control," *New York Times*, January 11, 1935.

"The New Fatalism," *New York Times*, January 14, 1935.

"Japan and the Tariff," *New York Times*, January 14, 1935.

"Great Britain's Foreign Trade," *New York Times*, January 16, 1935.

"The Metrical Service," *New York Times*, January 17, 1935.

"Defining an 'Amateur'," *New York Times*, January 18, 1935.

"Public Works: A Case Study," *New York Times*, January 19, 1935.

"Mr. Krutch Reaffirms the Liberal Creed," *New York Times*, January 20, 1935.

"Work of the RFC," *New York Times*, January 21, 1935.

"Stable Currencies," *New York Times*, January 21, 1935.

"Depreciation and Trade," *New York Times*, January 22, 1935.

"Shirts and Wage Rates," *New York Times*, January 23, 1935.

"The Price of Credit," *New York Times*, January 24, 1935.

"Mr. Wallace's Proposal," *New York Times*, January 26, 1935.

"Blaming the Banks," *New York Times*, January 28, 1935.

"Capitalism not Suicidal," *New York Times*, January 30, 1935.

"If The Court Turn Thumbs Down," *The Nation*, January 30, 1935.

"Why Noise Continues," *New York Times*, January 31, 1935.

"German Debts and Trade," *New York Times*, February 1, 1935.

"The New Gold Deal," *New York Times*, February 2, 1935.

"Who Reads the Classics?" *New York Times*, February 3, 1935.

"A Bombardment of the New Deal," *New York Times*, February 3, 1935.

"Labor Betrayed," *New York Times*, February 4, 1935.

"Compelling Waste," *New York Times*, February 5, 1935.

"Literary Snobbery," *New York Times*, February 6, 1935.

"Of Their Own Choosing," *New York Times*, February 7, 1935.

"Debating Work Relief," *New York Times*, February 8, 1935.

"Canada's Insurance Plan," *New York Times*, February 9, 1935.

"Automobile and Labor," *New York Times*, February 9, 1935.

"Banking Improvement," *New York Times*, February 11, 1935.

"Tariff Lobbies," *New York Times*, February 12, 1935.

"1/8 of 1 Per Cent," *New York Times*, February 13, 1935.

"Credit Control," *New York Times*, February 14, 1935.

"Flat British Novels," *New York Times*, February 15, 1935.

"British Banks," *New York Times*, February 17, 1935.

"The 'Fixing' Evil," *New York Times*, February 18, 1935.

"Tearing Down Wages?" *New York Times*, February 19, 1935.

"The French Deficit," *New York Times*, February 23, 1935.

"Helping the Railroads," *New York Times*, February 25, 1935.

"The Too Improbable," *New York Times*, February 25, 1935.

"Up to the Country," *New York Times*, February 28, 1935.

"Circumstantial Evidence," *New York Times*, February 28, 1935.

"The German Boycott," *New York Times*, March 1, 1935.

"What It Will Cost," *New York Times*, March 4, 1935.

"Our Murder Record," *New York Times*, March 5, 1935.

"John Strachey on 'The Nature of the Capitalist Crisis'," *New York Times Book Review*, March 3, 1935.

"Argentina Prospers," *New York Times*, March 6, 1935.

"The Valley of Indecision," *New York Times*, March 8, 1935.

"Bank Liquidity," *New York Times*, March 11, 1935.

"Mr. Hull on Tariffs," *New York Times*, March 25, 1935.

"Kinds of Stabilization," *New York Times*, March 25, 1935.

"The NRA at Sea," *New York Times*, March 28, 1935.

"How to Swim," *New York Times*, March 29, 1935.

"The Byrne-Killgrew Bill," *New York Times*, March 30, 1935.

"The Railway Decision," *New York Times*, April 1, 1935.

"Dilemma of the NRA," *New York Times*, April 2, 1935.

"Tangle in Fire Hose," *New York Times*, April 3, 1935.

"Sunday on Broadway," *New York Times*, April 5, 1935.

"The Japanese 'Menace'," *New York Times*, April 5, 1935.

"Edwin Robinson," *New York Times*, April 7, 1935.

"Social Insurance Again," *New York Times*, April 8, 1935.

"State Job Insurance," *New York Times*, April 11, 1935.

"An Udder Question," *New York Times*, April 12, 1935.

"Title II," *New York Times*, April 12, 1935.

"Setback for Utopia," *New York Times*, April 13, 1935.

"The Thirty-Hour Week," *New York Times*, April 13, 1935.

"The 'Barbarous Relic'," *New York Times*, April 14, 1935.

"AAA in the Courts," *New York Times*, April 15, 1935.

"Art, Crime, and Profit," *New York Times*, April 17, 1935.

"South American Trade," *New York Times*, April 18, 1935.

"Japan and Cotton," *New York Times*, April 19, 1935.

"Locking the Stable," *New York Times*, April 20, 1945.

"Intemperate Retorts," *New York Times*, April 22, 1935.

"Meaning of Freedom," *New York Times*, April 23, 1945.

"Refusal of Credit," *New York Times*, April 25, 1935.

"Psychology of Deficits," *New York Times*, April 26, 1935.

"Workers' Insurance," *New York Times*, April 27, 1935.

"Politics and Banking," *New York Times*, April 29, 1935.

"Two Policies," *New York Times*, April 30, 1935.

"Tidying Up," *New York Times*, May 1, 1935.

"Mysteries of the Mind," *New York Times*, May 2, 1935.

"Wingless Blue Eagle," *New York Times*, May 3, 1935.

"British Taxes and Ours," *New York Times*, May 5, 1935.

"Kenneth Burke's Metaphysics," *New York Times Book Review*, May 5, 1935.

"Foreign Loans in Default," *New York Times*, May 6, 1935.

"Another Peek Scare," *New York Times*, May 7, 1935.

"Russia 'Plans'," *New York Times*, May 8, 1935.

"A Friendly Policy," *New York Times*, May 9, 1935.

"What Waitresses Get," *New York Times*, May 10, 1935.

"The Banking Bill," *New York Times*, May 11, 1935.

"Indexing of Labor Gains," *New York Times*, May 13, 1945.

"Relief and Work," *New York Times*, May 15, 1935.

"Social Security," *New York Times*, May 18, 1935.

"The Giant Airplane," *New York Times*, May 20, 1935.

"Memories of Holmes," *New York Times*, May 22, 1935.

"NRA at Bay," *New York Times*, May 23, 1935.

"Governing in Hard Times," *New York Times*, May 25, 1935.

"Pareto's Picture of Society: His Monumental Work Covers an Enormous Field of Knowledge" (on *The Mind and Society*), *New York Times*, May 26, 1935.

"Another Conference," *New York Times*, May 27, 1935.

"The Workers' Part," *New York Times*, May 30, 1935.

"Estimating Revenues," *New York Times*, June 1, 1935.

"Hopwood Awards," Speech at the University of Michigan, *New York Times*, June 1, 1935.

"Time for Faith" (from "As for the effect . . . " to "NIRA to a mere shell of its former self"), *New York Times*, June 2, 1935.

"Air Conditioning," *New York Times*, June 4, 1935.

"Ownership of Wealth," *New York Times*, June 5, 1935.

"Implacable Critics," *New York Times*, June 7, 1935.

"Taxing Inheritances," *New York Times*, June 8, 1935.

"Monopoly Under NIRA," *New York Times*, June 10, 1935.

"The Bank of France," *New York Times*, June 11, 1935.

"Hope for Pitts," *New York Times*, June 13, 1935.

"The Forty-Hour Week," *New York Times*, June 14, 1935.

"Color on the Screen," *New York Times*, June 15, 1935.

"The Social Security Bill," *New York Times*, June 17, 1933.

"The Payroll Tax," *New York Times*, June 18, 1935.

"Pitts May Play," *New York Times*, June 19, 1935.

"Collision 'Repeaters'," *New York Times*, June 19, 1935.

"What is 'Chiseling'?" *New York Times*, June 20, 1935.

"Tax Principles," *New York Times*, June 22, 1935.

"*The New America: The New World* by H.G. Wells," *New York Times Book Review, June 23, 1935.*

"Forty Hours in Principle," *New York Times*, June 25, 1935.

"Codes and the New NRA," *New York Times*, June 25, 1935.

"The Tax on Payrolls," *New York Times*, June 25, 1935.

"Abolishing Tax-Free Bonds," *New York Times*, June 26, 1935.

"Tax Yield 'Estimates'," *New York Times*, June 27, 1935.

"Regaining First Place," *New York Times*, June 27, 1935.

"Literature vs. Opinion," *Michigan Alumnus Quarterly Review*, June 29, 1935 (Summer).

"No More 'Hicks'," *New York Times*, June 29, 1935.

"Not a Revenue Measure," *New York Times*, June 29, 1935.

"Invention is a Trade," *New York Times*, June 30, 1935.

"What to Invent," *New York Times*, June 30, 1935.

"Prefabricated Housing," *New York Times*, July 1, 1935.

"Mr. Ritchie's Warning," *New York Times*, July 1, 1935.

"A Narrow Class Tax," *New York Times*, July 2, 1935.

"Vanishing American Tourists," *New York Times*, July 2, 1935.

"A Senseless Crime," *New York Times*, July 3, 1935.

"The Labor Disputes Bill," *New York Times*, July 3, 1935.

"Prevailing Wage Again," *New York Times*, July 4, 1935.

"Esperanto in Verse," *New York Times*, July 5, 1935.

"Wage Fixing," *New York Times*, July 5, 1935.

"Divorce in Russia," *New York Times*, July 7, 1945.

"The Two Helens," *New York Times*, July 8, 1935.

"Production for Use," *New York Times*, July 8, 1935.

"The 'Wealth Taxes'," *New York Times*, July 9, 1935.

"A Forest of Ifs," *New York Times*, July 9, 1935.

"Who Has Recovered Most?" *New York Times*, July 11, 1935.

"Rates and Yields," *New York Times*, July 12, 1935.

"The Crime of Consorting," *New York Times*, July 13, 1935.

"Dividends and Wages," *New York Times*, July 15, 1935.

"What Will Be Left," *New York Times*, July 16, 1935.

"Dilemma of Big Business," *New York Times*, July 17, 1935.

"The Jobless 'On Strike'," *New York Times*, July 18, 1935.

"An Invasion Repelled," *New York Times*, July 19, 1935.

"Another Gold Decision," *New York Times*, July 20, 1935.

"Start Them Young," *New York Times*, July 22, 1935.

"It's Dogged as Does It," *New York Times*, July 22, 1935.

"Retaliation," *New York Times*, July 22, 1935.

"The Morals of Lobbying," *New York Times*, July 23, 1935.

"Nuisance Coins," *New York Times*, July 24, 1935.

"Lewis Douglas Dissects The New Deal" (on *The Liberal Tradition*), *New York Times Book Review*, July 28, 1935.

"Italian Finances," *New York Times*, July 25, 1935.

"Shaw at 79," *New York Times*, July 26, 1935.

"The Import Alarmists," *New York Times*, July 26, 1935. Also *The Chattanooga Times*.

"Steel and the Tariff," *New York Times*, July 27, 1935.

"How Wealth is Shared," *New York Times*, July 28, 1935.

"Windows Should Open," *New York Times*, July 29, 1935.

"The Crisis in Holland," *New York Times*, July 30, 1935.

"The Tax Bill," *New York Times*, July 31, 1935.

"Taxing Corporations," *New York Times*, August 1, 1935.

"The Discount Rate," *New York Times*, August 2, 1935.

"Taxing Inheritances," *New York Times*, August 3, 1935.

"The New Encyclopedia," *New York Times*, August 5, 1935.

"A Timely Warning," *New York Times*, August 5, 1935.

"Childless Couples," *New York Times*, August 7, 1935.

"Our Income Tax," *New York Times*, August 7, 1935.

"A Lawyer's Defense," *New York Times*, August 8, 1935.

"The Tom Thumb Money," *New York Times*, August 9, 1935.

"If A Escapes, Hit B," *New York Times*, August 9, 1935.

"The Strike and Relief," *New York Times*, August 10, 1935.

"The Security Bill," *New York Times*, August 11, 1935.

"War on Noise," *New York Times*, August 13, 1935.

"The National Income," *New York Times*, August 14, 1935.

"Tax-Free Securities," *New York Times*, August 15, 1935.

"No Inheritance Tax," *New York Times*, August 16, 1935.

"Where Nations Buy," *New York Times*, August 17, 1935.

"What Labor Gets," *New York Times*, August 19, 1935.

"Dr. Schacht's Warning," *New York Times*, August 20, 1935.

"The Banking Bill," *New York Times*, August 21, 1935.

"The Tax Bill," *New York Times*, August 22, 1935.

"Training Relief Workers," *New York Times*, August 23, 1935.

"The Dilemma in Cotton," *New York Times*, August 24, 1935.

"Recovery Through Saving," *New York Times*, August 26, 1935.

"Reviving NRA?" *New York Times*, August 27, 1935.

"The Cotton Compromise," *New York Times*, August 28, 1935.

"An Expensive Tax," *New York Times*, August 29, 1935.

"Social Security Explained," *New York Times*, August 30, 1945.

"Budget Prophecy," *New York Times*, August 31, 1935.

"After Labor Day," *New York Times*, September 2, 1935.

"John Dewey's History and Analysis of 'Liberalism'," *New York Times Book Review*, September 1, 1935.

"Social Credit in Utopia," *New York Times*, September 2, 1935.

"A Difficult Assignment," *New York Times*, September 4, 1935.

"Our Dual Bank System," *New York Times*, September 5, 1935.

"Potato Control," *New York Times*, September 6, 1935.

"Depreciation and Exports," *New York Times*, September 7, 1935.

"The Secret of Happiness," *New York Times*, September 8, 1935.

"The Railroad Problem," *New York Times*, September 9, 1935.

"Relativity in Sports," *New York Times*, September 17, 1935.

"Parity Prices," *New York Times*, September 18, 1935.

"Prevailing Wages,"*New York Times*, September 21, 1935.

"The Government's Role in Business" (on Stuart Chase), *New York Times Book Review*, September 22, 1935.

"PWA and Employment," *New York Times*, September 22, 1935.

"Super-Natural?" *New York Times*, September 24, 1935.

"Inflation Not Imminent," *New York Times*, September 24, 1935.

"Recovery in Literature," *New York Times*, September 25, 1935.

"Protecting the Unfit," *New York Times*, September 27, 1935.

"Mr. Dawes's Discovery," *New York Times*, September 28, 1935.

"Employment Rises," *New York Times*, September 30, 1935.

"Fall of King Cotton," *Current History*, October 1935.

"Rising World Prices," *New York Times*, October 1, 1935.

"Licenses for Living," *New York Times*, October 2, 1935.

"Why Men Are Put to Work," *New York Times*, October 2, 1935.

"Fingerprinting for All," *New York Times*, October 4, 1935.

"Nazi Sleight-of-Hand," *New York Times*, October 5, 1935.

"Profits and Wages," *New York Times*, October 7, 1935.

"Dilemma of Relief Work," *New York Times*, October 8, 1935.

"Bertrand Russell's Essays," *New York Times*, October 8, 1935.

"Trade Control Flounders," *New York Times*, October 12, 1935.

"Diamonds," *New York Times*, October 13, 1935.

"Labor Savers," *New York Times*, October 15, 1935.

"The Week's Wage," *New York Times*, October 15, 1935.

"The Thirty-Hour Mirage," *New York Times*, October 16, 1935.

"$5,000,000 for Potatoes," *New York Times*, October 17, 1935.

"Subsidizing Exports," *New York Times*, October 19, 1935.

"*Our Enemy, The State*, by Albert Jay Nock," *New York Times Book Review*, October 20, 1935.

"Sphere of the State," *New York Times*, October 21, 1935.

"Questions About Indian Summer," *New York Times*, October 22, 1935.

"Creator of Andy Gump," *New York Times*, October 22, 1935.

"War and Economics," *New York Times*, October 22, 1935.

"Cities of Light," *New York Times*, October 23, 1935.

"Trade Contradictions," *New York Times*, October 25, 1935.

"Legend vs. the Camera," *New York Times*, October 26, 1935.

"Gains in Employment," *New York Times*, October 26, 1935.

"The Corn-Hog Vote," *New York Times*, October 28, 1935.

"Test Labor Cases," *New York Times*, October 29, 1935.

"Criminal Usurers," *New York Times*, October 30, 1935.

"English at Bay," *New York Times*, October 31, 1935.

"Subtleties," *New York Times*, November 1, 1935.

"Ever-Normal Granaries," *New York Times*, November 3, 1935.

" 'Helping' China," *New York Times*, November 4, 1935.

"Troubles of the WPA," *New York Times*, November 4, 1935.

"Letting the Rich Pay," *New York Times*, November 5, 1935.

"Death on the Highway," *New York Times*, November 6, 1935.

"No New NRA," *New York Times*, November 7, 1935.

"A Bank Under Fire," *New York Times*, November 9, 1935.

"The Silver Rainbow," *New York Times*, November 10, 1935.

"Crowds for Art," *New York Times*, November 11, 1935.

"Loaded Questions," *New York Times*, November 12, 1935.

"Little NRA in Court,"*New York Times*, November 16, 1935.

"Reciprocity," *New York Times*, November 18, 1935.

"Eternal Breathing," *New York Times*, November 19, 1935.

"Efficiency and Welfare," *New York Times*, November 20, 1935.

"Lumber, the Lamb," *New York Times*, November 23, 1935.

"Amateur Economists," *New York Times*, November 24, 1935.

"Which Form of Union?" *New York Times*, November 25, 1935.

"Budget Problems," *New York Times*, November 26, 1935.

"Legislating Lawsuits," *New York Times*, November 27, 1935.

"Better Times and Workers," *New York Times*, November 29, 1935.

"Social Insurance Defects," *New York Times*, December 1, 1935.

"Census of Unemployed Needed for Planning," *New York Times*, December 1, 1935.

"Wages of Waitresses," *New York Times*, December 2, 1935.

"Incidence of a Tax," *New York Times*, December 3, 1935.

"Imports and Revival," *New York Times*, December 4, 1935.

"Counting the Jobless," *New York Times*, December 5, 1935.

"Temperance in Criticism," *New York Times*, December 6, 1935.

"Incomes in 1934," *New York Times*, December 7, 1935.

"Mr. Peck as Historian," *New York Times*, December 9, 1935.

"The Scale of Errors," *New York Times*, December 10, 1935.

"German Trade and Debts," *New York Times*, December 11, 1935.

"Reprieve for Cotton," *New York Times*, December 13, 1945.

"Gold and Stabilization," *New York Times*, December 14, 1935.

"Social Security Cost," *New York Times*, December 15, 1935.

"What We Get For the Outlay," *New York Times*, December 16, 1935.

"An Unemployment Census," *New York Times*, December 17, 1935.

"Manual Workers," *New York Times*, December 22, 1935.

"Townsend's Plan Explained and Analyzed," *New York Times*, December 22, 1935.

"Bertrand Russell Challenges the New Intolerance," *New York Times Book Review*, December 29, 1935.

"Religions of Reform," *New York Times*, December 29, 1935.

"Warren on the AAA," *New York Times*, December 30, 1935.

1936

"The Scottsboro Case," *New York Times*, January 25, 1936.

"Ickes on Public Works," *New York Times*, January 27, 1936.

"A Portrait of Voltaire, Foe of All Bigots" (on Brailsford), *New York Times Book Review*, February 2, 1936.

"Industry's Refusal," *New York Times*, February 7, 1936.

"The Price of Favors," *New York Times*, February 10, 1936.

"A Senator 'Speaks Out'," *New York Times*, February 12, 1936.

"Consumer Protection," *New York Times*, February 13, 1936.

"Social Security Payments," *New York Times*, February 15, 1936.

"Morris and the AAA," *New York Times*, February 17, 1936.

"Pensions and Lobbyists," *New York Times*, February 18, 1936.

"The 'Chain-Store' Bill," *New York Times*, February 19, 1936.

"What the Court 'Obstructs'," *New York Times*, February 21, 1936.

"The 'Travel' Mark," *New York Times*, February 22, 1936.

"Machinery and Welfare," *New York Times*, February 23, 1936.

"Income by Legislation," *New York Times*, February 24, 1936.

"Mortgage Moratorium," *New York Times*, February 24, 1936.

"Utilities and the Law," *New York Times*, February 25, 1936.

"State Job Insurance," *New York Times*, February 27, 1936.

"Financial Home Rule," *New York Times*, February 28, 1936.

"The Slash in Rates," *New York Times*, February 29, 1936.

"William Gillette Returns," *New York Times*, February 29, 1936.

"Bus Regulation," *New York Times*, March 3, 1936.

"The New Farm Law," *New York Times*, March 3, 1936.

"Social Legislation," *New York Times*, March 4, 1936.

"The Minimum Wage Law," *New York Times*, March 5, 1936.

"Accidents and Speed," *New York Times*, March 6, 1936.

"Taxes vs. Expansion," *New York Times*, March 7, 1936.

"The 'Decay' of Congress," *New York Times*, March 9, 1936.

"Driving out Surpluses," *New York Times*, March 11, 1936.

"A Possible Compromise," *New York Times*, March 12, 1936.

"City Provincialism," *New York Times*, March 13, 1936.

"Punishing Prudence," *New York Times*, March 13, 1936.

"Advertising WPA," *New York Times*, March 14, 1936.

"Rentals for Paintings," *New York Times*, March 14, 1936.

"In Its Financial Section Today . . .," *New York Times*, March 15, 1936.

"Unemployment Insurance," *New York Times*, March 15, 1936.

"Reducing Accidents," *New York Times*, March 16, 1936.

"The New Tax Schedule," *New York Times*, March 17, 1936.

"Britain's Betting Industry," *New York Times*, March 18, 1936.

"Labor Facts and Theories," *New York Times*, March 18, 1936.

"The Townsendites," *New York Times Book Review*, March 22, 1936.

"Equality of Taxation," *New York Times*, March 20, 1936.

"Slums and Low Wages," *New York Times*, March 21, 1936.

"Old-Age Pensions," *New York Times*, March 22, 1936.

"Taxes in Deep Water," *New York Times*, March 22, 1936.

" 'Abstract' Art," *New York Times*, March 23, 1936.

"The Right to Privacy," *New York Times*, March 24, 1936.

"Answering Questions," *New York Times*, March 25, 1936.

"The Labor Disputes Act," *New York Times*, March 26, 1936.

"Election-Year Taxes," *New York Times*, March 27, 1936.

"Money Velocity," *New York Times*, March 28, 1936.

"Accident Compensation," *New York Times*, March 29, 1936.

"Job Insurance," *New York Times*, March 30, 1936.

"Politician's Paradise," *New York Times*, March 31, 1936.

"Prince-and-Pauper Tax," *New York Times*, April 1, 1936.

"Britain's Surplus," *New York Times*, April 2, 1936.

"The Surplus Tax," *New York Times*, April 3, 1936.

"The Lyons Bill," *New York Times*, April 4, 1936.

"Production and Jobs," *New York Times*, April 5, 1936.

"The Housing Bill," *New York Times*, April 6, 1936.

"Big Money from the AAA," *New York Times*, April 7, 1936.

"The Ship and the Rats," *New York Times*, April 8, 1936.

"The Spread of the Ghost," *New York Times*, April 8, 1936.

"The Relief Problem," *New York Times*, April 9, 1936.

"The Village Green," *New York Times*, April 9, 1936.

"Court and Committee," *New York Times*, April 19, 1936.

"Relief Still Rises," *New York Times*, April 13, 1936.

"Quest of the Davis Cup," *New York Times*, April 13, 1936.

"Tax Riddles," *New York Times*, April 15, 1936.

"Tariff 'Publicity'," *New York Times*, April 16, 1936.

"Job Insurance," *New York Times*, April 17, 1936.

"A Dangerous Measure," *New York Times*, April 18, 1936.

"The Liggett Case," *New York Times*, April 18, 1936.

"Governments and Prices," *New York Times*, April 19, 1936.

"German Private Bonds," *New York Times*, April 20, 1936.

"The Dismissal Wage," *New York Times*, April 22, 1936.

"Simplified Taxes," *New York Times*, April 23, 1936.

"Another 'Death Penalty'," *New York Times*, April 25, 1936.

"Private Pension Plans," *New York Times*, April 26, 1936.

"Unemployment Amid Recovery: Vast Riddle," *New York Times*, April 26, 1936.

"Corporations and Labor," *New York Times*, April 27, 1936.

"What is 'Unemployment'?" *New York Times*, April 28, 1936.

"Railroad Advance," *New York Times*, April 30, 1936.

"On the Senate's Lap," *New York Times*, April 30, 1936.

"Job Insurance Taxes," *New York Times*, May 1, 1936.

"A 1924 Tax Bill," *New York Times*, May 2, 1936.

"Against Chain Stores," *New York Times*, May 3, 1936.

"A Compromise Tax Bill," *New York Times*, May 4, 1936.

"Refusing Federal Funds," *New York Times*, May 6, 1936.

"Reserves for the Future," *New York Times*, May 7, 1936.

"A Huge Gamble," *New York Times*, May 8, 1936.

"Oswald Spengler," *New York Times*, May 9, 1936.

"How Many Jobless," *New York Times*, May 10, 1936.

"Franchise Tax Due May 15," *New York Times*, May 11, 1936.

"Do We Save Too Much?" *New York Times*, May 12, 1936.

"The Governor's Program," *New York Times*, May 13, 1936.

"Revising the Tax Bill," *New York Times*, May 14, 1936.

"Senate Tax Changes," *New York Times*, May 18, 1936.

"Jobs, Profits, Output," *New York Times*, May 20, 1936.

"High Hourly Wages," *New York Times*, May 21, 1936.

"Twilight of Utopia," *New York Times*, May 22, 1936.

"A Backward Step," *New York Times*, May 23, 1936.

"Biography as an Art," *New York Times*, May 24, 1936.

"Taxes and Votes," *New York Times*, May 25, 1936.

"Progress and Jobs," *New York Times*, May 27, 1936.

"A Ruinous Principle," *New York Times*, May 28, 1936.

"Rising Employment," *New York Times*, May 29, 1936.

"The Senate Tax Bill," *New York Times*, May 30, 1936.

"Lower Railroad Fares," *New York Times*, June 1, 1936.

"The Minimum Wage Case," *New York Times*, June 2, 1936.

"How Not to Levy Taxes," *New York Times*, June 3, 1936.

"Principles and Yields," *New York Times*, June 4, 1936.

"Time to Consider," *New York Times*, June 5, 1936.

"Subsidized Exports," *New York Times*, June 6, 1936.

"The Perils That Face Social Security," *New York Times Book Review*, June 7, 1936.

"Hopkins on the Critics," *New York Times*, June 8, 1936.

"Tax Bill Compromise," *New York Times*, June 9, 1936.

"Future of the Franc," *New York Times*, June 10, 1936.

"An Unplanned Shortage," *New York Times*, June 11, 1936.

"How Many Unemployed?" *New York Times*, June 12, 1936.

"G. K. Chesterton," *New York Times*, June 15, 1936.

"The Small Corporation," *New York Times*, June 16, 1936.

"Labor As a Commodity," *New York Times*, June 17, 1936.

"Compromising A Compromise," *New York Times*, June 18, 1936.

"Penalizing Production," *New York Times*, June 20, 1936.

"Consequences of Congress," *New York Times*, June 22, 1936.

"Reversing a Price Policy," *New York Times*, June 23, 1936.

"Gains in Employment," *New York Times*, June 24, 1936.

"The Back-Door NRA," *New York Times*, June 25, 1936.

"Agricultural 'Slums'," *New York Times*, June 28, 1936.

"Future Federal Taxes," *New York Times*, July 5, 1936.

"Deathbed Repentance?" *New York Times*, July 8, 1936.

"The Number of Jobs," *New York Times*, July 11, 1936.

"New York's Fiscal Maze," *New York Times*, July 11, 1936.

"The Capital Gains Tax," *New York Times*, July 12, 1936.

"Low Fares Succeeding," *New York Times*, July 15, 1936.

"Sun-spots Again," *New York Times*, July 16, 1936.

"Sun in the News," *New York Times*, July 16, 1936.

"The Costs of Housing," *New York Times Book Review*, July 12, 1936.

"Death on the Road," *New York Times*, July 19, 1936.

"'Anti Chain-Store' Law," *New York Times*, July 19, 1936.

"Bank of France Reforms," *New York Times*, July 20, 1936.

"The Long Island Loses," *New York Times*, July 29, 1936.

"Two-Sided Trade," *New York Times*, July 21, 1936.

"Barbarous Barter," *New York Times*, July 25, 1936.

"The All-Steel Home," *New York Times*, July 25, 1936.

"World Wheat Shortage?" *New York Times*, July 27, 1936.

"The 'New' Economics," *New York Times*, July 27, 1936.

"England Retains the Cup," *New York Times*, July 29, 1936.

"Hand and Brain," *New York Times*, July 30, 1936.

"Governments Bailing Out," *New York Times*, July 31, 1936.

"On Being Misunderstood," *New York Times*, August 1, 1936.

"Is England Against Gold?" *New York Times*, August 3, 1936.

"The Ill Wind Blows Good," *New York Times*, August 3, 1936.

"A Pioneer 'Birdman'," *New York Times*, August 4, 1936.

"Limiting Incomes," *New York Times*, August 5, 1936.

"Murder in Minneapolis," *New York Times*, August 7, 1936.

"Here Comes the Trailer," *New York Times*, August 8, 1936.

"Unfit for Automobiles," *New York Times*, August 9, 1936.

"Our Trade With Germany," *New York Times*, August 9, 1936.

"'P. R.' For New York," *New York Times*, August 10, 1936.

"Germany's Olympic Triumph," *New York Times*, August 18, 1936.

"Social Security Problems," *New York Times*, August 19, 1936.

"Crop Insurance," *New York Times*, August 22, 1936.

"The Japanese Bugaboo," *New York Times*, August 23, 1936.

"Alberta's Stage Money," *New York Times*, August 23, 1936.

"Governor Olson," *New York Times*, August 24, 1936.

"The Housing Problem," *New York Times*, August 24, 1936.

"The Patman Law Fog," *New York Times*, August 26, 1936.

"Landon on Taxation," *New York Times*, August 27, 1936.

"Jersey Justice?" *New York Times*, August 28, 1936.

"International Wage Pacts," *New York Times*, August 28, 1936.

"New Plants—And a New Tax," *New York Times*, August 29, 1936.

"Motor Deaths Rise Again," *New York Times*, August 29, 1936.

"The 'Truth' about Taxes," *New York Times*, August 31, 1936.

"Some WPA Achievements," *New York Times*, September 1, 1936.

"Mechanical Cotton Picker," *New York Times*, September 2, 1936.

"The Budget Problem," *New York Times*, September 3, 1936.

"The Surplus Tax," *New York Times*, September 5, 1936.

"Our 'National Income'," *New York Times*, September 6, 1936.

"Labor: The Two Roads," *New York Times*, September 7, 1936.

"How Many Unemployed," *New York Times*, September 8, 1936.

"The 'Prevailing Wage'," *New York Times*, September 10, 1936.

"Not Fit for the Ears of Queens," *New York Times*, September 11, 1936.

"Machines and Jobs," *New York Times*, September 13, 1936.

"New Queen of the Courts," *New York Times*, September 14, 1936.

"Mr. Laski Moves Left" (on *The Rise of Liberalism*), *New York Times Book Review*, September 13, 1936.

"The Anatomy of Fascism," *New York Times*, September 15, 1936.

"New Jersey's Own Plan," *New York Times*, September 16, 1936.

"Charting Our Abilities," *New York Times*, September 19, 1936.

"Tablecloth Writing Analyzed," *New York Times*, September 19, 1936.

"Another Liberty Threatened," *New York Times*, September 19, 1936.

"Left-Handed Regulation," *New York Times*, September 20, 1936.

"A Case for Capitalism," *New York Times*, September 20, 1936.

"Gold vs. Gold Coin," *New York Times*, September 21, 1936.

"Uniform Traffic Fines," *New York Times*, September 22, 1936.

"The Banker and Reform," *New York Times*, September 23, 1936.

"Employment Slowly Gains," *New York Times*, September 24, 1936.

"A Lot of Smoking," *New York Times*, September 23, 1936.

"Economists Keep 'Failing'," *New York Times*, September 23, 1936.

"Architecture as Our 'Chief Art'," *New York Times*, September 25, 1936.

"Cost of Old-Age Pensions," *New York Times*, September 27, 1936.

"Production for Use," *New York Times*, September 27, 1936.

"And Production for Profit," *New York Times*, September 27, 1936.

"Landon on Social Security," *New York Times*, September 28, 1936.

"An Instructive Reply," *New York Times*, September 28, 1936.

"Before Stabilization," *New York Times*, September 30, 1936.

"Security in Politics," *New York Times*, October 2, 1936.

"Restoring Monetary Order," *New York Times*, October 4, 1936.

"Low Fares Spread,' *New York Times*, October 4, 1936.

"France Cuts Tariffs," *New York Times*, October 5, 1936.

"Lehman's Budget Estimates," *New York Times*, October 7, 1936.

"The Return to Gold," *New York Times*, October 8, 1936.

"Rectifying a Bad Tax," *New York Times*, October 14, 1936.

"Uniform Fines," *New York Times*, October 15, 1936.

"Models in the Schools," *New York Times*, October 17, 1936.

"Hourly vs. Annual Wages," *New York Times*, October 17, 1936.

"Liberal and Communist," *New York Times*, October 18, 1936.

"The Outlook for Jobs," *New York Times*, October 18, 1936.

"Driving Markets Abroad?" *New York Times*, October 19, 1936.

"The President on Taxes," *New York Times*, October 23, 1936.

"That 'Pay Deduction'," *New York Times*, October 27, 1936.

"Crop Insurance," *New York Times*, October 28, 1936.

"Debt and National Income," *New York Times*, October 28, 1936.

"Case for 'Telepathy'," *New York Times*, October 28, 1936.

"Fatigue a Factor," *New York Times*, October 28, 1936.

"Self-Imposed Quotas," *New York Times*, October 31, 1936.

"Who Pays Taxes," *New York Times*, November 1, 1936.

"The Odds on the Odds," *New York Times*, November 2, 1936.

"The Genius of George Santayana," *New York Times Book Review*, November 1, 1936.

"Punishing Chain Stores," *New York Times*, November 6, 1936.

"Old-Age Insurance Begins," *New York Times*, November 8, 1936.

"More Factories," *New York Times*, November 9, 1936.

"Militarism and Trade," *New York Times*, November 10, 1936.

"Perry As a 'Pro'," *New York Times*, November 11, 1936.

"Investment Trust Control," *New York Times*, November 12, 1936.

"Automobile-Making Jobs," *New York Times*, November 14, 1936.

"Foreign Money Here," *New York Times*, November 16, 1936.

"The Capital Gains Tax and the Market," *New York Times*, November 17, 1936.

"A Census of the Jobless," *New York Times*, November 18, 1936.

"The Chosen Half," *New York Times*, November 19, 1936.

"What Farmers Get," *New York Times*, November 21, 1936.

"Rising World Prices," *New York Times*, November 22, 1936.

"Stolen Coal," *New York Times*, November 24, 1936.

"The Gold Policy," *New York Times*, November 25, 1936.

"What is 'Telepathy'?" *New York Times*, November 28, 1936.

"Mr. Green's Proposals," *New York Times*, November 28, 1936.

"Concerning the Future of Liberty" (on George Soule), *New York Times Book Review*, November 29, 1936.

"Labor Since the NRA," *New York Times*, November 30, 1936.

"State vs. Federal Taxes," *New York Times*, December 1, 1936.

"Hangmen's Economics," *New York Times*, December 3, 1936.

"The Capital Gains Tax," *New York Times*, December 5, 1936.

"State Job Insurance," *New York Times*, December 8, 1936.

"Books of the Times" (on H. F. Armstong's defense of Mussolini), *New York Times*, December 8, 1936.

"Books of the Times" (on J. Strachey's *Theory and Practice of Socialism*), *New York Times*, December 9, 1936.

"Books of the Times" (on Dorothy Parker), *New York Times*, December 11, 1936.

"Books of the Times" (on Charles M. Andrews's historical work), *New York Times*, December 15, 1936.

"Books of the Times," (on Paul Gauguin's journals), *New York Times*, December 16, 1936.

"Books of the Times" (on Sheldon and Martha Cheney's *Art and the Machine*), December 18, 1936.

"Books of the Times" (on E. S. West's biography of Thomas De Quincey), *New York Times*, December 19, 1936.

"The Rate Decision," *New York Times*, December 21, 1936.

"Where Were the Police?" *New York Times*, December 23, 1936.

"Mrs. Einstein," *New York Times*, December 23, 1936.

"The Job Problem," *New York Times*, December 24, 1936.

"Wheat Insurance," *New York Times*, December 25, 1936.

"At Least $3,600 A Year," *New York Times*, December 28, 1936.

"The Surplus Tax," *New York Times*, December 28, 1936.

"Unjust and Needless," *New York Times*, December 29, 1936.

"I.C.C. vs. the Treasury," *New York Times*, December 30, 1936.

"An Unemployment Cure," *New York Times*, December 30, 1936.

"Curtailing Public Works," *New York Times*, December 31, 1936.

1937

"Mr. Huxley's Message," *The Modern Monthly*, January 1937.

"Enforcing Labor Agreements," *New York Times*, January 1, 1937.

"Sit-Down," *New York Times*, January 2, 1937.

"The Case of Glenn Frank," *New York Times*, January 4, 1937.

"The Surplus Tax," *New York Times*, January 5, 1937.

"An Angry Labor Board," *New York Times*, January 6, 1937.

"Mortgage Moratorium," *New York Times*, January 8, 1937.

"Books of the Times" (on J. P. Senning on the *One-House Legislature*), *New York Times*, January 7, 1937.

"The Glenn Frank Case," *New York Times*, January 10, 1937.

"Social Awareness," *New York Times*, January 11, 1937.

"Hours, Jobs, and Welfare," *New York Times*, January 13, 1937.

"The 'Modern' Mind," *New York Times*, January 13, 1937.

"The Salary List," *New York Times*, January 15, 1937.

"Bury the Gold Down Deep," *New York Times*, January 16, 1937.

"Cheap Power and Fair Play," *New York Times*, January 18, 1937.

"'Amateur' Snobbery," *New York Times*, January 20, 1937.

"One-Man Townsend Plan," *New York Times*, January 24, 1937.

"Child Labor," *New York Times*, January 22, 1937.

"Freedom of Assembly," *New York Times*, January 23, 1937.

"Surreal Insanity," *New York Times*, January 24, 1937.

"1929 Employment Reached," *New York Times*, January 25, 1937.

"Up to Albany," *New York Times*, January 26, 1937.

"An Agreement with Japan," *New York Times*, January 22, 1937.

"Business Concentration," *New York Times*, January 29, 1937.

"Communism and Socialism," *New York Times*, January 30, 1937.

"Controlling Credit," *New York Times*, February 1, 1937.

"The Mayor's Ambiguous Praise," *New York Times*, February 1, 1937.

"Death by Automobile," *New York Times*, February 2, 1937.

"Wage and Hour Laws," *New York Times*, February 3, 1937.

"Courses in 'Living'," *New York Times*, February 3, 1937.

"Our Dual Banking System," *New York Times*, February 4, 1937.

"Two Kinds of 'Winter'," *New York Times*, February 4, 1937.

"Restoring City Salaries," *New York Times*, February 5, 1937.

"Profits in Britain," *New York Times*, February 6, 1937.

"Brookings Report on Recovery," *New York Times Book Review*, February 7, 1937.

"Cures for Slumps,"*New York Times*, February 7, 1937.

"Mussolini vs. Capitalism," *New York Times*, February 8, 1937.

"State Social Security," *New York Times*, February 12, 1937.

"Tenant Farm Problem," *New York Times*, February 14, 1937.

"Wage Increases," *New York Times*, February 16, 1937.

"City's Capital Outlays," *New York Times*, February 17, 1937.

"The Here-And-There NRA," *New York Times*, February 18, 1937.

"Crop Insurance," *New York Times*, February 19, 1937.

"175,000 Tax Units," *New York Times*, February 20, 1937.

"Keeping Genius Out," *New York Times*, February 21, 1937.

"New Traffic Code," *New York Times*, February 22, 1937.

"The Empire's 'Supreme' Court," *New York Times*, February 23, 1937.

"Child Labor," *New York Times*, February 24, 1937.

"Wages and the Railroads," *New York Times*, February 25, 1937.

"British-American Trade," *New York Times*, February 26, 1937.

"Metaphysics of Traffic," *New York Times*, February 27, 1937.

"Child Labor Powers," *New York Times*, February 28, 1937.

"Altering Old Tenements," *New York Times*, March 1, 1937.

"Gold Bullion Contracts," *New York Times*, March 2, 1937.

"Bad Food, Bad Temper," *New York Times*, March 2, 1937.

"Regulating Sugar," *New York Times*, March 3, 1937.

"Germany's Economy," *New York Times*, March 4, 1937.

"Population Circle," *New York Times*, March 5, 1937.

"A Desirable Change," *New York Times*, March 5, 1937.

"The Wage-Price Spiral," *New York Times*, March 7, 1937.

"Method of Amendment" *New York Times*, March 7, 1937.

"Protecting Our Children," *New York Times*, March 8, 1937.

"Another 'Franc Crisis'," *New York Times*, March 9, 1937.

"Australia's Constitution," *New York Times*, March 9, 1937.

"Mortgage Moratorium," *New York Times*, March 10, 1937.

"Resale Price Fixing," *New York Times*, March 12, 1937.

"Child Labor: What Now?" *New York Times*, March 12, 1937.

"Price-Fixing in Coal," *New York Times*, March 13, 1937.

"Dykstra at Wisconsin," *New York Times*, March 14, 1937.

"Child Labor Laws," *New York Times*, March 15, 1937.

"Economics of Sugar," *New York Times*, March 16, 1937.

"Preventing Inflation," *New York Times*, March 17, 1937.

"Railroad Pensions," *New York Times*, March 18, 1937.

"Revising Job Insurance," *New York Times*, March 19, 1937.

"The Control of Inflation," *New York Times*, March 21, 1937.

"Politics and the Schools," *New York Times*, March 23, 1937.

"The Dilemmas of Relief," *New York Times*, March 24, 1937.

"Boom-and-Slump Control," *New York Times*, March 25, 1937.

"To End Child Labor," *New York Times*, March 26, 1937.

"Stretching the Postal Power," *New York Times*, March 27, 1937.

"Scattered Disaster," *New York Times*, March 29, 1937.

"The Future of Unemployment," *New York Times*, March 29, 1937.

"Legalizing the Sit-Down," *New York Times*, March 30, 1937.

"Mr. Vandenberg's Amendment," *New York Times*, March 30, 1937.

"Why Factories Leave," *New York Times*, April 2, 1937.

"A 'Boom' in Durable Goods," *New York Times*, April 3, 1937.

"The Egg, the Tack and the Fair," *New York Times*, April 3, 1937.

"Court Reversals," *New York Times*, April 4, 1937.

"Discretion for Juries," *New York Times*, April 5, 1937.

"The Business of Relief," *New York Times*, April 5, 1937.

"A Permanent CCC," *New York Times*, April 6, 1937.

"Clarity on the Sit-Down," *New York Times*, April 7, 1937.

"To Diminish Labor Disputes," *New York Times*, April 8, 1937.

"That Gasoline Tax," *New York Times*, April 9, 1937.

"Divided Policies," *New York Times*, April 11, 1937.

"Sauce for Goose Only," *New York Times*, April 12, 1937.

"The Creation of Jobs," *New York Times*, April 14, 1937.

"State Relief Taxes," *New York Times*, April 14, 1937.

"Freedom of the Press," *New York Times*, April 15, 1937.

"Red Baiting," *New York Times*, April 17, 1937.

"To Settle Labor Disputes," *New York Times*, April 18, 1937.

"Purchasing Power," *New York Times*, April 19, 1937.

"Why Not a Census," *New York Times*, April 20, 1937.

"Britain's Budget," *New York Times*, April 21, 1937.

"The World's Fair," *New York Times*, April 22, 1937.

"Politics in Education," *New York Times*, April 24, 1937.

"Labor Relations," *New York Times*, April 26, 1937.

"Taxing Corporations," *New York Times*, April 23, 1937.

"An Employment Census," *New York Times*, April 27, 1937.

"Two Experiments in Coal," *New York Times*, April 28, 1937.

"A Check on Peeping Toms," *New York Times*, April 29, 1931.

"The Minimum Wage Law," *New York Times*, April 30, 1937.

"Barring Child Labor," *New York Times*, April 30, 1937.

"The Need for Stability," *New York Times*, May 2, 1937.

"Mediation Boards," *New York Times*, May 3, 1937.

"The Sugar Quotas," *New York Times*, May 4, 1937.

"Labor Arbitrators," *New York Times*, May 4, 1937.

"The Guggenheim Committee," *New York Times*, May 6, 1937.

"The Wheeler-Johnson Bill," *New York Times*, May 6, 1937.

"Higher Than in 1929," *New York Times*, May 7, 1937.

"The Sugar Agreement," *New York Times*, May 8, 1937.

"The Capital Gains Tax," *New York Times*, May 9, 1937.

"The Record at Albany," *New York Times*, May 10, 1937.

"Mortgage Banks," *New York Times*, May 11, 1937.

"Reforming Relief," *New York Times*, May 12, 1937.

"A Threat to the Stage," *New York Times*, May 13, 1937.

"Measuring 'Unemployment'," *New York Times*, May 15, 1937.

"A Private Pension Plan," *New York Times*, May 15, 1937.

"To End Poverty," *New York Times*, May 17, 1937.

"One-Man Censorship," *New York Times*, May 18, 1937.

"Taxing Chain Stores," *New York Times*, May 19, 1937.

"An Admirable Veto," *New York Times*, May 20, 1937.

"For Improving Tenements," *New York Times*, May 20,1937

"That Ever-Normal Granary," *New York Times*, May 21, 1937.

"Milk Price Fixing," *New York Times*, May 22, 1937.

"Capital-Gains Tax," *New York Times*, May 22, 1937.

"Madariaga's View of Aristocracy," *New York Times Book Review*, May 23, 1937.

"Labor and Management," *New York Times*, May 24, 1937.

"Federal Wage-and-Hour Controls," *New York Times*, May 25, 1937.

"The New NRA" (parts II and II only), *New York Times*, May 26, 1937.

"Security Reforms," *New York Times*, May 27, 1937.

"Tax Evasion," *New York Times*, May 29, 1937.

"Delegation—and Pressure," *New York Times*, May 31, 1937.

"Separate Child-Labor Bill," *New York Times*, June 7, 1937.

"How to Pay for Housing," *New York Times*, June 10, 1937.

"Our Farm Policy" (except "3"), *New York Times*, June 13, 1937.

"The Reform of Relief," *New York Times*, June 14, 1937.

"War Debt Day," *New York Times*, June 15, 1937.

"National Income," *New York Times*, June 15, 1937.

"Regulate Everything," *New York Times*, June 16, 1937.

"Income and the Budget," *New York Times*, June 17, 1937.

"Socializing War Plants," *New York Times*, June 20, 1937.

"High Taxes vs. Revenues," *New York Times*, June 22, 1937.

"More Blank-Check Relief," *New York Times*, June 23, 1937.

"Senators and Relief," *New York Times*, June 4, 1937.

"To End Child Labor," *New York Times*, June 24, 1937.

"How Not to Levy Taxes," *New York Times*, June 25, 1937.

"Railroad Pensions," *New York Times*, June 26, 1937.

"Labor and Production," *New York Times*, June 27, 1937.

"Mexico 'Socializes'," *New York Times*, June 28, 1937.

"France's Financial Crisis," *New York Times*, June 30, 1937.

"A Disappointing Statement," *New York Times*, July 1, 1937.

"Frank A. Vanderlip," *New York Times*, July 1, 1937.

"More for Milk," *New York Times*, July 2, 1937.

"Mr. Donald Budge," *New York Times*, July 3, 1937.

"Riots and Relief," *New York Times*, July 3, 1937.

"To Revise the Labor Law," *New York Times*, July 5, 1937.

"The Ethics of Taxation," *New York Times*, July 6, 1937.

"The Need for Building," *New York Times*, July 7, 1937.

"An Ever-Political Granary," *New York Times*, July 8, 1937.

"Personal Depreciation," *New York Times*, July 9, 1937.

"Life in the A. F. of L.," *New York Times*, July 9, 1937.

" 'Burlesque' into ' Variety'," *New York Times*, July 12, 1937.

"The New Wage-Hour Bill," *New York Times*, July 12, 1937.

"Our Bumper Wheat Crop," *New York Times*, July 13, 1937.

"A Good Veto," *New York Times*, July 13, 1937.

"Penalizing Sound Management," *New York Times*, July 14, 1937.

"Economy Loses Again," *New York Times*, July 15, 1937.

"Plugging the Loopholes," *New York Times*, July 18, 1937.

"Minimum Wage and the Tariff," *New York Times*, July 19, 1937.

"H. Parker Willis" (on his death), *New York Times*, July 20, 1937.

"Machines and Jobs," *New York Times*, July 20, 1937.

"Nearing the Cup," *New York Times*, July 21, 1937.

"Labor-Rackets and the Law," *New York Times*, July 22 1937.

"The Memorial Day Riot," *New York Times*, July 24, 1937.

"Mr. Wagner and Labor," *New York Times*, July 25, 1937.

"Housing in France," *New York Times*, July 31, 1937.

"Economic Planning as a Panacea" (on Lionel Robbins), *New York Times Book Review*, August 1, 1937.

"A Count of the Jobless," *New York Times*, August 10, 1937.

"Fixing Wages in the Dark," *New York Times*, August 11, 1937.

"The Dread of Plenty," *New York Times*, August 12, 1937.

"Bitterness in Sugar," *New York Times*, August 13, 1937.

"Time for Thought," *New York Times*, August 15, 1937.

"WPA in New York City," *New York Times*, August 16, 1937.

"A Dangerous Program," *New York Times*, August 16, 1937.

"Another Unsound Tax," *New York Times*, August 17, 1937.

"The Two Housing Bills," *New York Times*, August 18, 1937.

"A Timely Warning," *New York Times*, August 19, 1937.

"New York's Hands Are Tied," *New York Times*, August 20, 1937.

"Do or Die—Or Default," *New York Times*, August 21, 1937.

"Congress Between Sessions," *New York Times*, August 23, 1937.

"A New Start on Housing," *New York Times*, August 24, 1937.

"New York Regains Power," *New York Times*, August 25, 1937.

"Milk Goes Up Again," *New York Times*, August 25, 1937.

"A 'Census'—of What?" *New York Times*, August 26, 1937.

"Railway Wage Demands," *New York Times*, August 27, 1937.

"Our Cotton Revolution," *New York Times*, August 29, 1937.

"Mass Purchasing Power," *New York Times*, August 30, 1937.

"An Encouraging Veto," *New York Times*, August 30, 1937.

Stilt Under Cotton," *New York Times*, August 31, 1937.

"A Worthless 'Census'," *New York Times*, September 1, 1937.

"Victims of Propaganda," *New York Times*, September 1, 1937.

"Toward Better Housing," *New York Times*, September 3, 1937.

"Sugar Under Control," *New York Times*, September 3, 1937.

"Tax Penalty on Marriage," *New York Times*, September 4, 1937.

"Subsidizing Scarcity," *New York Times*, September 6, 1937.

"The Right to Strike," *New York Times*, September 8, 1937.

"Germany's Planned Economy," *New York Times*, September 9, 1937.

"Jobless Poll Day," *New York Times*, September 11, 1937.

"American Imports Genius," *New York Times*, September 12, 1937.

"The Labor Board Disposes," *New York Times*, September 19, 1937.

"The Mayor States the Issue," *New York Times*, September 14, 1937.

"The Load of Taxation," *New York Times*, September 15, 1937.

"Why the Franc Falls," *New York Times*, September 17, 1937.

"More Crop Reduction," *New York Times*, September 19, 1937.

"Communism in Practice," *New York Times*, September 20, 1937.

"Competition vs. Control," *New York Times*, September 21, 1937.

"B.M.T. and the Public," *New York Times*, September 18, 1937.

"Courageous Resignations," *New York Times*, September 18, 1937.

" 'Census' By Mail," *New York Times*, September 24, 1937.

"Parity Income," *New York Times*, September 24, 1937.

"Stock Market Regulation," *New York Times*, September 25, 1937.

"Walter Lippmann's Prescription for the Good Society," *New York Times Book Review*, September 26, 1937.

"Labor and the Law," *New York Times*, September 26, 1937.

"A Business Barometer?" *New York Times*, September 27, 1937.

"The Profits Tax," *New York Times*, September 29, 1937.

"Argumentum Ad Hominem," *New York Times*, October 1, 1937.

"More Light Needed," *New York Times*, October 1, 1937.

"Mr. Lewis's Program," *New York Times*, October 2, 1937.

"Right Hand vs. Left Hand," *New York Times*, October 8, 1937.

" 'Insiders' and the Market," *New York Times*, October 11, 1937.

"The Farm Program," *New York Times*, October 11, 1937.

"If We Boycott Japan," *New York Times*, October 12, 1937.

"The Autarchic Mentality," *New York Times*, October 13, 1937.

"Balanced Abundance," *New York Times*, October 14, 1937.

"Security Regulation," *New York Times*, October 15, 1937.

"Rule vs. Discretion," *New York Times*, October 17, 1937.

"Stock Market Controls," *New York Times*, October 21, 1937.

"More Subsidies," *New York Times*, October 22, 1937.

"The Rate Increase," *New York Times*, October 23, 1937.

"Commission Government," *New York Times*, October 24, 1937.

"Charity and Relief," *New York Times*, October 25, 1937.

"A Budget Principle," *New York Times*, October 26, 1937.

"Exit the Wizard," *New York Times*, October 28, 1937.

"Wages and the States," *New York Times*, October 29, 1937.

"Spending for Spending's Sake," *New York Times*, October 30, 1937.

"The Planned Economy: Have We Too Much?," *New York Times Magazine*, October 31, 1937. Reply to criticisms, November 5, 1937.

"No Real 'Budget Balance'," *New York Times*, November 1, 1937.

"Annually Balanced," *New York Times*, November 2, 1937.

"That Pseudo-Reserve Fund," *New York Times*, November 3, 1937.

"Brazil Gives Up," *New York Times*, November 5, 1937.

"The New Deal Power Plan," *New York Times*, November 7, 1937.

"A Federal Wage-Hour Law," *New York Times*, November 8, 1937.

"Kennedy on Shipping," *New York Times*, November 10, 1937.

"A Record Cotton Crop," *New York Times*, November 10, 1937.

"Sectional Wage Tariffs," *New York Times*, November 11, 1937.

"Eat Your Cake Three Times," *New York Times*, November 13, 1937.

"How to Fix Utility Rates," *New York Times*, November 13, 1937.

"Wages and Autarchy," *New York Times*, November 14, 1937.

"Mr. Wallace's 'Balance'," *New York Times*, November 15, 1937.

"Temper of the Wage-Hour Bill," *New York Times*, November 15, 1937.

"The Unemployment Census," *New York Times*, November 16, 1937.

"The TVA in Court," *New York Times*, November 17, 1937.

"Britain Nationalizes Coal," *New York Times*, November 18, 1937.

"Taxing Capital Gains," *New York Times*, November 20, 1937.

"Unemployment Reserves," *New York Times*, November 21, 1937.

"Farm Aid vs. Tax Aid," *New York Times*, November 25, 1937.

"Market Regulation," *New York Times*, November 25, 1937.

"With the Prince Left Out," *New York Times*, November 26, 1937.

"Wage Bill vs. Farm Labor," *New York Times*, December 9, 1937.

"Before Congress Votes," *New York Times*, December 10, 1937.

"The SEC and the Exchange," *New York Times*, December 11, 1937.

"Pump-Priming Again?" *New York Times*, December 12, 1937.

"A $500,000,000 Limit," *New York Times*, December 13, 1937.

"Recovery vs. the Wage Bill," *New York Times*, December 13, 1937.

"Aldous Huxley's New Credo," *New York Times Book Review*, December 12, 1937.

"More Light," *New York Times*, December 14, 1937.

"Another Gold-Clause Case," *New York Times*, December 15, 1937.

"Unlimited Spending," *New York Times*, December 16, 1937.

"France's Forty-Hour Week," *New York Times*, December 16, 1937.

"I Am the Law," *New York Times*, December 17, 1937.

"'Saving' the Farmer," *New York Times*, December 20, 1937.

"The Labor Spy," *New York Times*, December 23, 1937.

"Hair-Trigger Charges," *New York Times*, December 24, 1937.

"The NLRB and Henry Ford," *New York Times*, December 25, 1937.

"Limitation of Power," *New York Times*, December 26, 1937.

"Wages: the Next Step," *New York Times*, December 27, 1937.

"Firing on 'Monopoly'," *New York Times*, December 28, 1937.

"We Don't Want Them Here," *New York Times*, December 29, 1937.

"The Milk Problem," *New York Times*, December 29, 1937.

"Mr. Jackson's Broadside," *New York Times*, December 30, 1937.

1938

"The New Mythology," *New York Times*, January 2, 1938.

"The Jobless Census," *New York Times*, January 3, 1938.

"A Relief Proposal," *New York Times*, January 3, 1938.

"Press Censorship," *New York Times*, January 5, 1938.

"Wanted: A Trust Policy," *New York Times*, January 6, 1938.

"'Insurance' and Relief," *New York Times*, January 8, 1938.

"A Higher National Income," *New York Times*, January 9, 1938.

"A Revised Attack on Socialism" (Ludwig von Mises's *Socialism*), *New York Times Book Review*, January 9, 1938.

"The Need For Capital," *New York Times*, January 13, 1938.

"The Sixty-Headed Hydra," *New York Times*, January 14, 1938.

"Economic Programs" (Pigou's *Socialism vs. Capitalism*), *New York Times Book Review*, January 16, 1938.

"Fifty Years from Now," *New York Times*, January 17, 1938.

"Competition or Control?" *New York Times*, January 17, 1938.

"The Proposed Tax Bill," *New York Times*, January 18, 1938.

"Hard Coal vs. Soft," *New York Times*, January 19, 1938.

"To End Child Labor," *New York Times*, January 19, 1938.

"Motor Cars vs. Houses," *New York Times*, January 20, 1938.

"A Bad Tax Nears its End," *New York Times*, January 21, 1938.

"U.S. As the World Pivot," *New York Times*, January 22, 1938.

"No 'Prevailing-Wage' Joke," *New York Times*, January 22, 1938.

"The Oil Verdict," *New York Times*, January 25, 1938.

"Merely Moral," *New York Times*, January 25, 1938.

"On the Importance of Meanings" (on Stuart Chase's *Tyranny of Words*), *New York Times Book Review*, January 23, 1938.

"The 'Third Basket'," *New York Times*, January 27, 1938.

"Wages, Prices, and Recovery," *New York Times*, January 27, 1938.

"Sunlight and Traffic Fines," *New York Times*, January 28, 1938.

"Toward More Housing," *New York Times*, January 29, 1938.

"International Action," *New York Times*, January 30, 1938.

"Art at the Fair," *New York Times*, February 1, 1938.

"Extending Job Insurance," *New York Times*, February 1, 1938.

"The Corporate 'Person'," *New York Times*, February 2, 1938.

"A Program of Housing," *New York Times*, February 4, 1938.

"The Drive to Spend," *New York Times*, February 8, 1938.

"Art at the Fair," *New York Times*, February 9, 1938.

"Confidence and the A. F. of L.," *New York Times*, February 10, 1938.

"The Milk Audit," *New York Times*, February 10, 1938.

"The C.I.O. and Steel," *New York Times*, February 11, 1938.

"The Magic Chart," *New York Times*, February 11, 1938.

"The Momentum of Control," *New York Times*, February 13, 1938.

"Regimented Agriculture," *New York Times*, February 11, 1938.

"Wages, 'North' and 'South'," *New York Times*, February 15, 1938.

"The Capital Gains Tax," *New York Times*, February 16, 1938.

"In Vain the Net," *New York Times*, February 17, 1938.

"This 'Folklore' of Capitalism" (on Thurman W. Arnold), *New York Times Book Review*, February 13, 1938.

"The Child Labor Problem," *New York Times*, February 17, 1938.

"Balanced Prices," *New York Times*, February 19, 1938.

"The 'Third Basket'," *New York Times*, February 23, 1938.

"The Railroad Problem," *New York Times*, February 24 1938.

"Coal Control Cracks," *New York Times*, February 25, 1938.

"The Control of Radio," *New York Times*, February 27, 1938.

"Santayana Meditates on Truth," *New York Times Book Review*, February 27, 1938.

"What is Democracy?" *New York Times*, February 28, 1938.

"Pressure on the I.C.C.," *New York Times*, March 1, 1938.

"Savings Bank Life Insurance," *New York Times*, March 2, 1938.

"The Profits Tax," *New York Times*, March 3, 1938.

"Bank Holding Companies," *New York Times*, March 4, 1938.

"Mortgage Banks," *New York Times*, March 5, 1938.

"Replies to Thurman Arnold's Review of *Folklore of Capitalism*," *New York Times*, March 6, 1938.

"Relief in New York City," *New York Times*, March 7, 1938.

"Anti-Trust," *New York Times*, March 8, 1938.

"We Need the Money," *New York Times*, March 8, 1938.

"Mr. Hull Carries On," *New York Times*, March 9, 1938.

"A Bad Tax Defeated," *New York Times*, March 10, 1938.

"Labor and Stockholders," *New York Times*, March 10, 1938.

"Mysteries in Milk," *New York Times*, March 11, 1938.

"Making Taxes Clear," *New York Times*, March 14, 1938.

"Relief: Which Program?" *New York Times*, March 14, 1938.

"Your Income Tax," *New York Times*, March 15, 1938.

"On Being Subversive," *New York Times*, March 16, 1938.

"Financial Anemia," *New York Times*, March 16, 1938.

"Income Tax Reform," *New York Times*, March 17, 1938.

"Saving Bank Life Insurance," *New York Times*, March 18, 1938.

"A Dangerous Bill," *New York Times*, March 22, 1938.

"John Bates Clark," *New York Times*, March 23, 1938.

"Taxation and Power," *New York Times*, March 23, 1938.

"For Complete Repeal," *New York Times*, March 25, 1938.

"Advertising Protection," *New York Times*, March 26, 1938.

"Buying Power," *New York Times*, March 27, 1938.

"Proposing a Unicameral Legislature for New York State," *New York Times*, March 27, 1938.

"The Panacea of Spending," *New York Times*, March 28, 1938.

"Favoritism in Relief," *New York Times*, March 28, 1938.

"Silver From Mexico," *New York Times*, March 29, 1938.

"Registration Upheld," *New York Times*, March 29, 1938.

"Taxes on 'Gross'," *New York Times*, March 30, 1938.

"Real Tax Reform," *New York Times*, March 31, 1938.

"A Fine Veto," *New York Times*, April 1, 1938.

"We and Canada," *New York Times*, April 3, 1938.

"The Telephone Report," *New York Times*, April 5, 1938.

"No Railroad Subsidy," *New York Times*, April 6, 1938.

"The New City Taxes," *New York Times*, April 7, 1938.

"The New Wage Bill," *New York Times*, April 8, 1938.

"Still More Spending?" *New York Times*, April 9, 1938.

"A Reassuring Tax Bill," *New York Times*, April 11, 1938.

"Mr. La Guardia's Scheme," *New York Times*, April 13, 1938.

"The President Intervenes," *New York Times*, April 14, 1938.

"The Theory Behind Spending," *New York Times*, April 18, 1938.

"The One-Way Referee," *New York Times*, April 21, 1938.

"Taxes and Recovery," *New York Times*, April 23, 1938.

"New Names For Deficits," *New York Times*, April 24, 1938.

"Taxes Out of Conference," *New York Times*, April 25, 1938.

"Britain's Budget," *New York Times*, April 27, 1938.

"'Disappointing' Yields," *New York Times*, April 28, 1938.

"On the Way to the Fair," *New York Times*, April 28, 1938.

"The New Wage Bill," *New York Times*, April 29, 1938.

"Getting Together," *New York Times*, April 29, 1938.

"Monopoly," *New York Times*, April 30, 1938.

"Another NLRB Decision," *New York Times*, April 30, 1930.

"May Day," *New York Times*, May 1, 1938.

"Rudimentary Fair Play," *New York Times*, May 2, 1938.

"Queens and the Fair," *New York Times*, May 2, 1938.

"The Presidents Public Papers; Five Volumes Which Bring the Record Down to January, 1937," *New York Times Book Review*, May 1, 1938.

"The President's Letter," *New York Times*, May 3, 1938.

"Railroad Wage Scales," *New York Times*, May 4, 1938.

"Two French Decrees," *New York Times*, May 4, 1938.

"France Devalues Again," *New York Times*, May 5, 1938.

"Are You Better Off?" *New York Times*, May 6, 1938.

"The Real Danger," *New York Times*, May 7, 1938.

"Time to Reconsider," *New York Times*, May 8, 1938.

"Pump-Priming Has Failed," *New York Times*, May, 9 1938.

"Mr. Hague's Supporters," *New York Times*, May 9, 1938.

"Labor Leaders vs. Labor," *New York Times*, May 13, 1938.

"Scalpel—Or Axe?" *New York Times*, May 16, 1938.

"Private Capital and Public Housing," *New York Times*, May 16, 1938.

"Good and Bad Advice," *New York Times*, May 18, 1938.

"The Nazi Economy," *New York Times*, May 13, 1948.

"Mr. Madden's Defense," *New York Times*, May 20, 1983.

"Polling Public Opinion (sic)," *New York Times*, May 7, 1938.

"Not Popular," *New York Times*, May 21, 1938.

"Differentials in Wages," *New York Times*, May 21, 1938.

"The Question of Hours," *New York Times*, May 2, 1938.

"Railway Wages," *New York Times*, May 22, 1938.

"To Make It Workable," *New York Times*, May 23, 1938.

"Left-Wing Blueprint," *New York Times*, May 24, 1938.

"House vs. Senate Version," *New York Times*, May 25, 1938.

"Working Hours," *New York Times*, May 25, 1938.

"Minimum Wages and NRA," *New York Times*, May 27, 1938.

"Without Benefit of Signatures," *New York Times*, May 28, 1938.

"Behind Autarchy," *New York Times*, May 29, 1938.

"Capital Gain Taxation," *New York Times*, June 1, 1938.

"The Wage Bill Compromise," *New York Times*, June 2, 1938.

"Everybody's Liberties," *New York Times*, June 2, 1938.

"Standard Procedure," *New York Times*, June 3, 1938.

"Farmers and the Rest of Us," *New York Times*, June 3, 1938.

"The Verdict of Economists," *New York Times*, June 4, 1938.

"Cooperation from SEC," *New York Times*, June 4, 1938.

"The Method of Reform," *New York Times*, June 5, 1938.

"The Problem of Economic Accounting Under Socialism" (*On the Economic Theory of Socialism* by O. Lange and F. M. Taylor), *New York Times Book Review* , June 5, 1938.

"America, Inc.," *New York Times*, June 6, 1938.

"Free Speech in Jersey," *New York Times*, June 7, 1938.

" 'Principle' vs. Substance," *New York Times*, June 8, 1938.

"Taxes on Capital Gains," *New York Times*, June 8, 1938.

"Before Congress Adjourns," *New York Times*, June 9, 1938.

"A Test of the Wagner Act," *New York Times*, June 10, 1938.

"Raw Materials," *New York Times*, June 12, 1938.

"Investigating Monopoly," *New York Times*, June 12, 1938.

"High Wages Not Remedy," *New York Times*, June 12, 1938.

"The Method of Recovery," *New York Times*, June 13, 1938.

"British Wage Boards," *New York Times*, June 13, 1938.

"Hurting Railroad Workers," *New York Times*, June 13, 1938.

"The Final Wage-Hour Bill," *New York Times*, June 14, 1938.

"No Free Speech Issue," *New York Times*, June 15, 1938.

"A Potential Joker," *New York Times*, June 16, 1938.

"The Record of Congress," *New York Times*, June 16, 1938.

"Between Sessions," *New York Times*, June 19, 1938.

"Give a Dog an Ill Name," *New York Times*, June 20, 1938.

"The Appropriate Unit," *New York Times*, June 24, 1938.

"Worse Goods, Better Alibis," *New York Times*, June 25, 1938.

"Sound Counsel on Relief," *New York Times*, June 25, 1938.

"Low Prices, High Wages," *New York Times*, June 27, 1938.

"The 'Buy-and-Give' Scheme," *New York Times*, June 28, 1938.

"Relief in Politics," *New York Times*, June 29, 1938.

"WPA Wage—And Hours," *New York Times*, July 1, 1938.

"Psychology of Budgets," *New York Times*, July 3, 1938.

"If Mr. Williams Had His Way," *New York Times*, July 4, 1938.

"A Plea For Economic Isolation: Jerome Frank Offers a Plan to 'Save America First'," *New York Times Book Review*, July 3, 1938.

"Revolution in Steel Prices," *New York Times*, July 5, 1938.

"After Three Years," *New York Times*, July 6, 1938.

"No. 1 Economic Problem," *New York Times*, July 7, 1938.

"Higher Railroad Fares," *New York Times*, July 8, 1938.

"Just Beating the Gun?" *New York Times*, July 9, 1938.

"Our Experiment in Cotton," *New York Times*, July 11, 1938.

"The President on Wages," *New York Times*, July 12, 1938.

"Protection Against Plenty," *New York Times*, July 13, 1938.

"Civil Liberties for Labor," *New York Times*, July 15, 1938.

"Government Loans on Wheat," *New York Times*, July 16, 1938.

"Relief Wages," *New York Times*, July 18, 1938.

"The Need for 'Big Business'," *New York Times*, July 18, 1938.

"The Varied Heresies of J. A. Hobson" (on *Confessions of an Economic Heretic* by J. A. Hobson), *New York Times Book Review*, July 24, 1938.

"Slavery and 'Wealth'," *New York Times*, July 24, 1938.

"Mr. Hull's Trade Treaties," *New York Times*, August 2, 1938.

"Not Our Problem," *New York Times*, August 3, 1938.

"The Battle of Newton," *New York Times*, August 4, 1938.

"America's Income," *New York Times*, August 7, 1938.

"The Result in Kentucky," *New York Times*, August 8, 1938.

"The Power to Tax," *New York Times*, August 8, 1938.

"The Mexican Episode," *New York Times*, August 9, 1938.

"Preview of Taxpayers," *New York Times*, August 10, 1938.

"Lights on the Roads," *New York Times*, August 11, 1938.

"Mind vs. Matter," *New York Times*, August 11, 1938.

"The Relief Machine," *New York Times*, August 12, 1938.

"That No. 1 Problem," *New York Times*, August 13, 1938.

"State 'Tariff Walls'," *New York Times*, August 14, 1938.

"Curbing Bureaucracy," *New York Times*, August 15, 1938.

"The Brandenburg Flight," *New York Times*, August 15, 1938.

"Interpreting the Wage Act," *New York Times*, August 16, 1938.

"Democracy in Art?" *New York Times*, August 16, 1938.

"Price-Fixing in Milk," *New York Times*, August 18, 1938.

"Another Subsidy," *New York Times*, August 19, 1938.

"The 'Monopoly' Problem," *New York Times*, August 20, 1938.

"Social Security," *New York Times*, August 21, 1938.

"Two Economic Worlds," *New York Times*, August 22, 1938.

"Frances's Forty-Hour Week," *New York Times*, August 23, 1938.

"WPA in Politics," *New York Times*, August 24, 1938.

"Victory vs. the Game," *New York Times*, August 24, 1938.

"Labor Relations," *New York Times*, August 25, 1938.

"Democratic Process," *New York Times*, August 26, 1938.

"American Recovery," *New York Times*, August 26, 1938.

"The Note To Mexico," *New York Times*, August 27, 1938.

"War Has No Victor," *New York Times*, August 29, 1938.

"$30-Every-Thursday," *New York Times*, August 30, 1938.

"The Forty-Hour Week," *New York Times*, August 31, 1938.

"Labor Relations," *New York Times*, September 3, 1938.

"Three-Thirds of a Nation," *New York Times*, September 4, 1938.

"The Reserve Fund," *New York Times*, September 5, 1938.

"Dangers From Within," *New York Times*, September 6 1938.

"Comparisons," *New York Times*, September 6, 1938.

"No Regimentation for Labor," *New York Times*, September 7, 1938.

"The League on the New Deal," *New York Times*, September 7, 1938.

" 'Hot' Pension Money," *New York Times*, September 10, 1938.

"What Women Think of Relief," *New York Times*, September 12, 1938.

"Red Bating and Black Baiting," *New York Times*, September 13, 1938.

"Problem in 'Coercion'," *New York Times*, September 13, 1938.

"Taxes on Business," *New York Times*, September 16, 1938.

"Pensions and Solvency," *New York Times*, September 15, 1938.

"Some Rough C's," *New York Times*, September 17, 1938.

"Germany's Economic Outlook," *New York Times*, September 17, 1938.

"Curbs on Picketing," *New York Times*, September 19, 1938.

"Creating Jobs," *New York Times*, September 19, 1938.

"Unionizing WPA," *New York Times*, September 20, 1938.

"Investment Trusts," *New York Times*, September 23, 1938.

"Insuring the Future," *New York Times*, September 24, 1938.

"Blood Givers Union," *New York Times*, September 25, 1938.

"Their Social Duty," *New York Times*, September 25, 1938.

"Part of the Whole," *New York Times*, September 25, 1938.

"Dictatorship and War," *New York Times*, September 25, 1938.

"Labor Relations in Sweden," *New York Times*, September 25, 1938.

"Don Budge's Record," *New York Times*, September 26, 1938.

"The Wagner Act Again," *New York Times*, September 27, 1938.

"WPA Politics," *New York Times*, September 27, 1938.

"A Good Commission," *New York Times*, September 28, 1938.

"Germany's Money," *New York Times*, September 28, 1938.

"Republican Keynote," *New York Times*, September 29, 1938.

"State Mortgage Reform," *New York Times*, October 1, 1938.

"Heigh-Ho, Silver!" *New York Times*, October 1, 1938.

"Honest Cost Finding," *New York Times*, October 2, 1938.

"After the Amputation," *New York Times*, October 2, 1938.

"Four Capitals," *New York Times*, October 3, 1938.

"Power and the Modern World" (on Bertrand Russell), *New York Times Book Review*, October 2, 1938.

"Economic Saber-Rattling," *New York Times*, October 6, 1938.

"Old Capital—and New," *New York Times*, October 7, 1938.

"Toward Peace at Home," *New York Times*, October 8, 1938.

"Women Workers," *New York Times*, October 10, 1938.

"Appeasement No Nearer," *New York Times*, October 10, 1938.

"The King and Queen Here?" *New York Times*, October 10, 1938.

"The Strachey Affair," *New York Times*, October 12, 1938.

"The 'Monopoly' Probe," *New York Times*, October 13, 1938.

"The Governor Acts," *New York Times*, October 14, 1938.

"The 'Two-Price' Scheme," *New York Times*, October 14, 1938.

"Buy Dear, Sell Cheap," *New York Times*, October 14, 1938.

"A New 'Railroad Cure'," *New York Times*, October 15, 1938.

"The One-Way Nazi Mind," *New York Times*, October 17, 1938.

"Warning From Colorado," *New York Times*, October 17, 1938.

"Farm Program Under Fire," *New York Times*, October 18, 1938.

"The Railway Wage Dispute," *New York Times*, October 19, 1938.

"Two Kinds of Restriction," *New York Times*, October 22, 1938.

"$30-Every-Thursday," *New York Times*, October 23, 1938.

"The Wage-Hour Law," *New York Times*, October 24, 1938.

"Education Eats Up Life," *New York Times*, October 24, 1938.

"Lop-Sided Justice," *New York Times*, October 24, 1938.

"The Wage Act Joker," *New York Times*, October 25, 1938.

"A Brief History of Economic Thought" (on J. H. Ferguson), *New York Times Book Review*, October 30, 1938.

"Relief Load Rises in Chicago Upturn," *New York Times*, November 1, 1938.

"Free Speech in Jersey City," *New York Times*, November 9, 1938.

"Germany Forgets History," *New York Times*, November 12, 1938.

"Wage-Hour Law Effects," *New York Times*, November 12, 1938.

"Advice to Republicans," *New York Times*, November 13, 1938.

"Profit from Persecution," *New York Times*, November 14, 1938.

"The Wagner Act," *New York Times*, November 14, 1938.

"Stabilizing Income," *New York Times*, November 16, 1938.

"WPA and National Defense," *New York Times*, November 16, 1938.

"Inspecting Tax Returns," *New York Times*, November 17, 1938.

"Two-Class Relief System," *New York Times*, November 18, 1938.

"Crop Control for 1939," *New York Times*, November 19, 1938.

"Foreign Trade: Two Systems," *New York Times*, November 19, 1938.

"Future of Trade Treaties," *New York Times*, November 21, 1938.

"Commendable Restraint," *New York Times*, November 21, 1938.

"To Take a Great National Question Out of Politics," *New York Times*, November 23, 1938.

"Toward Conciliation," *New York Times*, November 23, 1938.

"The Rockefellers," *New York Times*, November 24, 1938.

"Our Dual Relief System," *New York Times*, November 25, 1938.

"Cotton Policy," *New York Times*, November 25, 1938.

"National Unity," *New York Times*, November 26, 1938.

"Wallace Weighs Our Changing Farm Problem," *New York Times Magazine*, November 27, 1938.

"Production and Jobs," *New York Times*, November 27, 1938.

"No 'Withering' Away," *New York Times*, November 27, 1938.

"The Monopoly Probe," *New York Times*, November 28, 1938.

"Freedom On the Air," *New York Times*, November 29, 1938.

"All Eyes on France," *New York Times*, November 30, 1938.

"Daladier's Victory," *New York Times*, December 1, 1938.

"A World Trade War," *New York Times*, December 2, 1938.

"The Opening Gun," *New York Times*, December 3, 1938.

"No 'Perfect' Competition," *New York Times*, December 5, 1938.

"Europe's Crisis Factories," *New York Times*, December 5, 1938.

"Wagner Act in Court," *New York Times*, December 6, 1938.

"Business Mortality," *New York Times*, December 7, 1938.

"New Industries," *New York Times*, December 8, 1938.

"A Relief Formula," *New York Times*, December 9, 1938.

"Out of the Red," *New York Times*, December 9, 1938.

"Grounds for Suspicion," *New York Times*, December 9, 1938.

"Japan Closes the Door," *New York Times*, December 10, 1938.

"The Farmers Vote," *New York Times*, December 10, 1938.

"What the Farm Vote Means," *New York Times*, December 13, 1938.

"For Human Rights," *New York Times*, December 13, 1938.

"Patents and Monopoly," *New York Times*, December 14, 1938.

"Mr. Wallace Reports," *New York Times*, December 16, 1938.

"Incentive Taxation," *New York Times*, December 18, 1938.

"Revising Social Security," *New York Times*, December 19, 1938.

"Cost of Social Insurance," *New York Times*, December 20, 1938.

"Railway Rate-Making," *New York Times*, December 21, 1938.

"Oregon's Labor Law," *New York Times*, December 21, 1938.

"For Further Study," *New York Times*, December 22, 1938.

"Wage Discrimination," *New York Times*, December 23, 1938.

"Transportation Reform," *New York Times*, December 24, 1938.

"Wages and Profits," *New York Times*, December 24, 1938.

"Mr. Hopkins's Appointment," *New York Times*, December 24, 1938.

"Salvation Through Deficits," *New York Times*, December 27, 1938.

"Deficits Made Easy," *New York Times*, December 28, 1938.

"The Reform of Relief," *New York Times*, December 28, 1938.

"Congress on Its Own," *New York Times*, December 30, 1938.

"A Drop of Ten Billions," *New York Times*, December 30, 1938.

"The Small End of the Funnel," *New York Times*, December 31, 1938.

1939

"Governor Murphy," *New York Times*, January 2, 1939.

"The Problem of Relief," *New York Times*, January 2, 1939.

"The Task Before Congress," *New York Times*, January 2, 1939.

"Silver on the Dole," *New York Times*, January 3, 1939.

"Relief in Politics," *New York Times*, January 4, 1939.

"Mr. Dies Reports," *New York Times*, January 5, 1939.

"Relief Reform in Sight," *New York Times*, January 6, 1939.

"Relief from Relief: Proposed Reform of the Chaotic Home-Relief-WPA System," *The Annalist*, January 4, 1939.

"England's Government Today" (on Harold J. Laski), *New York Times Book Review*, January 8, 1939.

"Spending for Relief," *New York Times*, January 9, 1939.

"A 'Formula' for Relief," *New York Times*, January 10, 1939.

"Why Credit Lags," *New York Times*, January 11, 1939.

"Herman Oliphant," *New York Times*, January 12, 1939.

"WPA Expenditures," *New York Times*, January 13, 1939.

"Defending States' Rights," *New York Times*, January 14, 1939.

"A New Relief Program," *New York Times*, January 16, 1939.

"Punitive Deprivation," *New York Times*, January 16, 1939.

"Controlling Bureaucracy," *New York Times*, January 16, 1939.

"The President's Message," *New York Times*, January 17, 1939.

"Stop, Look and Listen," *New York Times*, January 19, 1939.

"The Method of Relief," *New York Times*, January 20, 1939.

"For Foreign Markets," *New York Times*, January 20, 1939.

"Crops and Income," *New York Times*, January 21, 1939.

"The Power Over Money," *New York Times*, January 23, 1939.

"Deficits vs. Responsibility," *New York Times*, January 24, 1939.

"Borrower's Logic," *New York Times*, January 25, 1939.

"The Bridges Case," *New York Times*, January 25, 1939.

"Against Six-Year Terms," *New York Times*, January 26, 1939.

"German Debt Evasion," *New York Times*, January 26, 1939.

"Amending the Wagner Act," *New York Times*, January 27, 1939.

"Six Years of Hitler," *New York Times*, January 29, 1939.

"Working to Music," *New York Times*, January 30, 1939.

"Administration of Relief," *New York Times*, January 30, 1939.

"TVA—and Recovery," *New York Times*, January 31, 1939.

"Rising Relief Load," *New York Times*, February 1, 1939.

"War Insurance," *New York Times*, February 2, 1939.

"Export or Die," *New York Times*, February 5, 1939.

"Failure of Pump-Priming," *New York Times*, February 5, 1939.

"Daylight for Utilities," *New York Times*, February 6, 1939.

"WPA Wages," *New York Times*, February 6, 1939.

"A Two-Sided Victory," *New York Times*, February 7, 1939.

"Motives Under Communism," *New York Times*, February 7, 1939.

"The Amlie Appointment," *New York Times*, February 8, 1939.

"Interpreting the Election," *New York Times*, February 9, 1939.

"Mr. Amlie's Own Reason," *New York Times*, February 9, 1939.

"The Silver Folly," *New York Times*, February 9, 1939.

"Miss Perkins's Defense," *New York Times*, February 10, 1939.

"Reforming Relief," *New York Times*, February 11, 1939.

"The Power to Appoint," *New York Times*, February 13, 1939.

"The Dogma of Buying Power," *New York Times*, February 13, 1939.

"Why Congress Marks Time," *New York Times*, February 14, 1939.

"Self-Perpetuating Relief," *New York Times*, February 15, 1939.

"Toward Recovery," *New York Times*, February 16, 1939.

"President vs. Congress," *New York Times*, February 17, 1939.

"Emergency Powers," *New York Times*, February 18, 1939.

"Business, Big and Little," *New York Times*, February 18, 1939.

"New Ideas," *New York Times*, February 19, 1939.

"National Incomes," *New York Times*, February 19, 1939.

"France Acts," *New York Times*, February 10, 1939.

"Business and Taxes," *New York Times*, February 21, 1939.

"Trading with Germany," *New York Times*, February 23, 1939.

"Prices and Production," *New York Times*, February 24, 1939.

"Mr. Hopkins on Recovery," *New York Times*, February 25, 1939.

"A. F. of L. and C.I.O.," *New York Times*, February 27, 1939.

"Taxes vs. Production," *New York Times*, February 28, 1939.

"Interpretation or Amendment?" *New York Times*, March 1, 1939.

"Needed Clarification," *New York Times*, March 2, 1939.

"On the Trail of Monopoly," *New York Times*, March 6, 1939.

"Toward a Balanced Budget," *New York Times*, March 8, 1939.

"Red Tape at Albany," *New York Times*, March 9, 1939.

"'P.R.' for Labor," *New York Times*, March 10, 1939.

"Good Neighbors," *New York Times*, March 11, 1939.

"The Food Scrip Plan," *New York Times*, March 11, 1939.

"A Coordinated Program," *New York Times*, March 12, 1939.

"On Revising the Labor Act," *New York Times*, March 13, 1939.

"Industry by Industry," *New York Times*, March 13, 1939.

"Cooperative Regulation," *New York Times*, March 14, 1939.

"America and the European Crisis" (on L. Mumford and S. Chase), *New York Times Book Review*, March 12, 1939.

"Misleading Index," *New York Times*, March 14, 1939.

"The Relief Appropriation," *New York Times*, March 15, 1939.

"Reform or Relief," *New York Times*, March 16, 1939.

"Unifying Relief," *New York Times*, March 17, 1939.

"Power to Print Greenbacks," *New York Times*, March 17, 1939.

"SEC and the Exchanges," *New York Times*, March 18, 1939.

"Stronger then Mere Words," *New York Times*, March 20, 1939.

"Mr. Douglas to the Court," *New York Times*, March 21, 1939.

"Shadow and Substance," *New York Times*, March 23, 1939.

"Punishing Ourselves," *New York Times*, March 23, 1939.

"Ironclad Guarantee," *New York Times*, March 24, 1939.

"Investigating WPA," *New York Times*, March 24, 1939.

"Mr. Eccles and the Budget," *New York Times*, March 25, 1939.

"End of the Huge 'Reserve'," *New York Times*, March 25, 1939.

"An Emotional Gesture," *New York Times*, March 27, 1939.

"Is Money Too Easy?" *New York Times*, March 27, 1939.

"Reciprocal Tax Powers," *New York Times*, March 28, 1939.

"Investigation and Reform," *New York Times*, March 29, 1939.

"Collapse of a Program," *New York Times*, March 30, 1939.

"Revising the Wage-Hour Act," *New York Times*, March 31, 1939.

"Back-Door Tariff Increase," *New York Times*, April 1, 1939.

"The New Pension Scale," *New York Times*, April 1, 1939.

"Income vs. Taxes," *New York Times*, April 2, 1939.

"Franco's Spain," *New York Times*, April 3, 1939.

"Cotton Problem," *New York Times*, April 5, 1939.

" 'Rider' Legislation," *New York Times*, April 6, 1939.

"The Record on Cotton," *New York Times*, April 6, 1939.

"Need of Tax Revision," *New York Times*, April 7, 1939.

"Albanian Seizure," *New York Times*, April 10, 1939.

"On the Way to the Fair," *New York Times*, April 8, 1939.

"Farmers and the Treasury," *New York Times*, April 10, 1939.

"American Trade Policy," *New York Times*, April 11, 1939.

"A New Barter Plan," *New York Times*, April 12, 1939.

"Mr. Wagner on the Wagner Act," *New York Times*, April 13, 1939.

"Merit Rating," *New York Times*, April 15, 1939.

"Machiavelli in Our Time," *New York Times*, April 16, 1939.

"The Soft Coal Tie Up," *New York Times*, April 17, 1939.

"Federal Aid," *New York Times*, April 17, 1939.

"The Strecker Decision," *New York Times*, April 18, 1939.

"The New AAA Upheld," *New York Times*, April 19, 1939.

"Power Over Money," *New York Times*, April 20, 1939.

"One Man Admits It," *New York Times*, April 20, 1939.

"Advice to Democrats," *New York Times*, April 21, 1939.

"A New Relief Bill," *New York Times*, April 22, 1939.

"The $80,000,000,000 Income," *New York Times*, April 24, 1939.

"Then Why Not Give Pledges?" *New York Times*, April 24, 1939.

"Amending Social Security," *New York Times*, April 24, 1939.

"Appointment to the SEC," *New York Times*, April 25, 1939.

"Real Tax Revision," *New York Times*, April 25, 1939.

"A Revised Wage-Hour Act," *New York Times*, April 26, 1939.

"Incentive for Expansion," *New York Times*, April 26, 1939.

"The Relief Message," *New York Times*, April 28, 1939.

"No Relief Economy," *New York Times*, April 29, 1939.

"Cotton Economics," *New York Times*, May 1, 1939.

"Every Tax a Deterrent," *New York Times*, May 16, 1939.

"Tax Revision," *New York Times*, May 17, 1939.

"Idle Money and Men," *New York Times*, May 18, 1939.

"Need for Free Enterprise," *New York Times*, May 19, 1939.

"What Retards Recovery," *New York Times*, May 20, 1939.

"Labor Relations," *New York Times*, May 21, 1939.

"National Debt Week," *New York Times*, May 22, 1939.

"For Human Rights," *New York Times*, May 23, 1939.

"The Merit-Rating Bill," *New York Times*, May 24, 1939.

"Radio Control," *New York Times*, May 25, 1939.

"Green Light for Tax Reform," *New York Times*, May 26, 1939.

"The Great Illusion," *New York Times*, May 26, 1939.

"Which Road to Freedom?" (on F. A. Hayek on "Freedom and the Economic System"), *New York Times Book Review*, May 28, 1939.

"To Make Taxes Fair," *New York Times*, May 29, 1939.

"The Case Against Isolation," *New York Times*, May 30, 1939.

"New Labor Acts," *New York Times*, May 31, 1939.

"Lower Railroad Fares," *New York Times*, June 1, 1939.

"The Townsend Plan Vote," *New York Times*, June 2, 1939.

"Supervising Local Relief," *New York Times*, June 3, 1939.

"Selling Below Cost," *New York Times*, June 3, 1939.

"Labor Rackets at the Fair," *New York Times*, June 3, 1939.

"One Factor Overlooked," *New York Times*, June 4, 1939.

"Justice for Sale," *New York Times*, June 5, 1939.

"Child Labor Amendment," *New York Times*, June 6, 1939.

"The Young Bill Veto," *New York Times*, June 6, 1939.

"Loans to 'Small Business'," *New York Times*, June 7, 1939.

"Revising Social Security," *New York Times*, June 8, 1939.

"'Unenforceable' Price Fixing," *New York Times*, June 10, 1939.

"A Wider Social Security," *New York Times*, June 12, 1939.

"Reforming Relief," *New York Times*, June 13, 1939.

"Tax Reform Under Way," *New York Times*, June 14, 1939.

"Restricting TVA," *New York Times*, June 15, 1939.

"The New Relief Bill," *New York Times*, June 16, 1939.

"Tires Are Too Good," *New York Times*, June 17, 1939.

"Complicating State Aid," *New York Times*, June 18, 1939.

"The Politics of Spending," *New York Times*, June 18, 1939.

"Relief Reform," *New York Times*, June 19, 1939.

"Profit Sharing," *New York Times*, June 20, 1939.

"The New Mood of Congress," *New York Times*, June 2, 1939.

"That $47,000,000,000 Reserve," *New York Times*, June 22, 1939.

"Employer Petitions," *New York Times*, June 23, 1939.

"Still More Spending," *New York Times*, June 23, 1939.

"Sad Dilemma," *New York Times*, June 23, 1939.

"Spend and Spend," *New York Times*, June 25, 1939.

"The Silver Hold-Up," *New York Times*, June 26, 1939.

"Federal Theatre Project," *New York Times*, June 26, 1939.

"The Senate Makes a Trade," *New York Times*, June 27, 1939.

"Flank Attack," *New York Times*, June 28, 1939.

"Silver and Mexico," *New York Times*, June 29, 1939.

"More Teeth Than Justice," *New York Times*, June 30, 1939.

"The New Relief Bill," *New York Times*, July 1, 1939.

"Battle of the Dollar," *New York Times*, July 2, 1939.

"The Federal Theatre," *New York Times*, July 3, 1939.

"The Ninth Deficit," *New York Times*, July 3, 1939.

"The New Relief System," *New York Times*, July 4, 1939.

"The O'Mahoney Bill," *New York Times*, July 5, 1939.

"Strike Against Work Relief," *New York Times*, July 7, 1939.

"The WPA 'Strike'," *New York Times*, July 8, 1939.

"Germany's 'Cannon Boom'," *New York Times*, July 9, 1939.

"Our Hybrid WPA," *New York Times*, July 10, 1939.

"Drive on Building Costs," *New York Times*, July 11, 1939.

"What Are the Facts?" *New York Times*, July 12, 1939.

"The WPA Strike," *New York Times*, July 13, 1939.

"The New Broadcasting Code," *New York Times*, July 13, 1939.

"No WPA 'Strike'," *New York Times*, July 14, 1939.

"Boosting Pensions," *New York Times*, July 14, 1939.

"Revising Social Security," *New York Times*, July 15, 1939.

"Mr. Roosevelt and the Strike," *New York Times*, July 15, 1939.

"The Dilemma of WPA," *New York Times*, July 17, 1939.

"A Bad Amendment," *New York Times*, July 19, 1939.

"The 'Monopoly' Report," *New York Times*, July 19, 1939.

"A New Dispute in Congress," *New York Times*, July 21, 1939.

"For Better Labor Relations," *New York Times*, July 22, 1939.

"Mr. Andrews Changes His Mind," *New York Times*, July 22, 1939.

"Continuity in Congress," *New York Times*, July 23, 1939.

"Spending Masquerades," *New York Times*, July 24, 1939.

"Illusions About Relief," *New York Times*, July 25, 1939.

"Collapse of Farm 'Planning'," *New York Times*, July 27, 1939.

"A.M.A. In Court," *New York Times*, July 28, 1939.

"Unemployment Insurance," *New York Times*, July 28, 1939.

"Relief and the Cities," *New York Times*, July 29, 1939.

"Yes, But—," *New York Times*, July 31, 1939.

"Wages on Relief," *New York Times*, July 31, 1939.

"Restricting Civil Liberties," *New York Times*, August 1, 1939.

"The Fair for 50 Cents," *New York Times*, August 2, 1939.

"The Lending Plan Scotched," *New York Times*, August 2, 1939.

"Housing," *New York Times*, August 3, 1939.

"The 'Clean Politics' Law," *New York Times*, August 3, 1939.

"Industrial Warfare," *New York Times*, August 4, 1939.

"An End of Pump-Priming," *New York Times*, August 6, 1939.

"The Record of Congress," *New York Times*, August 7, 1939.

"In Place of Pump-Priming," *New York Times*, August 8, 1939.

"Objectives and Methods," *New York Times*, August 9, 1939.

"Who is the Gambler?" *New York Times*, August 10, 1939.

"The Meaning of Money," *New York Times*, August 12, 1939.

"Budge Speaks of Tennis" (on J. D. Budge), *New York Times Book Review*, August 13, 1939.

"The New Social Security," *New York Times*, August 14, 1939.

"Mexican Oil Problem," *New York Times*, August 16, 1939.

"Relief Wage Scales," *New York Times*, August 17, 1939.

"The Seizure of Slovakia," *New York Times*, August 19, 1939.

"The Milk Strike," *New York Times*, August 21, 1939

"The SEC and German Bonds," *New York Times*, August 23, 1939.

"Stabilizing Milk Prices," *New York Times*, August 23, 1939.

"Government By Definition," *New York Times*, August 24, 1939.

"An Argentine Trade Treaty," *New York Times*, August 25, 1939.

"The American Attitude," *New York Times*, August 27, 1939.

"The Real Issue," *New York Times*, August 28, 1939.

"Mr. Hitler's Argument," *New York Times*, August 29, 1939.

"The Attack on Poland," *New York Times*, September 3, 1939.

"New Light on Economic Fundamentals" (on J. R. Hicks's *Value and Capital*), *New York Times Book Review*, September 3, 1939.

"War Guilt," *New York Times*, September 3, 1939.

"The Cup Leaves," *New York Times*, September 4, 1939.

"The Economic Aspect," *New York Times*, September 9, 1939.

"The War of Words," *New York Times*, September 10, 1939.

"The British Answer," *New York Times*, September 11, 1939.

"War News on the Radio," *New York Times*, September 13, 1939.

"Broadcaster in Trouble," *New York Times*, September 14, 1939.

"Price-Fixing in Milk," *New York Times*, September 16, 1939.

"Literature as Propaganda," *Saturday Review of Literature*, September 16, 1939.

"The Economic Alignment," *New York Times*, September 17, 1939.

"The Russian Betrayal," *New York Times*, September 18, 1939.

"'Profiteering," *New York Times*, September 18, 1939.

"Economic War Strength," *New York Times*, September 20, 1939.

"The British Blue Book," *New York Times*, September 23, 1939.

"Private Initiative," *New York Times*, September 23, 1939.

"Russian 'Help' to Germany," *New York Times*, September 25, 1939.

"Economic Power," *New York Times*, September 26, 1939.

"The Government Payroll," *New York Times*, September 27, 1939.

"The Cost of War," *New York Times*, September 28, 1939.

"Unemployment Falling," *New York Times*, September 29, 1939.

"Russian-German Alliance," *New York Times*, October 1, 1939.

"An Audit for Relief," *New York Times*, October 2, 1939.

"The Struggle for Allies," *New York Times*, October 2, 1939.

"Walsh-Healey Wages," *New York Times*, October 5, 1939.

"War and the Deficit," *New York Times*, October 6, 1939.

"Business Recovery," *New York Times*, October 9, 1939.

"Social Security Funds," *New York Times*, October 9, 1939.

"Controlling Economic Life," *New York Times*, October 10, 1939.

"Power Over Labor," *New York Times*, October 12, 1939.

"Curbs On Our Own Shipping," *New York Times*, October 13, 1939.

"Propaganda in Reverse," *New York Times*, October 15, 1939.

"Corporate Profits in America" *New York Times Book Review*, October 15, 1939.

"Economics of the War," *New York Times*, October 10, 1939.

"The Royal Oak," *New York Times*, October 16, 1939.

"Financial Preparedness," *New York Times*, October 17, 1939.

"Lionel Robbins on Class Conflict," *New York Times Book Review*, October 22, 1939.

"Mr. Hazlitt Replies," *New York Times Book Review*, October 29, 1939.

"Andrews Out, Fleming In," *New York Times*, October 29, 1939.

"Milk Prices and the Mayor," *New York Times*, October 19, 1939.

"The Ban of Submarines," *New York Times*, October 20, 1939.

"The Loss in Idle Ships," *New York Times*, October 21, 1939.

"A Victory for the A.M.A.," *New York Times*, October 24, 1939.

"The Wage-Hour Act," *New York Times*, October 23, 1939.

"Mr. Browder's Indictment," *New York Times*, October 24, 1939.

"The Ohio Pension Scheme," *New York Times*, October 25, 1939.

"Shotgun Publicity," *New York Times*, October 27, 1939.

"An Interim Congress," *New York Times*, October 29, 1939.

"Grotesquely Drastic," *New York Times*, October 30, 1939.

"The Flint Affair," *New York Times*, October 30, 1939.

"'Ham and Eggs' Again," *New York Times*, October 31, 1939.

"Art in America," *New York Times*, November 1, 1939.

"Withholding Federal Funds," *New York Times*, November 1, 1939.

"Ham and Eggs—For Whom?" *New York Times*, November 2, 1939.

"A United Nation," *New York Times*, November 4, 1939.

"What Kind of Democracy?" *New York Times*, November 5, 1939.

"Recovery and Confidence," *New York Times*, November 6, 1939.

"Democracy and Security," *New York Times*, November 7, 1939.

"Life and Freedom," *New York Times*, November 12, 1939.

"Central War Aim," *New York Times*, November 13, 1939.

"Democratic Machinery," *New York Times*, November 12, 1939.

"$60 at 60," *New York Times*, November 14, 1939.

"Our Financial Weakness," *New York Times*, November 15, 1939.

"The Theory Behind Spending," *New York Times, November 16, 1939.*

"The America That is Enduring" (on *The Living Tradition* by S. Strunsky), *New York Times Book Review*, November 19, 1939.

"Reflections on P. R.," *New York Times*, November 20, 1939.

"Labor Under the Trust Laws," *New York Times*, November 21, 1939.

"Common Sense About Taxes," *New York Times*, November 22, 1939.

"P. R. As a Scapegoat," *New York Times*, November 23, 1939.

"Case of Charles Boyer," *New York Times*, November 24, 1939.

"State Trade Barriers," *New York Times*, November 25, 1939.

"Union for Europe," *New York Times*, November 26, 1939.

"No Segregated Budget," *New York Times*, November 27, 1939.

"Why Germany Needs Exports," *New York Times*, November 29, 1939.

"The Double Budget," *New York Times*, November 30, 1939.

"What P. R. Accomplished," *New York Times*, December 2, 1939.

"Bombs Over Finland," *New York Times*, December 3, 1939.

"World Condemnation," *New York Times*, December 4, 1939.

"Why the Pension Panaceas?" *New York Times*, December 4, 1939.

"Ernest Sutherland Bates," *New York Times*, December 5, 1939.

"Labor Under the Law," *New York Times*, December 5, 1939.

"No Agricultural Exemption," *New York Times*, December 5, 1939.

"Mr. Dewey's Opening Gun," *New York Times*, December 7, 1939.

"TVA Problems," *New York Times*, December 8, 1939.

"Fate of Small Nations," *New York Times*, December 10, 1939.

"Supervising Life Insurance," *New York Times*, December 15, 1939.

"Inside Germany," *New York Times*, December 17, 1939.

"Relief: A Case Study," *New York Times*, December 18, 1939.

"Ciano Gives the Case Away," *New York Times*, December 18, 1939.

"A Policy of Peace," *New York Times*, December 19, 1939.

"The *Columbus* Scuttled," *New York Times*, December 20, 1939.

"The Processing Tax," *New York Times*, December 21, 1939.

"Reasons for Unemployment," *New York Times*, December 11, 1939.

"Stupid Lying," *New York Times*, December 22, 1939.

"Stalin's Birthday," *New York Times*, December 23, 1939.

"Unifying the Peace Seekers," *New York Times*, December 25, 1939.

"High Tariffs Are 'Planning'," *New York Times*, December 29, 1939.

"Old-Age Insurance," *New York Times*, December 29, 1939.

"The Russian Censorship," *New York Times*, December 30, 1939.

"Man Against Nature," *New York Times*, December 30, 1939.

"An Excellent Guide to the Second World War" (on J. D. de Wilde, et al.), *New York Times Book Review*, December 31, 1939.

1940

"Hitler's New Year Threat," *New York Times*, January 1, 1940.

"Clarity About Deficits," *New York Times*, January 2, 1940.

"The Task Before Congress," *New York Times*, January 3, 1940.

"Labor Board Powers," *New York Times*, January 4, 1940.

"The Dies Committee," *New York Times*, January 5, 1940.

"The Democratic Process," *New York Times*, January 7, 1940.

"A Wide-Ranging History of Political Thought" (on G. Catlin), *New York Times Book Review*, January 7, 1940.

"1933 and 1940: Two Views," *New York Times*, January 8, 1940.

"Toward a Real Budget," *New York Times*, January 9, 1940.

"Advice to Republicans," *New York Times*, January 12, 1940.

"The Tax Tangle," *New York Times*, January 12, 1940.

"Mr. Hull States His Case," *New York Times*, January 13, 1940.

"Shadow vs. Substance," *New York Times*, January 15, 1940.

"The Neutrals Wait," *New York Times*, January 15, 1940.

"An Essential Study," *New York Times*, January 18, 1940.

"A Bad Precedent," *New York Times*, January 19, 1940.

"Government Price Fixing," *New York Times*, January 20, 1940.

"Trade With Japan," *New York Times*, January 21, 1940.

"On Business Cycles" (on L. Ayres, *Turning Points in Business Cycles*), *New York Times Book Review*, January 21, 1940.

"Pump-Priming vs. Recovery," *New York Times*, January 22, 1940.

"Britain's Mail Search," *New York Times*, January 22, 1940.

"The Silver Folly," *New York Times*, January 23, 1940.

"The Browder Case," *New York Times*, January 23, 1940.

"Continuing the Dies Case," *New York Times*, January 24, 1940.

"Restraints by Unions," *New York Times*, January 25, 1940.

"A Good Veto," *New York Times*, January 25, 1940.

"A Verdict Upheld," *New York Times*, January 27, 1940.

"A New Liberalism," *New York Times*, January 28, 1940.

"Capital is Still Wanted," *New York Times*, January 30, 1940.

"New Capital and Profits," *New York Times*, January 31, 1940.

"Economy Reaches Farm Aid," *New York Times*, February 1, 1940

"Old-Age Checks Flow Out," *New York Times*, February 2, 1940.

"Profits Make Jobs," *New York Times*, February 2, 1940.

"Jobs and the Machine," *New York Times*, February 3, 1940.

"'Have' and 'Have'-Nots," *New York Times*, February 4, 1940.

"What Farm and Costs?" *New York Times*, February 5, 1940.

"Labor and Industry," *New York Times*, February 6, 1940.

"The President's Dilemma," *New York Times*, February 8, 1940.

"The Need for Capital," *New York Times*, February 8, 1940.

"More Farm Aid Costs," *New York Times*, February 9, 1940.

"The Rate of Failure," *New York Times*, February 10, 1940.

"If it Were Really So," *New York Times*, February 11, 1940.

"The Economics of Debt," *New York Times*, February 12, 1940.

"Revising Job Insurance," *New York Times*, February 13, 1940.

"The Silver Folly," *New York Times*, February 15, 1940.

"Revising the Wagner Act," *New York Times*, February 17, 1940.

"Our Tariff Wall," *New York Times*, February 19, 1940.

"The Unsolved Relief Problem," *New York Times*, February 20, 1940.

"Inventions Make Jobs," *New York Times*, February 21, 1940.

"On Dangerous Thoughts" (on L. Hogben), *New York Times Book Review*, March 3, 1940.

"Amending the Wagner Act," *New York Times*, March 8, 1940.

"The Trade Agreements," *New York Times*, March 9, 1940.

"Between the Acts," *New York Times*, March 11, 1940.

"The Twilight of Economy," *New York Times*, March 11, 1940.

"The Test Case," *New York Times*, March 12, 1940.

"The New Hatch Bill," *New York Times*, March 13, 1940.

"A Penalty on Progress," *New York Times*, March 14, 1940.

"Wagner Act Changes," *New York Times*, March 15, 1940.

"Overdue Regulation," *New York Times*, March 16, 1940.

"Farm Aid and Relief," *New York Times*, March 17, 1940.

"The Hatch Bill," *New York Times*, March 18, 1940.

"A 'Real Peace'," *New York Times*, March 18, 1940.

"The $200,000,000 Handout," *New York Times*, March 19, 1940.

"A Letter to the SEC," *New York Times*, March 20, 1940.

"Election Year Finance," *New York Times*, March 22, 1940.

"Back-Door Health Insurance," *New York Times*, March 22, 1940.

"To Encourage New Capital," *New York Times*, March 23, 1940.

"Santayana on the German Philosophy of Egotism" (on George Santayana), *New York Times Book Review*, March 31, 1940

"Studies in Money and Power" (on H. R. Fairchild, E. Pound, H. B. Parlees, C. Snyder), *New York Times Book Review*, April 7, 1940.

"The Trees vs. the Forest," New York Times, April 9, 1940.

"With Back Pay," *New York Times*, April 10, 1940.

"Mr. Hughes at 78," *New York Times*, April 11, 1940.

"The Note to Mexico," *New York Times*, April 11, 1940.

"Amending the Wage-Hour Act," *New York Times*, April 12, 1940.

"Defense of the Wagner Act," *New York Times*, April 13, 1940.

"A Good Veto," *New York Times*, April 14, 1940.

"The Crime Against Norway," *New York Times*, April 15, 1940.

"Income is Production," *New York Times*, April 15, 1940.

"Regulating the Regulators," *New York Times*, April 16, 1940.

"Hitler's Excuses," *New York Times*, April 17, 1940.

"A Good Veto," *New York Times*, April 17, 1940.

"The Easiest Way," *New York Times*, April 19, 1940.

"A Protest from the House," *New York Times*, April 20, 1940.

"Tragedy at Little Falls," *New York Times*, April 22, 1940.

"Relief Probabilities," *New York Times*, April 22, 1940.

"Chain-Store Death Sentence," *New York Times*, April 22, 1940.

"The Menace of 'Easy Money'," *New York Times*, April 23, 1940.

"Britain's War Effort," *New York Times*, April 24, 1940.

"Wage-Hour Amendments," *New York Times*, April 25, 1940.

"The Taxi Cab Strike," *New York Times*, April 26, 1940.

"Wage-Hour Exemptions," *New York Times*, April 26, 1940.

"Investment Trust Control," *New York Times*, April 27, 1940.

"Mr. Willkie's Candor," *New York Times*, April 27, 1940.

"Machines on the Farm," *New York Times*, April 28, 1940.

"Wage-Hour Amendments," *New York Times*, April 29, 1940.

"Reform of Relief," *New York Times*, April 29, 1940.

"Risk Money," *New York Times*, April 30, 1930.

"Walsh-Healey Wages," *New York Times*, May 1, 1940.

"The Silver Folly," *New York Times*, May 2, 1940.

"Time for Responsibility," *New York Times*, May 6, 1940.

"While Il Duce Decides," *New York Times*, May 6, 1940.

"A Balanced Defense," *New York Times*, May 6, 1940.

"Progeny of the Deficit," *New York Times*, May 7, 1940.

"Crop Insurance," *New York Times*, May 8, 1940.

"In Restraint of Trade," *New York Times*, May 8, 1940.

"A Corn Export Subsidy," *New York Times*, May 8, 1940.

"What 'Restrains' Trade?" *New York Times*, May 9, 1940.

"Political Hand-Out," *New York Times*, May 11, 1940.

"A World in Flames," *New York Times*, May 12, 1940.

"Veterans' Pension Raid," *New York Times*, May 13, 1940.

"World Revolution," *New York Times*, May 13, 1940.

"A National Defense Program (Part I)," *New York Times*, May 15, 1940.

"A National Defense Program (Part II)," *New York Times*, May 16, 1940.

"Defending America," *New York Times*, May 19, 1940.

"Pegging Grain Prices," *New York Times*, May 10, 1940.

"The Line Still Holds," *New York Times*, May 20, 1940.

"A National Defense Program (Part VI)," *New York Times*, May 21, 1940.

"A National Defense Program (Part VII)," *New York Times*, May 22, 1940.

"An Obstacle to Defense," *New York Times*, May 23, 1940.

"Britain's 'Dictatorship'," *New York Times*, May 24, 1940.

"Defense of Democracy," *New York Times*, May 26, 1940.

"The President on Defense," *New York Times*, May 27, 1940.

"What Holds Back Business," *New York Times*, May 27, 1940.

"Production is the Problem," *New York Times*, May 28, 1940.

"Mr. Willkie on Defense," *New York Times*, May 31, 1940.

"Financing Defense," *New York Times*, June 1, 1940.

"Defending Our Hemisphere," *New York Times*, June 3, 1940.

"A Token Economy," *New York Times*, June 3, 1940.

"Guarding the Armories," *New York Times*, June 4, 1940.

"Mr. Stettinius Serves," *New York Times*, June 5, 1940.

"Symbolic Economy," *New York Times*, June 5, 1940.

"WPA vs. Defense," *New York Times*, June 6, 1940.

"WPA vs. Defense," *New York Times*, June 7, 1940.

"Training War Workers," *New York Times*, June 8, 1940.

"A Universal Income Tax," *New York Times*, June 8, 1940.

"A World Explores," *New York Times*, June 9, 1940.

"Defense Dollar," *New York Times*, June 10, 1940.

"Wagner Act Amendments," *New York Times*, June 11, 1940.

"Why Congress Must Stay in Session," *New York Times*, June 13, 1940.

"Rumble in Brazil," *New York Times*, June 14, 1940.

"A Bill Aimed at One Man," *New York Times*, June 15, 1940.

"Congress Must Stay," *New York Times*, June 15, 1940.

"WPA vs. Defense," *New York Times*, June 15, 1940.

"A Need to be Ready," *New York Times*, June 16, 1940.

"Lindbergh's Blind Spots," *New York Times*, June 17, 1940.

"Congress Must Stay," *New York Times*, June 18, 1940.

"Congress Must Stay," *New York Times*, June 19, 1940.

"Advice to Republicans," *New York Times*, June 19, 1940.

"Inter-American Trade," *New York Times*, June 20, 1940.

"Hasty Tax Plans," *New York Times*, June 21, 1940.

"A Good Rejection," *New York Times*, June 22, 1940.

"Controlled Labor," Speech at Tamiment Economic and Social Institute, *New York Times*, June 23, 1940.

"The Republican Opportunity," *New York Times*, June 24, 1940.

"Congress So Far," *New York Times*, June 25, 1940.

"Political Miracle," *New York Times*, June 30, 1940.

"A Tribute to V. F. Calverton," *The Modern Quarterly*, Fall 1940 (vol. XI, no. 7).

"Confusion in Defense," *New York Times*, July 1, 1940.

"Ships and Planes," *New York Times*, July 2, 1940.

"Taxing Excess Profits," *New York Times*, July 3, 1940.

"The Tenth Deficit," *New York Times*, July 4, 1940.

"Dollars for Defense," *New York Times*, July 7, 1940.

"The End of Maginot Lines," *New York Times*, July 8, 1940.

"A Budget Policy," *New York Times*, July 8, 1940.

"Regional 'Monroe Doctrines'," *New York Times*, July 8, 1940.

"Flow of Capital," *New York Times*, July 9, 1940.

"WPA vs. Defense," *New York Times*, July 10, 1940.

"Mr. Roosevelt and Defense," *New York Times*, July 12, 1940.

"Ships and Planes," *New York Times*, July 13, 1940.

"New, But Obsolete," *New York Times*, July 15, 1940.

"Why a Vice-President?" *New York Times*, July 16, 1940.

"The Democratic Platform," *New York Times*, July 19, 1940.

"Defense Expenditures," *New York Times*, July 21, 1940.

"After the Convention," *New York Times*, July 21, 1940.

"The Second Hatch Act," *New York Times*, July 22, 1940.

"Pan-American Trade," *New York Times*, July 22, 1940.

"Congress Not Included," *New York Times*, July 22, 1940.

"The New Order," *New York Times*, July 22, 1940.

"Uses of the Telephone," *New York Times*, July 23, 1940.

"Inter-American Policies," *New York Times*, July 23, 1940.

"Britain's New Budget," *New York Times*, July 24, 1940.

"The Real American Interest," *New York Times*, July 27, 1940.

"American Planes," *New York Times*, July 27, 1940.

"Freedom and Control," *New York Times*, July 28, 1940.

"Unity at Havana," *New York Times*, July 29, 1940.

"Taxing Excess Profits," *New York Times*, July 30, 1940.

"Life and Death of a Policy," *New York Times*, July 31, 1940.

"State Help in Defense," *New York Times*, August 3, 1940.

"The President on Conscription," *New York Times*, August 3, 1940.

"Alarm of an Invasion," *New York Times*, August 4, 1940.

"Liberal Trade Principles," *New York Times*, August 5, 1940.

"While Defense Lags," *New York Times*, August 5, 1940.

"Confusing Export Policy," *New York Times*, August 7, 1940.

"To Combat Sedition," *New York Times*, August 7, 1940.

"The Excess Profits Tax," *New York Times*, August 8, 1940.

"Topics of the Times," *New York Times*, August 8, 1940.

"No Budget Policy," *New York Times*, August 11, 1940.

"Dangers of Bad Temper," *New York Times*, August 11, 1940.

"The Pork Barrel View," *New York Times*, August 12, 1940.

"Planning for Defense," *New York Times*, August 12, 1940.

"Haves and Have-Nots," *New York Times*, August 12, 1940.

"Excess Profits Tax Changes," *New York Times*, August 13, 1940.

"The Social Security Act," *New York Times*, August 14, 1940.

"Foolishly Handcuffed," *New York Times*, August 16, 1940.

"For Hemispheral Defense," *New York Times*, August 17, 1940.

"The State of Our Defense," *New York Times*, August 19, 1940.

"Face-to-Face Debate," *New York Times*, August 19, 1940.

"Walter P. Chrysler," *New York Times*, August 20, 1940.

"Campaign Mud," *New York Times*, August 21, 1940

"A Needless Yoke," *New York Times*, August 22, 1940.

"Loans to Latin America," *New York Times*, August 23, 1940.

"Fallacy of 'Defense'," *New York Times*, August 25, 1940.

"The Problem of Contracts," *New York Times*, August 26, 1940.

"Two Jobs for Mr. Jones?" *New York Times*, August 28, 1940.

"Excess Profits Taxes," *New York Times*, August 28, 1940.

"For Democratic Debate," *New York Times*, August 30, 1940.

"Information on Defense," *New York Times*, August 30, 1940.

"Taking Over Industry," *New York Times*, August 31, 1940.

"A Defense Report," *New York Times*, September 1, 1940.

"Congressional Jitters," *New York Times*, September 2, 1940.

"Conscripting Industry," *New York Times*, September 4, 1940.

"Airplane Figures," *New York Times*, September 4, 1940.

"Results of Plant Seizure," *New York Times*, September 5, 1940.

"Our New Bases," *New York Times*, September 5, 1940.

"Democratic Process," *New York Times*, September 6, 1940.

"The Excess Profits Tax," *New York Times*, September 6, 1940.

"The Excess Profits Tax," *New York Times*, September 7, 1940.

"Casualties—War and Peace," *New York Times*, September 7, 1940.

"'Planning' and War," *New York Times*, September 8, 1940.

"Conscription of Wealth," *New York Times*, September 8, 1940.

"Conscription in Conference," *New York Times*, September 9, 1940.

"For Democratic Safeguards," *New York Times*, September 10, 1940.

"For A Planned Defense," *New York Times*, September 11, 1940.

"Housing for Defense," *New York Times*, September 12, 1940.

"Keeping 'Labor's Gain'," *New York Times*, September 13, 1940.

"Conscription Adopted," *New York Times*, September 15, 1940.

"Sacrifice—of What?" *New York Times*, September 15, 1940.

"How Much Control?" *New York Times*, September 16, 1940.

"Truth About 'Appeasement'," *New York Times*, September 17, 1940.

"Mr. Wilkie at Coffeyville," *New York Times*, September 17, 1940.

"Taxing Normal Profits," *New York Times*, September 18, 1940.

"Economic Defense," *New York Times*, September 20, 1940.

"The Need Is Production," *New York Times*, September 21, 1940.

"Mr. Willkie's Foreign Views," *New York Times*, September 23, 1940.

"To Permit British Enlistment," *New York Times*, September 23, 1940.

"Congress Should Stay," *New York Times*, September 23, 1940.

"Congress Should Stay," *New York Times*, September 26, 1940.

"A Hurried Tax Bill," *New York Times*, September 24, 1940.

"The Dangers of Haste," *New York Times*, September 25, 1940.

"Curbing the Regulators," *New York Times*, September 25, 1940.

"Wildcat Legislation," *New York Times*, September 26, 1940.

"Mr. Norris's Dilemma," *New York Times*, September 26, 1940.

"Short-Circuit Legislation," *New York Times*, September 27, 1940.

"Democratic Processes," *New York Times*, September 27, 1940.

"Mr. Norris's Reversal," *New York Times*, September 28, 1940.

"The Strategy of Terror," *New York Times*, September 29, 1940.

"The Tax Agreement," *New York Times*, October 1, 1940.

"The NLRB Vacancy," *New York Times*, October 3, 1940.

"Mr. Willkie on Defense," *New York Times*, October 4, 1940.

"An Astonishing 'Opinion'," *New York Times*, October 5, 1940.

"Air Policy Criticized," *New York Times*, October 6, 1940.

"Labor Policy vs. Defense," *New York Times*, October 7, 1940.

"Administration Labor Policy," *New York Times*, October 9, 1940.

"Nothing Left But the Grin," *New York Times*, October 10, 1940.

"An Interim Committee," *New York Times*, October 11, 1940.

"Why the NLRB Vacancy?" *New York Times*, October 11, 1940.

"No Press Exemption," *The Chattanooga Times*, September 12, 1940.

"No Press Exemption," *New York Times*, September 13, 1940.

"Party Leadership," *New York Times*, October 14, 1940.

"Bases in South America," *New York Times*, October 15, 1940.

"Register Today," *New York Times*, October 15, 1940.

"Wage-Hour Rulings," *New York Times*, October 16, 1940.

"A Poor Third-Term Argument," *New York Times*, October 17, 1940.

"Within the Law," *New York Times*, October 19, 1940.

"Presidents, Prime Ministers and Third Terms," *New York Times*, October 21, 1940.

"The Third Term Issue," *New York Times*, October 23, 1940.

"The Wage-Hour Law," *New York Times*, October 24, 1940.

"Mr. Roosevelt on Production," *New York Times*, October 25, 1940.

"The Third Term," *New York Times*, October 25, 1940.

"The Third Term," *New York Times*, October 26, 1940.

"Third-Term Background," *New York Times*, October 27, 1940.

"Can America Grow?" *New York Times*, October 28, 1940.

"The Third Term," *New York Times*, October 28,1940.

"Cooper Union," *New York Times*, October 28, 1940.

"Foreign Policy and Defense," *New York Times*, October 30, 1940.

"The Third Term," *New York Times*, October 30, 1940.

"The Third Term," *New York Times*, October 31, 1940.

"Warning the Farmers," *New York Times*, October 31, 1940.

"The Road to Bankruptcy," *New York Times*, November 1, 1940.

"The Third Term," *New York Times*, November 1, 1940.

"Mr. Roosevelt on Defense," *New York Times*, November 2, 1940.

"The Third Term," *New York Times*, November 4, 1940.

"Electoral vs. Popular Vote," *New York Times*, November 5, 1940.

"Wage Regulation," *New York Times*, November 6, 1940.

"Mr. Roosevelt's 'Mandate'," *New York Times*, November 7, 1940.

"The New Congress," *New York Times*, November 8, 1940.

"President and Congress," *New York Times*, November 8, 1940.

"For a Budget Policy," *New York Times*, November 9, 1940.

"Congress Should Stay," *New York Times*, November 19, 1940.

"Defense Work Strikes," *New York Times*, November 20, 1940.

"Congress Votes to Stay," *New York Times*, November 21, 1940.

"The Logan-Walter Bill," *New York Times*, November 21, 1940.

"V. F. Calverton," *New York Times*, November 22, 1940.

"Toward A Budget Policy," *New York Times*, November 22, 1940.

"Britain's Need for Credit," *New York Times*, November 25, 1940.

"Regulating the Regulators," *New York Times*, November 26, 1940.

"WPA vs. Defense," *New York Times*, November 25, 1940.

"To Prevent Strikes," *New York Times*, November 27, 1940.

"Non-Defense Spending," *New York Times*, November 28, 1940.

"The Inside Story," *New York Times*, November 29, 1940.

"How Shall We Organize To Meet Today's Crisis?" *Independent Woman*, December 1940.

"The Level of Discussion," *New York Times*, December 2, 1940.

"A Sound Budget Policy," *New York Times*, December 2, 1940.

"Our Alternative To War" (partial authorship), *New York Times*, December 4, 1940.

"Credit for Britain," *New York Times*, December 5, 1940.

"Dollars for Argentina," *New York Times*, December 7, 1940.

"Help for Greece," *New York Times*, December 9, 1940.

"The Truth About Defense," *New York Times*, December 9, 1940.

"Advice to Taxpayers," *New York Times*, December 10, 1940.

"An Obstacle to Defense," *New York Times*, December 10, 1940.

"The Basis of Unity," *New York Times*, December 11, 1490.

"Taxing Government Bonds," *New York Times*, December 11, 1940.

"Food and the Blockade," *New York Times*, December 12, 1940.

"Defense and the Wagner Act," *New York Times*, December 14, 1940.

"The Truth About Defense," *New York Times*, December 15, 1940.

"Air Corps Students," *New York Times*, December 16, 1940.

"The Thirty-Nine Steps—Plus," *New York Times*, December 17, 1940.

"Machine Tools for Defense: A Lesson in Economics," *New York Times*, December 18, 1940.

"The Logan-Walter Bill Dies," *New York Times*, December 19, 1940.

"Priorities," *New York Times*, December 20, 1940.

"Aid to Britain" (from "The President gave . . ."), *New York Times*, December 22, 1940.

"Housing for Defense," *New York Times*, December 23, 1940.

"Our Aid in Aircraft," *New York Times*, December 26, 1940.

"The War in the Air," *New York Times*, December 29, 1940.

"A Call to Action," *New York Times*, December 30, 1940.

"Wagner Act Revision," *New York Times*, December 30, 1940.

"Non-Defense Economy," *New York Times*, December 31, 1940.

1941

"The Hopson Verdict," *New York Times*, January 1, 1941.

"Prefabricated Housing," *New York Times*, January 2, 1941.

"To Prevent Inflation," *New York Times*, January 3, 1941.

"The New American Fleet," *New York Times*, January 4, 1941.

"Roll Out the Bombers," *New York Times*, January 4, 1941.

"To Speed Up Our Aid," *New York Times*, January 6, 1941.

"Henri Bergson," *New York Times*, January 7, 1941.

"A General Income Tax," *New York Times*, January 8, 1941.

"Written Labor Agreements," *New York Times*, January 8, 1941.

"New Defense Set-Up," *New York Times*, January 9, 1941.

"Debt-Limit," *New York Times*, January 10, 1941.

"The Need Is Planes," *New York Times*, January 12, 1941.

"Thomas Davidson," *New York Times*, January 13, 1941.

"Credit to Britain Proposed" (signed under "Stuart Piebes"), *New York Times*, January 16, 1941.

"The Facts About Airplanes," *New York Times*, January 20, 1941.

"Britain's Draft of Workers," *New York Times*, January 22, 1941.

"Industrial Synchronization," *New York Times*, January 23, 1941.

"A Justice Steps Down," *New York Times*, January 23, 1941.

"The Mortgage Moratorium," *New York Times*, January 25, 1941.

"The Truth About Defense," *New York Times*, January 26, 1941.

"Regulating the Regulators," *New York Times*, January 27, 1941.

"War Tax Policy," *New York Times*, January 28, 1941.

"Hitler As Wizard," *New York Times*, January 30, 1941.

"Mr. Willkie's Dilemma," *New York Times*, January 30, 1941.

"Debt Limit and Budget," *New York Times*, January 31, 1941.

"500 Planes a Day," *New York Times*, January 31, 1941.

"National Income," *New York Times*, February 2, 1941.

"Labor's Share," *New York Times*, February 2, 1941.

"Milk Control," *New York Times*, February 4, 1941.

"A Veto Power for Congress," *New York Times*, February 4, 1941.

"An Historic Decision," *New York Times*, February 5, 1941.

"The Facts About Defense," *New York Times*, February 6, 1941.

"Unions and the Sherman Act," *New York Times*, February 8, 1941.

"The Wave of the Future . . .," *New York Times*, February 8, 1941.

"The African Campaign," *New York Times*, February 9, 1941.

"Mr. Churchill's Confidence," *New York Times*, February 10, 1941.

"Two Picketing Decisions," *New York Times*, February 12, 1941.

"The Dies Committee," *New York Times*, February 13, 1941.

"Aluminum 'Bottleneck'," *New York Times*, February 16, 1941.

"Diplomacy of Terror," *New York Times*, February 16, 1941.

"The Bill Before the Senate," *New York Times*, February 17, 1941.

"Airplane Production," *New York Times*, February 17, 1941.

"No Immunity," *New York Times*, February 18, 1941.

"Strategy in the Balkans," *New York Times*, February 18, 1941.

"On Doing Without," *New York Times*, February 19, 1941.

"Defense Production," *New York Times*, February 20, 1941.

"Limiting Delegated Powers" (signed under "Stuart Piebes"), *New York Times*, February 20, 1941.

"Business Jitters," *New York Times*, February 22, 1941.

"Defense Organization," *New York Times*, February 23, 1941.

"Defense Information," *New York Times*, February 24, 1941.

"Discredited Dictator," *New York Times*, February 25, 1941.

"Light on Our Defenses," *New York Times*, February 26, 1941.

"Corporate Tax Relief," *New York Times*, February 26, 1941.

"A Defense Inquiry," *New York Times*, February 27, 1941.

"Strike Prevention," *New York Times*, February 28, 1941.

"Two Ends of the Axis," *New York Times*, March 1, 1941.

"More 'Bloodless' Victories," *New York Times*, March 3, 1941.

"Enforcing Blue Laws," *New York Times*, March 4, 1941.

"Cost of Farm Aid," *New York Times*, March 5, 1941.

"Airplane Engines," *New York Times*, March 5, 1941.

"Reductio Ad Absurdum," *New York Times*, March 5, 1941.

"Defense Strikes," *New York Times*, March 6, 1941.

"Russia—Late Again," *New York Times*, March 6, 1941.

"The Threat to Greece," *New York Times*, March 7, 1941.

"Defense Strikes," *New York Times*, March 8, 1941.

"The Economic Choice," *New York Times*, March 11, 1941.

"Termination Clause Upheld," *New York Times*, March 11, 1941.

"Defense Standardization," *New York Times*, March 12, 1941.

"Snow White and the WPA," *New York Times*, March 12, 1941.

"The TNEC Concludes," *New York Times*, March 13, 1941.

"Communist Teachers," *New York Times*, March 14, 1941.

"Strike Mediation," *New York Times*, March 15, 1941.

"Facts About Airplanes," *New York Times*, March 15, 1941.

"America's Decision," *New York Times*, March 17, 1941.

"Psychology of Billions," *New York Times*, March 18, 1941.

"France's Food Shortage," *New York Times*, March 18, 1941.

"Communists in Education," *New York Times*, March 19, 1941.

"What a Strike May Mean," *New York Times*, March 20, 1941.

"The New Mediation Board," *New York Times*, March 20, 1941.

"The Bridge of Ship," *New York Times*, March 21, 1941.

"Extortionate Union Fees," *New York Times*, March 24, 1941.

"Stalin's Diplomacy," *New York Times*, March 24, 1941.

"Mortgage Moratorium," *New York Times*, March 25, 1941.

"Strikes: The Next Step," *New York Times*, March 27, 1941.

"Seizing Plants Won't Help," *New York Times*, March 28, 1941.

"Not A Solution," *New York Times*, March 29, 1941.

"Not Beyond the Law," *New York Times*, March 30, 1941.

"Nondefense Extravagance," *New York Times*, March 31, 1941.

"The TNEC Report," *New York Times*, April 1, 1941.

"The Soft-Coal Strike," *New York Times*, April 2, 1941.

"A Fair Trial For Mediation," *New York Times*, April 3, 1941.

"The Walsh-Healey Act," *New York Times*, April 4, 1941.

"A Labor Code for the Crisis," *New York Times*, April 4, 1941.

"Wage-Hour Act Revision," *New York Times*, April 5, 1941.

"Labor and Defense," *New York Times*, April 6, 1941.

"Extending a Bad Law," *New York Times*, April 6, 1941.

"A Dangerous 'Cure'," *New York Times*, April 8, 1941.

"Labor and the Trust Laws," *New York Times*, April 10, 1941.

"The Strike Problem," *New York Times*, April 11, 1941.

"A 'Cooling-Off' Period," *New York Times*, April 12, 1941.

"Clarity About Defense," *New York Times*, April 12, 1941.

"The Japanese-Russian Pact," *New York Times*, April 14, 1941.

"Why Yugoslavia Fought," *New York Times*, April 14, 1941.

"Unions in the Courts," *New York Times*, April 15, 1941.

"The Wage-Price Spiral," *New York Times*, April 16, 1941.

"The Farm 'Parity' Slogan," *New York Times*, April 17, 1941.

"Money Into Man-Hours," *New York Times*, April 18, 1941.

"Government Price Policy," *New York Times*, April 18, 1941.

"A Courageous Rejection," *New York Times*, April 19, 1941.

"The Yugoslav Decision," *New York Times*, April 20, 1941.

"On Appeasing Stalin," *New York Times*, April 21, 1941.

"The Vinson Labor Bill," *New York Times*, April 22, 1941.

"Committee Prerogatives," *New York Times*, April 26, 1941.

"What Air Power Means," *New York Times*, April 27, 1941.

"Today's Decision," *New York Times*, April 28, 1941.

"Hitler in Athens," *New York Times*, April 28, 1941.

"Let Us Face the Truth," *New York Times*, April 30, 1941.

"The Right Not to Hire," *New York Times*, May 1, 1941.

"For A Cooling Off Period," *New York Times*, May 2, 1941.

"The Right Not to Hire," *New York Times*, May 3, 1941.

"New Tax Plans," *New York Times*, May 4, 1941.

"A Reversal in Budget Policy," *New York Times*, May 5, 1941.

"The Choice Before Us," *New York Times*, May 7, 1941.

"Roll out the Bombers!" *New York Times*, May 8, 1941.

"A Regrettable Veto," *New York Times*, May 8, 1941.

"Using Our Labor Resources," *New York Times*, May 9, 1941.

"A Year of Awakening," *New York Times*, May 11, 1941.

"How Can the War Be Won?" *New York Times*, May 12, 1941.

"Another Needless Strike," *New York Times*, May 13, 1941.

"To Discourage Strikes," *New York Times*, May 14, 1941.

"Farm Grab," *New York Times*, May 15, 1941.

"A Bomber Patrol," *New York Times*, May 16, 1941.

"The Spiral of Wages," *New York Times*, May 17, 1941.

"Sacrifices—By Whom?" *New York Times*, May 20, 1941.

"WPA vs. Defense," *New York Times*, May 22, 1941.

"To Make Democracy Effective," *New York Times*, May 23, 1941.

"Buy Something British," *New York Times*, May 24, 1941.

"Does It 'Diminish Disputes'?" *New York Times*, May 24, 1941.

"A Lesson From Crete," *New York Times*, May 24, 1941.

"Sea Power vs. Air Power," *New York Times*, May 26, 1941.

"Labor Racketeering," *New York Times*, May 27, 1941.

"The Lesson of the Bismarck," *New York Times*, May 28, 1941.

"For Offensive 'Defense'," *New York Times*, May 29, 1941.

"Federal Wage Corporations," *New York Times*, May 30, 1941.

"The Meaning of Crete," *New York Times*, May 31, 1941.

"Labor, Goods, and Time," *New York Times*, June 3, 1941.

"Property Seizure," *New York Times*, June 4, 1941.

"A Plea of Guilty," *New York Times*, June 5, 1941.

"Double Standard," *New York Times*, June 5, 1941.

"Our Inflexible Government" (signed under "Stuart Piebes"), *New York Times*, June 5, 1941.

"France at the Crossroads," *New York Times*, June 6, 1941.

"Defense Strikes," *New York Times*, June 8, 1941.

"The Wrong Solution," *New York Times*, June 9, 1941.

"Communist-Inspired Strikes," *New York Times*, June 10, 1941.

"The Labor Crisis," *New York Times*, June 11, 1941.

"Settling Future Strikes," *New York Times*, June 12, 1941.

"Under the Wagner Act," *New York Times*, June 13, 1941.

"Senatorial Politics," *New York Times*, June 14, 1941.

"Stalin's Bankrupt Diplomacy," *New York Times*, June 17, 1941.

"New Strategy in the Pacific," *New York Times*, June 19, 1941.

"To Protect Our Ships," *New York Times*, June 20, 1941.

"A New Labor Program," *New York Times*, June 21, 1941.

"Hitlerian Strategy," *New York Times*, June 21, 1941.

"Hitler Invades Russia," *New York Times*, June 23, 1941.

"The Time to Act is Now," *New York Times*, June 24, 1941.

"A Better Bill," *New York Times*, June 25, 1941.

"The Right to Work," *New York Times*, June 27, 1941.

"Stalin's Bankrupt Diplomacy," *New York Times*, June 28, 1941.

"A Lesson From Hitler," *New York Times*, June 29, 1941.

"Topsy-Turvy Price-Fixing," *New York Times*, June 30, 1941.

"A Strike Averted," *New York Times*, June 30, 1941.

"Defense Needs Planning," *New York Times*, July 3, 1941.

"Strike Aftermath," *New York Times*, July 4, 1941.

"The American Communists," *New York Times*, July 5, 1941.

"The Milk Strike," *New York Times*, July 8, 1941.

"Iceland Must Be Held," *New York Times*, July 9, 1941.

"What Next for Japan?" *New York Times*, July 10, 1941.

"A Policy of Drift," *New York Times*, July 12, 1941.

"Germany Tastes Real War," *New York Times*, July 14, 1941.

"On Voting for Defense," *New York Times*, July 15, 1941.

"Mr. Henderson's Warning," *New York Times*, July 16, 1941.

"Communist Candor," *New York Times*, July 16, 1941.

"Why Power is Needed," *New York Times*, July 19, 1941.

"Penalizing Marriage," *New York Times*, July 19, 1941.

"Canada's Wage Plan," *New York Times*, July 22, 1941.

"Plant Seizure Demands," *New York Times*, July 22, 1941.

"Joint Tax Returns," *New York Times*, July 23, 1941.

"Newspaper-Owned Radio," *New York Times*, July 23, 1941.

"Joint Tax Returns" (signed under "Stuart Piebes"), *New York Times*, July 23, 1941.

"Taxing 'Excess' Profits" (to . . . earned on invested capital), *New York Times*, July 24, 1941.

"The Vice of 'Seniority'," *New York Times*, July 29, 1941.

"The Control of Prices," *New York Times*, July 31, 1941.

"Helicopters for Defense," *New York Times*, August 3, 1941.

"What Causes Inflation," *New York Times*, August 19, 1941.

"Defense and WPA," *New York Times*, August 20, 1941.

"The Kearny Strike," *New York Times*, August 21, 1941.

"Defense Lag," *New York Times*, August 22, 1941.

"The New Reign of Terror," *New York Times*, August 23, 1941.

"One-Sided Compulsion," *New York Times*, August 25, 1941.

"The Right to Manage," *New York Times*, August 26, 1941.

"Adopting a Labor Policy," *New York Times*, August 27, 1941.

"Unjudicial Mr. Smith," *New York Times*, August 28, 1941.

"Relations With Japan," *New York Times*, August 29, 1941.

"Defense Organization," *New York Times*, August 30, 1941.

"Regulating Radio," *New York Times*, August 30, 1941.

"More Pensioneering," *New York Times*, September 1, 1941.

"No Retreat," *New York Times*, September 2, 1941.

"Bankers Up in the Air," *New York Times*, September 2, 1941.

"Taxing Capital Gains," *New York Times*, September 5, 1941.

"Airplane Production Rises," *New York Times*, September 6, 1941.

"Money for Defense," *New York Times*, September 7, 1941.

"Revolution in Strategy," *New York Times*, September 8, 1941.

"Stabilizing Prices," *New York Times*, September 9, 1941.

"To Protect Workers," *New York Times*, September 10, 1941.

"First Things First," *New York Times*, September 11, 1941.

"Over-All Planning," *New York Times*, September 12, 1941.

"Price-Fixing Puzzles," *New York Times*, September 14, 1941.

"On the March," *New York Times*, September 14, 1941.

"The Fallacy of 'Defense'," *New York Times*, September 15, 1941.

"A Balanced Steel Output," *New York Times*, September 15, 1941.

" 'Voices' of Europe," *New York Times*, September 16, 1941.

"Hitler Behind Napoleon," *New York Times*, September 16, 1941.

"Two Septembers," *New York Times*, September 17, 1941.

"Dilemma at Kearny," *New York Times*, September 19, 1941.

"The Eastern Front," *New York Times*, September 20, 1941.

"The Race Against Time," *New York Times*, September 21, 1941.

"Government Ship Seizures," *New York Times*, September 23, 1941.

"The Editor of Harper's," *New York Times*, September 24, 1941.

"Participants as Mediators," *New York Times*, September 25, 1941.

"The Treasury's Proposals," *New York Times*, September 26, 1941.

"Argument for Delay," *New York Times*, September 27, 1941.

"The Closed Shop," *New York Times*, September 28, 1941.

"The People's of Czechoslovakia . . .," *New Yorksky Dennik*, October 28, 1941.

"The Battle of the Atlantic," *New York Times*, September 29, 1941.

"Kings in Exile" (co-authored), *New York Times*, September 29, 1941.

"The Bridges Case," *New York Times*, September 30, 1941.

"Not a War Profits Tax," *New York Times*, October 2, 1941.

"Revising Social Security," *New York Times*, October 2, 1941.

"Labor's Immunity," *New York Times*, October 4, 1941.

"Double Standard," *New York Times*, October 5, 1941.

"Social Security Reforms," *New York Times*, October 7, 1941.

"A Bill Aimed at One Man," *New York Times*, October 8, 1941.

"Words and Acts About Labor," *New York Times*, October 9, 1941.

"State Security Payments," *New York Times*, October 10, 1941.

"The Strange Case of the Currier Bid," *New York Times*, October 10, 1941.

"The Ban on New Building," *New York Times*, October 11, 1941.

"Encouraging Labor Chaos," *New York Times*, October 13, 1941.

"New Rules for Radio," *New York Times*, October 14, 1941.

"To Study Social Security," *New York Times*, October 15, 1941.

"A. F. L. vs. Mr. Arnold," *New York Times*, October 16, 1941.

"Why An Elected Controller?" *New York Times*, October 18, 1941.

"The Role of the R.A.F.," *New York Times*, October 19, 1941.

"A Program for Victory," *New York Times*, October 20, 1941.

"Heavy Tax But No Revenue," *New York Times*, October 20, 1941.

"One-Way Compulsion," *New York Times*, October 21, 1941.

"The New Double Standard," *New York Times*, October 22, 1941.

"NDMB Dilemma," *New York Times*, October 23, 1941.

"Oil and the War in Russia," *New York Times*, October 24, 1941.

"Uncle Sam Buys 'Protection'," *New York Times*, October 24, 1941.

"Cooper Union," *New York Times*, October 24, 1941.

"To Protect the Worker," *New York Times*, October 26, 1941.

"A Labor Program—Now," *New York Times*, October 27, 1941.

"New Voting Method Proposed to Remedy Present Faults," *New York Times*, October 26, 1941.

"The Power of Labor Leaders," *New York Times*, October 28, 1941.

"The Crisis in Labor," *New York Times*, October 29, 1941.

"The Next Step," *New York Times*, October 30, 1941.

"A Crucial Choice," *New York Times*, October 31, 1941.

"Behind Our Labor Laws," *New York Times*, November 2, 1941.

"Voter's Headache," *New York Times*, November 4, 1941.

"Coercing the Government," *New York Times*, November 5, 1941.

"We Must Work Longer Hours," *New York Times*, November 6, 1941.

"Our Policy Toward Finland," *New York Times*, November 6, 1941.

"Russia's Resistance," *New York Times*, November 7, 1941.

"The Railway Wage Decision," *New York Times*, November 7, 1941.

"To Curb Labor Racketeers," *New York Times*, November 8, 1941.

"Hitler's Latest Lie," *New York Times*, November 10, 1941.

"Defying the Government," *New York Times*, November 11, 1941.

"Toward a Showdown," *New York Times*, November 12, 1941.

"P. R. and the Council," *New York Times*, November 14, 1941.

"The President Speaks Out," *New York Times*, November 15, 1941.

"Mountain Mothers Mouse," *New York Times*, November 15, 1941.

"Biography of a Board," *New York Times*, November 18, 1941.

"A Muddled Decision," *New York Times*, November 18, 1941.

"The President's Proposal," *New York Times*, November 20, 1941.

"The Closed Shop Issue," *New York Times*, November 21, 1941.

"The Administration and Labor," *New York Times*, November 22, 1941.

"A Crucial Precedent," *New York Times*, November 24, 1941.

"Destroying Labor Boards," *New York Times*, November 25, 1941.

"Compulsory Arbitration?" *New York Times*, November 26, 1941.

"The Real Issue," *New York Times*, November 26, 1941.

"The New Labor Bill," *New York Times*, November 27, 1941.

"Too Much For One Man," *New York Times*, November 27, 1941.

"Higher Taxi Fares?" *New York Times*, November 28, 1941.

"Class Legislation," *New York Times*, November 30, 1941.

"Ineffective Labor Bills," *New York Times*, December 1, 1941.

"We Are A Funny People," *New York Times*, December 2, 1941.

"The Railway Settlement," *New York Times*, December 3, 1941.

"The Anti-Strike Bill," *New York Times*, December 4, 1941.

"The House Labor Bill," *New York Times*, December 5, 1941.

"An Ominous Delay," *New York Times*, December 6, 1941.

"One-Way Economics," *New York Times*, December 7, 1941.

"Amend the Wagner Act," *New York Times*, December 8, 1941.

"The Captive Mine Case," *New York Times*, December 10, 1941.

"Russia, Japan, and the United States," *New York Times*, December 11, 1941.

"This is an Air War," *New York Times*, December 11, 1941.

"The War Declarations," *New York Times*," December 12, 1941.

"This is an Air War," *New York Times*, December 13, 1941.

"To Hold the Philippines," *New York Times*, December 16, 1941.

"For Labor Peace," *New York Times*, December 17, 1941.

"Beginning With Me," *New York Times*, December 18, 1941.

"Air Power and Sea Power," *New York Times*, December 20, 1941.

"The End of 'Disunity'," *New York Times*, December 21, 1941.

"Six Months: The German Russian War Calendar," *New York Times*, December 21, 1941.

"Wartime Labor Relations," *New York Times*, December 22, 1941.

"The Welders' Strike," *New York Times*, December 23, 1941.

"The Labor Agreement," *New York Times*, December 24, 1941.

"Free Speech For Employers," *New York Times*, December 26, 1941.

"For Anglo-American Unity," *New York Times*, December 27, 1941.

"Congress in Wartime," *New York Times*, December 28, 1941.

"The Lessons of Air Power," *New York Times*, December 29, 1941.

"A War Labor Board," *New York Times*, December 31, 1941.

1942

"Fifty Billion a Year," *New York Times*, January 1, 1942.

"Labor Policy," *New York Times*, January 2, 1942.

"Civil Liberties in War," *New York Times*, January 4, 1942.

"The New League," *New York Times*, January 4, 1942.

"Congress in Wartime," *New York Times*, January 6, 1942.

"War News and the Censor," *New York Times*, January 7, 1942.

"The First War Budget," *New York Times*, January 8, 1942.

"Finland's Dilemma," *New York Times*, January 10, 1942.

"Political Price-Fixing," *New York Times*, January 12, 1942.

"The Strategy of Islands," *New York Times*, January 13, 1942.

"The New War Labor Board," *New York Times*, January 14, 1942.

"Legislating Inflation," *New York Times*, January 14, 1942.

"Report on Defense," *New York Times*, January 16, 1942.

"The Closed Union," *New York Times*, January 16, 1942.

"Organizing for War," *New York Times*, January 17, 1942.

"Wartime Labor Policy," *New York Times*, January 18, 1942.

"Blaming the Motor Industry," *New York Times*, January 19, 1942.

"A Union of Unions," *New York Times*, January 20, 1942.

"What Kind of Navy?" *New York Times*, January 21, 1942.

"The Vinson Report," *New York Times*, January 22, 1942.

"A Lucidly Written Introduction to Semantics" (on S. I. Hayakawa), *New York Times Book Review*, January 18, 1942.

"Moral of the Fare Increase," *New York Times*, January 23, 1942.

"Estimate vs. Actuality," *New York Times*, January 26, 1942.

"Travesty of Price Control," *New York Times*, January 24, 1942.

"The Report on Pearl Harbor," *New York Times*, January 26, 1942.

"For a Joint Committee," *New York Times*, January 27, 1942.

"A Veto Needed," *New York Times*, January 28, 1942.

"The Chain of Responsibility," *New York Times*, January 29, 1942.

"The Place of the Air Force," *New York Times*, January 29, 1942.

"Dollar-A-Year Men," *New York Times*, January 30, 1942.

"Reports to the Nation," *New York Times*, February 1, 1942.

"The Nation's Income," *New York Times*, February 2, 1942.

"Double Pay for Sundays?" *New York Times*, February 3, 1942.

"Sunday Wage Rates," *New York Times*, February 4, 1942.

"Price-Control Policies," *New York Times*, February 5, 1942.

"For A Wartime Labor Policy," *New York Times*, February 7, 1942.

"More Flexible Constitution Viewed as National Need," *New York Times*, February 8, 1942.

"This War Winter," *New York Times*, February 8, 1942.

"This is an Air War," *New York Times*, February 9, 1942.

"'Co-Prosperity' in Action," *New York Times*, February 11, 1942.

"Wartime Wage Policy," *New York Times*, February 11, 1942.

"Russian Winter Still," *New York Times*, February 13, 1942.

"The Ford Strike," *New York Times*, February 13, 1942.

"Virginia Senator," *New York Times*, February 14, 1942.

"Wages in Wartime," *New York Times*, February 15, 1942.

"Fighting the War on a Forty-Hour Week," *New York Times*, February 16, 1942.

"The Time is Now," *New York Times*, February 16, 1942.

"Mr. Churchill's Warning," *New York Times*, February 16, 1942.

"Chaos in Relief," *New York Times*, February 17, 1942.

"To Protect the Worker," *New York Times*, February 19, 1942.

"Wartime Labor Policy," *New York Times*, February 20, 1942.

"Chaotic Relief," *New York Times*, February 21, 1942.

"How Can I Help?" *New York Times*, February 23, 1942.

"Mr. Henderson on Wages," *New York Times*, February 23, 1942.

"War Displacement Benefits," *New York Times*, February 23, 1942.

"A Lesson in Diplomacy," *New York Times*, February 24, 1942.

"War Displacement Benefits," *New York Times*, February 25, 1942.

"The Turtle Policy," *New York Times*, February 25, 1942.

"Exemptions From Sacrifice," *New York Times*, February 28, 1942.

"The Los Angeles Mystery," *New York Times*, February 28, 1942.

"Who is 'Labor'?" *New York Times*, February 28, 1942.

"Fate of the Smith Bill," *New York Times*, March 3, 1942.

"Invitation to Racketeering," *New York Times*, March 5, 1942.

"The Public and the War," *New York Times*, March 6, 1942.

"Three Months of War," *New York Times*, March 7, 1942.

"This Forty-Hour Week War," *New York Times*, March 8, 1942.

"This Forty-Hour Week War," *New York Times*, March 9, 1942.

"Hitler in March," *New York Times*, March 10, 1942.

"Inviting Labor Racketeering," *New York Times*, March 12, 1942.

"This Forty-Hour Week War," *New York Times*, March 13, 1942.

"The Dies Committee," *New York Times*, March 13, 1942.

"Ordinary Union Activities," *New York Times*, March 15, 1942.

"Defense Will Not Win the War" (on W. F. Kernan), *New York Times Book Review*, March 15, 1942.

"A Great Naval Defeat," *New York Times*, March 16, 1942.

"War Production Must Be Synchonized," *New York Times*, March 17, 1942.

"MacArthur in Australia," *New York Times*, March 18, 1942.

"Toward the Closed Shop," *New York Times*, March 19, 1942.

"Unity of Command," *New York Times*, March 20, 1942.

"To Protect the Worker," *New York Times*, March 20, 1942.

"This Forty-Hour Week War," *New York Times*, March 21, 1942.

"Figuring War Profits," *New York Times*, March 22, 1942.

"This Forty-Hour Week War," *New York Times*, March 23, 1942.

"New York City's Budget," *New York Times*, March 23, 1942.

"For a Forty-Eight-Hour Week," *New York Times*, March 25, 1942.

"Education Defined," *New York Times*, March 25, 1942.

"Uncurbed Unions," *New York Times*, March 27, 1942.

"The Wage-Hour Act," *New York Times*, March 28, 1942.

"Unemployment Insurance," *New York Times*, March 28, 1942.

"For a 48-Hour Week," *New York Times*, March 29, 1942.

"Anti-Trust War Policy," *New York Times*, March 30, 1942.

"Reasons for Doing Nothing," *New York Times*, April 1, 1942.

"For a Forty-Eight-Hour Week," *New York Times*, April 4, 1942.

"40 Hours vs. 48" *New York Times*, April 5, 1942.

"Victory Needs Timing," *New York Times*, April 6, 1942.

"The President On Overtime," *New York Times*, April 8, 1942.

"Our Information Policy," *New York Times*, April 11, 942.

"Strategy of Attack," *New York Times*, April 12, 1942.

"Toward the Closed Shop," *New York Times*, April 13, 1942.

"Sleepwalking in India," *New York Times*, April 13, 1942.

"To Curb Inflation," *New York Times*, April 14, 1942.

"War Labor Board Economics," *New York Times*, April 15, 1942.

"The British Budget," *New York Times*, April 16, 1942.

"Regulating the Regulators," *New York Times*, April 18, 1942.

"A War Labor Program," *New York Times*, April 20, 1942.

"To Curb Labor Racketeering," *New York Times*, April 22, 1942.

"Curbing Inflation," *New York Times*, April 26, 1942.

"Stabilizing Wages," *New York Times*, April 27, 1942.

"Hitler's Admissions," *New York Times*, April 27, 1942.

"The President's Program," *New York Times*, April 29, 1942.

"A 94 Percent Tax," *New York Times*, May 2, 1942.

"The Anti-Inflation Program," *New York Times*, May 3, 1942.

"Wage Control," *New York Times*, May 6, 1942.

"Battle of the Coral Sea," *New York Times*, May 9, 1942.

"And the Days Are Passing," *New York Times*, May 1, 1942.

"The Rationale of Rationing," *New York Times*, May 16, 1942.

"To Curb Labor Racketeering," *New York Times*, May 20, 1942.

"On 'Dictatorial Powers'," *New York Times*, May 24, 1942.

"Knowledge and Morale," *New York Times*, May 25, 1942.

"Behind Schedule," *New York Times*, May 25, 1942.

"WPA vs. Defense," *New York Times*, May 27, 1942.

"Rationing Labor," *New York Times*, May 30, 1942.

"As June Begins," *New York Times*, June 1, 1942.

"City by City," *New York Times*, June 3, 1942.

"Six Months of War," *New York Times*, June 6, 1942.

"The Meaning of Midway," *New York Times*, June 9, 1942.

"200 Billion for War," *New York Times*, June 10, 1942.

"The Strategic Aleutians," *New York Times*, June 11, 1942.

"Wage-Hour Interpretations," *New York Times*, June 12, 1942.

"The Forty-Hour Week," *New York Times*, June 14, 1942.

"War Information," *New York Times*, June 15, 1942.

"Congress in Wartime," *New York Times*, June 17, 1942.

"Planning War Strategy," *New York Times*, June 20, 1942.

"The Lessons of Libya," *New York Times*, June 24, 1942.

"The Battle of the Atlantic," *New York Times*, June 26, 1942.

"Why Inflation is Winning," *New York Times*, July 8, 1942.

"Censorship in Reverse," *New York Times*, July 9, 1942.

"Mr. Petrillo Gives the Word," *New York Times*, July 10, 1942.

"Source of Complacency," *New York Times*, July 11, 1942.

"The German People," *New York Times*, July 13, 1942.

"Demagogy in Congress," *New York Times*, July 13, 1942.

"The Threat to Russia," *New York Times*, July 14, 1942.

"A Wage 'Compromise'," *New York Times*, July 16, 1942.

"Inflation Wins Again," *New York Times*, July 17, 1942.

"Two and Two Make Four," *New York Times*, July 18, 1942.

"A Diversion From Russia," *New York Times*, July 21, 1942.

"Russia: Thirteen Months," *New York Times*, July 22, 1942.

"Bomb German Railways," *New York Times*, July 24, 1942.

"The Case for a Sales Tax," *New York Times*, July 25, 1942.

"Can They Stop Petrillo?" *New York Times*, July 25, 1942.

"Bombing German Railroads," *New York Times*, July 27, 1942.

"An Anti-Inflation Program," *New York Times*, July 27, 1942.

"War Production," *New York Times*, July 28, 1942.

"Inflation is Taxation," *New York Times*, July 29, 1942.

"Balancing War Production," *New York Times*, July 30, 1942.

"Leadership in Strategy," *New York Times*, July 31, 1942.

"Mr. Taft's Five Points," *New York Times*, August 1, 1942.

"48 Hours vs. 40," *New York Times*, August 2, 1942.

"For a Unified Command," *New York Times*, August 4, 1942.

"Petrillo as a Case Study," *New York Times*, August 5, 1942.

"For a Unified Command," *New York Times*, August 7, 1942.

"Inflationary Wage Rises," *New York Times*, August 8, 1942.

"Counsel From the Left," *New York Times*, August 9, 1942.

"The Battle of Production," *New York Times*, August 10, 1942.

"Helicopters for Victory," *The Nation*, August 15, 1942.

"An Irresponsible Senator," *New York Times*, August 22, 1942.

"Attack and Counter-Attack," *New York Times*, August, 23, 1942.

"Revision of Counsel," *New York Times*, August 24, 1942.

"Brazil in the War," *New York Times*, August 24, 1942.

"The Labor Party," *New York Times*, August 25, 1942.

"Help for Russia," *New York Times*, August 26, 1942.

"Labor Plank," *New York Times*, August 26, 1942.

"The President on Inflation," *New York Times*, August 27, 1942.

"The Wage-Raising Machine," *New York Times*, August 28, 1942.

"Pay-As-You-Go Plan," *New York Times*, August 29, 1942.

"The President and Congress," *New York Times*, August 31, 1942.

"A 'Pending' Tax?" *New York Times*, September 1, 1942.

"Pay-As-You-Go Taxes," *New York Times*, September 3, 1942.

"The Invisible War," *New York Times*, September 4, 1942.

"Subsidizing High Wages," *New York Times*, September 5, 1942.

"The President's Ultimatum," *New York Times*, September 9, 1942.

"Petrillo Rides Again," *New York Times*, September 10, 1942.

"The Rubber Report," *New York Times*, September 11, 1942.

"A Lesson in Method," *New York Times*, September 12, 1942.

"Publicity Boon-Doggling," *New York Times*, September 13, 1942.

"The Anatomy of Inflation," *New York Times*, September 11, 1942.

"Freezing Prices and Wages," *New York Times*, September 15, 1942.

"Fighting Inflation," *New York Times*, September 16, 1942.

"A Lesson in Arithmetic," *New York Times*, September 17, 1942.

"Cracking Wage Ceilings," *New York Times*, September 18, 1942.

"Petrillo is Just One Man," *New York Times*, September 19, 1942.

"Price Control in France," *New York Times*, September 23, 1942.

"Lecturing the People," *New York Times*, September 26, 1942.

"Blocs Against Democracy," *New York Times*, September 27, 1942.

"The Profit Motive," *New York Times*, September 27, 1942.

"The War Against Inflation," *New York Times*, September 28, 1942.

"A's Income is B's Cost of Living," *New York Times*, September 29, 1942.

"Mercurial Farm Wages," *New York Times*, September 29, 1942.

"Farm Price Muddle," *New York Times*, September 30, 1942.

"A One-Way Bloc Program," *New York Times*, October 1, 1942.

"Parliament and Congress," *New York Times*, October 2, 1942.

"Reform of Congress," *New York Times*, October 5, 1942.

"The Futility of Conquest," *New York Times*, October 6, 1942.

"Petrillo Marches On," *New York Times*, October 7, 1942.

"Manpower," *New York Times*, October 10, 1942.

"England 56: America 43," *New York Times*, October 10, 1942.

"Cooper Union," *New York Times*, October 10, 1942.

"Incomes and Taxes," *New York Times*, October 11, 1942.

"Manpower Shortage," *New York Times*, October 12, 1942.

"Jeffers in the Lions' Den," *New York Times*, October 14, 1942.

"War Information," *New York Times*, October 15, 1942.

"Mr. Petrillo as a Test Case," *New York Times*, October 15, 1942.

"Size of the Army," *New York Times*, October 16, 1942.

"Alternatives in War," *New York Times*, October 19, 1942.

"Fighting For Bread," *New York Times*, October 20, 1942.

"The Value of Candor," *New York Times*, October 21, 1942.

"The Case for the Poll Tax" (signed under Henry Stuart Clark), *New York Times*, October 22, 1942.

"'Make Work' in Wartime," *New York Times*, October 23, 1942.

"France's Shadow Empire," *New York Times*, October 24, 1942.

"War Organization," *New York Times*, October 25, 1942.

"Tide of Battle," *New York Times*, October 26, 1942.

"Economic Freedom," *New York Times*, October 27, 1942.

"For a 48-Hour Week," *New York Times*, October 28, 1942.

"A $25,000 Ceiling," *New York Times*, October 281, 1942.

"A 33-Hour Week," *New York Times*, October 30, 1942.

"Twilight of WPA," *New York Times*, October 31, 1942.

"Choosing a Congress," *New York Times*, November 2, 1942.

"Tire Factory to Russia?" *New York Times*, November 2, 1942.

"Voter's Headache," *New York Times*, November 4, 1942.

"Don't Tie the Army's Hands," *New York Times*, November 6, 1942.

"A Wartime Labor Problem," *New York Times*, November 7, 1942.

"Using Our Labor Resources," *New York Times*, November 8, 1942.

"The Great Offensive," *New York Times*, November 9, 1942.

"Our Short Working Week," *New York Times*, November 10, 1942.

"The Manpower Problem," *New York Times*, November 11, 1942.

"Timid Manpower Policy," *New York Times*, November 12, 1942.

"America's Manpower," *New York Times*, November 14, 1942.

"Enough, and on Time," *New York Times*, November 15, 1942.

"Our 42-Hour Week," *New York Times*, November 16, 1942.

"Unified Control," *New York Times*, November 16, 1942.

"War Information," *New York Times*, November 16, 1942.

"Government Manpower Waste," *New York Times*, November 17, 1942.

"A War of Resources," *New York Times*, November 18, 1942.

"The 48-Hour Week," *New York Times*, November 20, 1942.

"The Yugoslavs," *New York Times*, November 21, 1942.

"Imperialistic Profit," *New York Times*, November 22, 1942.

"The Meaning of Africa," *New York Times*, November 23, 1942.

"War Censorship," *New York Times*, November 24, 1942.

"Compulsion Without Law," *New York Times*, November 25, 1942.

"War Organization," *New York Times*, November 26, 1942.

"Why Civilians Must Control," *New York Times*, November 27, 1942.

"The Glory of Toulon," *New York Times*, November 28, 1942.

"Churchill's Hint to Italy," *New York Times*, November 30, 1942.

"The Boston Disaster," *New York Times*, November 30, 1942.

"History of an Agreement," *New York Times*, November 30, 1942.

"An Offer to Italy?" *New York Times*, December 1, 1942.

"On Spiking Rumors," *New York Times*, December 2, 1942.

"The Choice Under Hitler," *New York Times*, December 3, 1942.

"The End of WPA," *New York Times*, December 5, 1942.

"The Beveridge Report," *New York Times*, December 5, 1942.

"The Truth About Pearl Harbor," *New York Times*, December 6, 1942.

"Increased Output," *New York Times*, December 8, 1942.

"To End Make-Work," *New York Times*, December 9, 1942.

"Make-Work on the Railroads," *New York Times*, December 12, 1942.

"To Limit Debate," *New York Times*, December 12, 1942.

"For a Balanced War Plan," *New York Times*, December 14, 1942.

"Mr. Arnold on Free Enterprise" (on T. W. Arnold), *New York Times Book Review*, December 13, 1942.

"Protection Against Fire," *New York Times*, December 15, 1942.

"Congress Adjourns," *New York Times*, December 16, 1942.

"Overtime in Government," *New York Times*, December 17, 1942.

"Conditions of Peace," *New York Times*, December 18, 1942.

"On the Offensive," *New York Times*, December 21, 1942.

"The C.I.O. on Manpower," *New York Times*, December 22, 1942.

"The End of Darlan," *New York Times*, December 25, 1942.

"The Danger of Subsidies," *New York Times*, December 25, 1942.

"The 'Backbone' of War," *New York Times*, December 27, 1942.

"Pay-As-You-Go Taxes," *New York Times*, December 28, 1942.

"Food Rationing," *New York Times*, December 29, 1942.

"To Pay Our Taxes," *New York Times*, December 31, 1942.

1943

"Pay-As-You-Go Taxes," *New York Times*, January 1, 1943.

"Protection Against Fire," *New York Times*, January 2, 1943.

"New York's 'Beveridge' Plan," *New York Times*, January 2, 1943.

"This Air-Land-Sea War," *New York Times*, January 3, 1943.

"To Set Men Free From Want" (on Beveridge's Plan for Social Security), *New York Times Book Review*, January 3, 1943.

"Pay-As-You-Go Taxes," *New York Times*, January 6, 1943.

"An 'Independent' Congress," *New York Times*, January 7, 1942.

"Pay-As-You-Go Taxes," *New York Times*, January 8, 1943.

"Black Markets," *New York Times*, January 9, 1943.

"Congress in Wartime," *New York Times*, January 10, 1943.

"How to Pay As We Go," *New York Times*, January 11, 1943.

"A Total-War Budget," *New York Times*, January 12, 1943.

"Pay-As-You-Go Taxes," *New York Times*, January 12, 1943.

"The Coal Strike," *New York Times*, January 14, 1943.

"State Job Insurance," *New York Times*, January 15, 1943.

"Pay-As-You-Go Taxes," *New York Times*, January 16, 1943.

"Why Mr. Petrillo Rules," *New York Times*, January 16, 1943.

"To Start Paying As We Go," *New York Times*, January 18, 1943.

"For Immediate Action," *New York Times*, January 19, 1943.

"A Revolving Door," *New York Times*, January 19, 1943.

"The Coal Strike," *New York Times*, January 20, 1943.

"The Submarine Menace," *New York Times*, January 21, 1943.

"Submarine Information," *New York Times*, January 22, 1943.

"Is Dynamiting Wrong?" *New York Times*, January 23, 1943.

"What Corporations Mean to Workers," *New York Times*, January 24, 1943.

"We Need A Tax Plan Now," *New York Times*, January 26, 1943.

"Congress in Time of Crisis" (on Roland Young), *New York Times*, January 24, 1943.

"The Debt Limit," *New York Times*, January 27, 1943.

"A Special Exemption," *New York Times*, January 28, 1943.

"Rationalizing Industry," *New York Times*, January 29, 1943.

"To Curb Racketeering," *New York Times*, January 30, 1943.

"Balanced War Production," *New York Times*, January 31, 1943.

"A Simplified Income Tax," *New York Times*, January 31, 1943.

"To Curb Racketeering," *New York Times*, February 1, 1943.

"Mr. Dewey's First Budget," *New York Times*, February 2, 1943.

"Some Fellow at the Top," *New York Times*, February 3, 1943.

"The Treasury in a Fog," *New York Times*, February 4, 1943.

"Two Years' Taxes in One," *New York Times*, February 5, 1943.

"Reforms Within Congress," *New York Times*, February 6, 1943.

"Pay-As-You-Go Taxes," *New York Times*, February 6, 1943.

"Reducing the Sources," *New York Times*, February 6, 1943.

"What Pay-As-You-Go Means," *New York Times*, February 7, 1943.

"The $25,000 Limit," *New York Times*, February 8, 1943.

"The Mayor Drops a Hint," *New York Times*, February 9, 1943.

"Two Years' Taxes in One," *New York Times*, February 9, 1943.

"Helicopter vs. Submarine," *New York Times*, February 9, 1943.

"Psychology of Rationing," *New York Times*, February 10, 1943.

"Inflation Wins Again," *New York Times*, February 11, 1943.

"Compulsory Inflation," *New York Times*, February 12, 1943.

"Incentive Wages," *New York Times*, February 13, 1943.

"Pay-As-You-Go Taxes," *New York Times*, February 14, 1943.

"The ABC of Pay-As-You-Go," *New York Times*, February 15, 1943.

"Mr. Petrillo's New Demands," *New York Times*, February 16, 1943.

"How We Cut Taxes in 1950," *New York Times*, February 17, 1943.

"Why Mr. Petrillo Rules," *New York Times*, February 17, 1943.

"Pay-And-A-Half As You Go," *New York Times*, February 18, 1943.

"The Domain of Congress," *New York Times*, February 19, 1943.

"Find the Lost Year," *New York Times*, February 20, 1943.

"The $25,000 Limit," *New York Times*, February 20, 1943.

"Congress's Two Glass Houses," *New York Times*, February 21, 1943.

"The Power to Confirm," *New York Times*, February 22, 1943.

"Pay-As-You-Go Taxes," *New York Times*, February 22, 1943.

"Taxing Tax-Exempts," *New York Times*, February 25, 1943.

"Size of the Army," *New York Times*, February 26, 1943.

"Senatorial Patronage," *New York Times*, February 26, 1943.

"War Strike Lessons," *New York Times*, February 27, 1943.

"Wage Policy," *New York Times*, March 2, 1943.

"The Helicopter Adopted," *New York Times*, March 2, 1943.

"A Withholding Tax," *New York Times*, March 3, 1943.

"A Pay-As-You-Go Solution," *New York Times*, March 4, 1943.

"Why the Ruml Plan?" *New York Times*, March 5, 1943.

"Retroactive Wage Increases," *New York Times*, March 5,1943.

"Payment by Results," *New York Times*, March 7, 1943.

"Undemocratic Process," *New York Times*, March 11, 1943.

"Post-War Planning," *New York Times*, March 12, 1943.

"A Bungled Tax Bill," *New York Times*, March 13, 1943.

"Proposals for Peace" (on A. C. Millspaugh), *New York Times Book Review*, March 14, 1943.

"Congress and the President," *New York Times*, March 15, 1943.

"Consent of the Senate," *New York Times*, March 17, 1943.

"Topsy-Turvy 'Democracy'," *New York Times*, March 18, 1943.

"Foremen in Unions," *New York Times*, March 20, 1943.

"Wage Stabilization," *New York Times*, March 21, 1943.

"Against Paying As We Go," *New York Times*, March 22, 1943.

"The Tripartite WLB," *New York Times*, March 23, 1943.

"A Spite Tax," *New York Times*, March 23, 1943.

"Hold That Line," *New York Times*, March 24, 1943.

"Petrillo's Arm in Florida," *New York Times*, March 24, 1943.

"Congress Makes it Clear," *New York Times*, March 25, 1943.

"Written on the Floor," *New York Times*, March 26, 1943.

"The Basic Problem," *New York Times*, March 26, 1943.

"Equality of Sacrifice," *New York Times*, March 27, 1943.

"The Tripartite WLB," *New York Times*, March 28, 1943.

"The Meat Shortage," *New York Times*, March 29, 1943.

"The Pay-As-You-Earn Plan," *New York Times*, March 30, 1943.

"The Committee Gets it Back," *New York Times*, March 31, 1943.

"What Mr. Doughton Says, Goes," *New York Times*, April 1, 1943.

"Up to the Treasury," *New York Times*, April 2, 1943.

"Chance for Leadership," *New York Times*, April 3, 1943.

"To Curb Inflation," *New York Times*, April 6, 1943.

"A Withholding Tax Now," *New York Times*, April 6, 1943.

"Stabilization: 1943 vs. 1933," *New York Times*, April 7, 1943.

"A Withholding Tax Now," *New York Times*, April 8, 1943.

"Why the Meat Shortage?" *New York Times*, April 9, 1943.

"To Hold the Line," *New York Times*, April 10, 1943.

"More Light on Wages," *New York Times*, April 12, 1943.

"End of the $25,000 Limit," *New York Times*, April 13, 1943.

"Two Budgets: A Contrast," *New York Times*, April 14, 1943.

"A Camouflaged Wage Rise?" *New York Times*, April 16, 1943.

"Looking for Loopholes," *New York Times*, April 17, 1943.

"Equality of Sacrifice," *New York Times*, April 18, 1943.

"A Tax Compromise," *New York Times*, April 19, 1943.

"End of Devaluation Powers," *New York Times*, April 19, 1943.

"The Greenback Power," *New York Times*, April 20, 1943.

"The Bombing of Tokyo," *New York Times*, April 20, 1943.

"Why Extend a Bad Act?" *New York Times*, April 21, 1943.

"Helicopter vs. Submarine," *New York Times*, April 22, 1943.

"Legalized Make-Work," *New York Times*, April 22, 1943.

"Tax Fiasco," *New York Times*, April 23, 1943.

"This Late Easter," *New York Times*, April 23, 1943.

"Show-Down," *New York Times*, April 24, 1943.

"A Camouflaged Tax Increase," *New York Times*, April 26, 1943.

"Soft-Coal Wages," *New York Times*, April 27, 1943.

"The Tax Bill Delay," *New York Times*, April 28, 1943.

"Manpower in the United States," Academy of Political Science, *Proceedings*, May 1943.

"Mr. Lewis's Defiance," *New York Times*, May 1, 1943.

"What is 'Civilian Defense'," *New York Times*, May 3, 1943.

"A Crucial Decision," *New York Times*, May 4, 1943.

"An Ambiguous Policy," *New York Times*, May 5, 1943.

"Pay-As-You-Go for Most," *New York Times*, May 6, 1943.

"Automatic Wage Inflation," *New York Times*, May 7, 1943.

"The Withholding Tax," *New York Times*, May 7, 1943.

"To Curb Strikes," *New York Times*, May 8, 1943.

"Subsidizing Inflation," *New York Times*, May 10, 1943.

"The Role of Subsidies," *New York Times*, May 11, 1943.

"Wages and Inflation," *New York Times*, May 12, 1943.

"Living Costs vs. Wages," *New York Times*, May 13, 1943.

"Foremen in Unions," *New York Times*, May 13, 1943.

"Hold What Line?" *New York Times*, May 14, 1943.

"Has the Administration an Anti-Inflation Policy?" *New York Times*, May 17, 1943.

"What the Issue Is," *New York Times*, May 18, 1943.

"The Cost of 'Beating Ruml'," *New York Times*, May 19, 1943.

"Wages vs. Living Costs," *New York Times*, May 21, 1943.

"The Tax Muddle," *New York Times*, May 22, 1943.

"A Tax Agreement," *New York Times*, May 24, 1943.

"The Facts About WLB," *New York Times*, May 24, 1943.

"Facts About Coal Wages," *New York Times*, May 25, 1943.

"The Akron Strike," *New York Times*, May 26, 1943.

"The Tax Compromise," *New York Times*, May 27, 1943.

"WLB Opens A Back Door," *New York Times*, May 27, 1943.

"That $50 Credit," *New York Times*, May 28, 1943.

"Toward a War Cabinet," *New York Times*, May 29, 1943.

"Wages and Prices," *New York Times*, May 31, 1943.

"Mr. Lewis's Defiance," *New York Times*, June 2, 1943.

"The Tax Compromise," *New York Times*, June 3, 1943.

"End of the Strike," *New York Times*, June 5, 1943.

"The Future of Food," *New York Times*, June 5, 1943.

"The Anti-Strike Bill," *New York Times*, June 7, 1943.

"The Showdown at Last," *New York Times*, June 4, 1943.

"Coal Wages: The Last Test," *New York Times*, June 8, 1943.

"Subsidies and Wages," *New York Times*, June 9, 1943.

"Up to the WLB," *New York Times*, June 11, 1943.

"Liaison with Congress," *New York Times*, June 11, 1943.

"The New Tax Law," *New York Times*, June 12, 1943.

"The Anti-Strike Bill," *New York Times*, June 14, 1943.

"Tax Responsibility," *New York Times*, June 15, 1943.

"Policy vs. Patronage," *New York Times*, June 16, 1943.

"Union Campaign Funds," *New York Times*, June 17, 1943.

"Shoe-Buying Panic," *New York Times*, June 17, 1943.

"Senator Aiken on Subsidies," *New York Times*, June 18, 1943.

"'Converted' Communists?" *New York Times*, June 18, 1943.

"What Subsides Mean," *New York Times*, June 19, 1943.

"Nationalizing for Mr. Lewis?" *New York Times*, June 22, 1943.

"The Issue is Drawn," *New York Times*, June 23, 1943.

"Does Mr. Lewis Give Orders to the Government?" *New York Times*, June 24, 1943.

"To Hold the Line," *New York Times*, June 25, 1943.

"Veto Overridden," *New York Times*, June 26, 1943.

"Disregarding Mr. Lewis?" *New York Times*, June 26, 1943.

"Subsides vs. Sales Taxes," *New York Times*, June 28, 1943.

"Congress and the President," *New York Times*, June 29, 1943.

"Accepting Mr. Lewis' Terms," *New York Times*, June 30, 1943.

"The Wallace-Jones Feud," *New York Times*, July 1, 1943.

"Meat Paradox," *New York Times*, July 2, 1943.

"Mr. Petrillo as a Symptom," *New York Times*, July 3, 1943.

"The Cost of Subsidies," *New York Times*, July 3, 1943.

"The Role of Subsidies," *New York Times*, July 5, 1943.

"Comparative Deficits," *New York Times*, July 6, 1943.

"Prepare a Tax Bill Now," *New York Times*, July 7, 1943.

"Accepting Mr. Lewis' Terms," *New York Times*, July 8, 1943.

"The Meat Shortage," *New York Times*, July 10, 1943.

"The Inflationary Gap," *New York Times*, July 11, 1943.

"End of the Guffey Coal Act," *New York Times*, July 12, 1943.

"War Bond Campaign," *New York Times*, July 13, 1942.

"To Return the Mines," *New York Times*, July 15, 1943.

"A Problem of Incomes," *New York Times*, July 16, 1943.

"The Smith-Connally Bill," *New York Times*, July 17, 1943.

"The Forgotten Man," *New York Times*, July 19, 1943.

"Inflation: the Alternative," *New York Times*, July 24, 1943.

"How to Provoke Strikes," *New York Times*, August 2, 1943.

"Mr. George on Taxes," *New York Times*, August 3, 1943.

"British Taxes and Ours," *New York Times*, August 4, 1943.

"Ballet Dancer as Economist," *New York Times*, August 4, 1943.

"More Light on Wages," *New York Times*, August 5, 1943.

"Mr. Wallace's Intolerance," *New York Times*, August 5, 1943.

"Invasion Money," *New York Times*, August 6, 1943.

"Where Income Taxes Fall," *New York Times*, August 7, 1943.

"Mr. Roosevelt and WLB," *New York Times*, August 7, 1943.

"Incentives to Produce," *New York Times*, August 8, 1943.

"A Union on the Closed Shop," *New York Times*, August 9, 1943.

"Begging Mr. Petrillo," *New York Times*, August 10, 1943.

"Providing Strike Ballots," *New York Times*, August 11, 1943.

"Diplomacy is Present Need," *New York Times*, August 12, 1943.

"To Simplify Taxes" (signed under "Philadius"), *New York Times*, August 13, 1943.

"Germany's Costly Education," *New York Times*, August 14, 1943.

"The Role of Air Power," *New York Times*, August 16, 1943.

"Taxes vs. Production," *New York Times*, August 16, 1943.

"Inflation vs. Insurance," *New York Times*, August 17, 1943.

"Inflation: Words vs. Acts," *New York Times*, August 18, 1943.

"America's Treaty Making," *New York Times*, August 19, 1943.

"Labor Board Weapons," *New York Times*, August 20, 1943.

"Forced Contributions," *New York Times*, August 21, 1943.

"The Lessons of Kiska," *New York Times*, August 23, 1943.

"Kharkov—and Cooperation," *New York Times*, August 24, 1943.

"Appeasing Mr. Lewis," *New York Times*, August 25, 1943.

"The Meaning of Quebec," *New York Times*, August 25, 1943.

"A Test Strike," *New York Times*, August 26, 1943.

"Sanctioning Strikes," *New York Times*, August 27, 1943.

"Lend-Lease," *New York Times*, August 27, 1943.

"The Separate Peace Bogey," *New York Times*, August 28, 1943.

"The Pro-and-Anti-Strike Act," *New York Times*, August 31, 1943.

"Mandatory Wage Increases," *New York Times*, September 1, 1943.

"The Stakes in Italy," *New York Times*, September 1, 1943.

"The Economist," *New York Times*, September 2, 1943.

"Fallacy of 'Parity'," *New York Times*, September 3, 1943.

"The Record on Gas," *New York Times*, September 5, 1943.

"Labor Day," *New York Times*, September 6, 1943.

"Definition of Intent Needed" (signed under "Henry Stuart Clark"), *New York Times*, September 6, 1943.

"Taxes and National Income," *New York Times*, September 8, 1943.

"General Marshall's Report," *New York Times*, September 9, 1943.

"How to Make A Petrillo," *New York Times*, September 10, 1943.

"A Historic 'If'," *New York Times*, September 12, 1943.

"Lend-Lease 'Repayment'," *New York Times*, September 12, 1943.

"American Peace Aims," *New York Times*, September 13, 1943.

"The Task Before Congress," *New York Times*, September 14, 1943.

"Price Rollback," *New York Times*, September 15, 1943.

"Income Tax Headache," *New York Times*, September 15, 1943.

"Failure on Taxes," *New York Times*, September 16, 1943.

"More Tax Delay," *New York Times*, September 17, 1943.

"The Lovett 'Rider'," *New York Times*, September 16, 1943.

"Mr. Doughton Calls for Help," *New York Times*, September 20, 1943.

"Criticisms From Russia," *New York Times*, September 21, 1943.

"Racial Discrimination," *New York Times*, September 22, 1943.

"The House Takes Its Stand," *New York Times*, September 22, 1943.

"Frank M. O'Brien," *New York Times*, September 23, 1943.

"Why Petrillo Wins," *New York Times*, September 23, 1943.

"Union Security," *New York Times*, September 25, 1943.

"The Bomb as Pedagogue," *New York Times*, September 26, 1943.

"Milk Subsidy," *New York Times*, September 27, 1943.

"Mr. Tugwell on Puerto Rico," *New York Times*, September 28, 1943.

"Union Coercion," *New York Times*, September 28, 1943.

"The Gold Standard," *New York Times*, September 29, 1943.

"A Needless Revision," *New York Times*, September 30, 1943.

"Tax Responsibility," *New York Times*, September 30, 1943.

"Petrillo's Victory," *New York Times*, October 1, 1943.

"Mr. Cox's Resignation," *New York Times*, October 2, 1943.

"Let the Senate Act," *New York Times*, October 4, 1943.

"The Treasury Tax Program," *New York Times*, October 5, 1943.

"A Shameful Strike," *New York Times*, October 6, 1943.

"For a Sales Tax," *New York Times*, October 7, 1943.

"What Limit to Taxes," *New York Times*, October 8, 1943.

"Why a Sales Tax?" *New York Times*, October 12, 1943.

"Income Tax Limits," *New York Times*, October 13, 1943.

"A New Ruml Plan," *New York Times*, October 14, 1943.

"The Connally Act Again," *New York Times*, October 14, 1943.

"Those Dim Traffic Lights," *New York Times*, October 14, 1943.

"Cooper Union," *New York Times*, October 16, 1943.

"The Future of Economic Nationalism," *New York Times*, October 18, 1943.

"Restoring World Trade," *New York Times*, October 19, 1943.

"Mr. Lewis and the Miners," *New York Times*, October 19, 1943.

"The Sales Tax," *New York Times*, October 19, 1943.

"For a Wage Policy," *New York Times*, October 20, 1943.

"Free Speech for Employers," *New York Times*, October 21, 1943.

"Taxes—or Inflation," *New York Times*, October 22, 1943.

"Mr. Petrillo Moves Ahead," *New York Times*, October 22, 1943.

"Approval of Treaties," *New York Times*, October 23, 1943.

"Up to the Senate," *New York Times*, October 25, 1943.

"Air Raid Signals," *New York Times*, October 28, 1943.

"Taxing War Profits," *New York Times*, October 29, 1943.

"On Seizing the Mines," *New York Times*, October 30, 1943.

"The Tax on Margarine," *New York Times*, October 31, 1943.

"Margarine Baiting," *New York Times*, November 1, 1943.

"Mr. Aurelio's Dilemma," *New York Times*, November 1, 1943.

"The Coal Strike," *New York Times*, November 2, 1943.

"Too Much Election," *New York Times*, November 3, 1943.

"Speaking of Precedents," *New York Times*, November 4, 1943.

"Surrender to Mr. Lewis," *New York Times*, November 5, 1943.

"The Forgotten Millions," *New York Times*, November 8, 1943.

"Mishandling Wage Disputes," *New York Times*, November 9, 1943.

"Reorganizing Congress," *New York Times*, November 11, 1943.

"Where the New Income Is," *New York Times*, November 12, 1943.

"Inflation is a Tax," *New York Times*, November 13, 1943.

"Does Congress Need a Rest?" *New York Times*, November 13, 1943.

"Wage Policy Chaos," *New York Times*, November 13, 1943.

"That Extra Fifteen Minutes," *New York Times*, November 15, 1943.

"What's In a Name?" *New York Times*, November 17, 1943.

"The Results of P. R.," *New York Times*, November 18, 1943.

"Stop, Look and Listen!" *New York Times*, November 19, 1943.

"Subsidies and Inflation," *New York Times*, November 22, 1943.

"Buried Statistics," *New York Times*, November 23, 1943.

"Results of Seniority," *New York Times*, November 24, 1943.

"The Subsidy Dilemma," *New York Times*, November 25, 1943.

"Subsidies: Two Kinds," *New York Times*, November 25, 1943.

"Railway Wages," *New York Times*, November 27, 1943.

"For an Executive Budget," *New York Times*, November 27, 1943.

"The Cabinet in Congress," *New York Times*, November 28, 1943.

"The Federal Deficit," *New York Times*, November 29, 1943.

"Treasury and Sales Tax," *New York Times*, December 1, 1943.

"A Congressional Error," *New York Times*, December 3, 1943.

"A New World Bank?" *New York Times*, December 4, 1943.

"Stabilizing Wages," *New York Times*, December 4, 1943.

"The Cabinet in Congress," *New York Times*, December 6, 1943.

"Railway Wages," *New York Times*, December 7, 1943.

"Holding the Line," *New York Times*, December 9, 1943.

"The Executive Budget," *New York Times*, December 12, 1943.

"The Senate's Blunder," *New York Times*, December 13, 1943.

"OPA vs. the Law," *New York Times*, December 13, 1943.

"OPA vs. the Law," *New York Times*, December 14, 1943.

"Blunder in the House," *New York Times*, December 15, 1943.

"The Vote to Strike," *New York Times*, December 16, 1943.

"The Victory Tax," *New York Times*, December 17, 1943.

"The Labor Crisis," *New York Times*, December 20, 1943.

"Equality of Treatment," *New York Times*, December 21, 1943.

"The Cabinet in Congress," *New York Times*, December 22, 1943.

"Mishandled Wage Disputes," *New York Times*, December 22, 1943.

"Renegotiation," *New York Times*, December 23, 1943.

"Labor Racketeering," *New York Times*, December 24, 1943.

"The Labor Crisis," *New York Times*, December 27, 1943.

"The 'No Contract' Argument," *New York Times*, December 28, 1943.

"Buying Off Strikes," *New York Times*, December 29, 1943.

"Severance Pay," *New York Times*, December 31, 1943.

1944

"We Owe It to Ourselves," *New York Times*, January 3, 1944.

"Money Grows on Trees," *New York Times*, January 4, 1944.

"Other People's Morale," *New York Times*, January 5, 1944.

"Responsible Spending," *New York Times*, January 6, 1944.

"For a Labor Policy," *New York Times*, January 8, 1944.

"Mishandling Wage Disputes," *New York Times*, January 9, 1944.

"The Task Before Congress," *New York Times*, January 10, 1944.

"Contract Settlement," *New York Times*, January 11, 1944.

"The Five-Point Program," *New York Times*, January 12, 1944.

"Budget for Victory," *New York Times*, January 14, 1944.

"Those Strike Statistics," *New York Times*, January 14, 1944.

"Safeguarding a Surplus," *New York Times*, January 19, 1944.

"After the Strike Threat," *New York Times*, January 20, 1944.

"Mustering Out Pay," *New York Times*, January 21, 1944.

"Permitted Violence," *New York Times*, January 22, 1944.

"To Protect Union Members," *New York Times*, January 24, 1944.

"The New Tax Bill," *New York Times*, January 25, 1944.

"WLB Under Fire," *New York Times*, January 27, 1944.

"After Discharge Pay," *New York Times*, January 28, 1944.

"Chinese Students," *New York Times*, January 28, 1944.

"One-Sided Legislation," *New York Times*, January 29, 1944.

"The State Budget," *New York Times*, February 1, 1944.

"Questions in Congress," *New York Times*, February 1, 1944.

"Wage Rise, Price Rise," *New York Times*, February 2, 1944.

"Bewildering Statistics," *New York Times*, February 3, 1944.

"An Unstable Court," *New York Times*, February 4, 1944.

"Post-War Democracy," *New York Times*, February 5, 1944.

"Gold vs. Coercion," *New York Times*, February 7, 1944.

"The Tax Bill," *New York Times*, February 8, 1944.

"The Future of OWI," *New York Times*, February 9, 1944.

"Independent Schools," *New York Times*, February 10, 1944.

"Mr. Wallace's 'Fascists'," *New York Times*, February 11, 1944.

"What Wage Policy?" *New York Times*, February 14, 1944.

"The Tripartite WLB," *New York Times*, February 15, 1944.

"Subsidy 'Savings'," *New York Times*, February 16, 1944.

"'Democracy,' New Style," *New York Times*, February 18, 1944.

"Conversion to Peace," *New York Times*, February 19, 1944.

"Enact the Tax Bill," *New York Times*, February 21, 1944.

"Revolt in Congress," *New York Times*, February 24, 1944.

"Tax Responsibility," *New York Times*, February 25, 1944.

"The New Tax Law," *New York Times*, February 26, 1944.

"Senator McNary," *New York Times*, February 26, 1944.

"The Subsidy Issue," *New York Times*, February 29, 1944.

"The Constitution vs. The Peace," *Yale Review*, March 1944.

"The Selection of Judges," *New York Times*, March 1, 1944.

"Republican Trend," *New York Times*, March 2, 1944.

"Residential Bugaboo," *New York Times*, March 3, 1944.

"Election Tabulation," *New York Times*, March 3, 1944.

"Helping the Veteran?" *New York Times*, March 3, 1944.

"Helping the Veteran?" *New York Times*, March 6, 1944.

"Setback for Mr. Petrillo," *New York Times*, March 14, 1944.

"Finland: A Test of the Peace," *New York Times*, March 16, 1944.

"For Simplified Taxes," *New York Times*, March 16, 1944.

"Deadlock in Government," *The New Leader*, March 18, 1944.

"To Halt Mr. Petrillo," *New York Times*, March 22, 1944.

"Disguised Wage Increases," *New York Times*, March 23, 1944.

"Wages and Subsidies," *New York Times*, March 24, 1944.

"Three-Dimensional War," *New York Times*, March 25, 1944.

"Who Makes Wage Policy?" *New York Times*, March 26, 1944.

"Make-Work vs. Labor," *New York Times*, March 27, 1944.

"Portal-to-Portal Pay," *New York Times*, March 29, 1944.

"The Vote of Confidence," *New York Times*, March 31, 1944.

"The Pacific War," *New York Times*, April 1, 1944.

"Principles for Peace," *New York Times*, April 2, 1944.

"Mr. Churchill's Leadership," *New York Times*, April 3, 1944.

"Post-War Democracy," *New York Times*, April 8, 1944.

"Wage Policy," *New York Times*, April 9, 1944.

"Mr. Wallace on 'Fascism'," *New York Times*, April 10, 1944.

"Calling in Congress," *New York Times*, April 11, 1944.

"New Wine, Old Bottle," *New York Times*, April 13, 1944.

"Post-War Plans," *New York Times*, April 14, 1944.

"What is Our Production?" *New York Times*, April 17, 1944.

"Approval of Treaties," *New York Times*, April 17, 1944.

"The Right to Discharge," *New York Times*, April 18, 1944.

"Our Hydra-Headed Congress," *New York Times*, April 20, 1944.

"The Pay Rise Campaign," *New York Times*, April 21, 1944.

"A World Monetary Plan," *New York Times*, April 24, 1944.

"Mr. Petrillo Marches On," *New York Times*, April 26, 1944.

"Approval of Treaties," *New York Times*, April 26, 1944.

"Britain's Budget—and Ours," *New York Times*, April 27, 1944.

"The Ward Case," *New York Times*, April 28, 1944.

"Gen. MacArthur's Withdrawal," *New York Times*, May 1, 1944.

"Mr. Biddle's Arguments," *New York Times*, May 2, 1944.

"Free Speech for Employers," *New York Times*, May 3, 1944.

"To Simplify Taxes, *New York Times*, May 5, 1944.

"Taxes—and Inflation," *New York Times*, May 6, 1944.

"Plant Seizure as Cure-All," *New York Times*, May 8, 1944.

"French Realities," *New York Times*, May 9, 1944.

"Approval of Treaties," *New York Times*, May 10, 1944.

"Ward Case Issues," *New York Times*, May 11, 1944.

"Gold?—Well, Hardly Ever," *New York Times*, May 12, 1944.

"Free Speech for Employers," *New York Times*, May 15, 1944.

"Mr. Landon on Tariffs," *New York Times*, May 17, 1944.

"Mr. Davis and the WLB," *New York Times*, May 18, 1944.

"Freedom with Efficiency," *New York Times*, May 20, 1944.

"Approval of Treaties," *New York Times*, May 22, 1944.

"What is Our Production?" *New York Times*, May 22, 1944.

"Keeping it One-Sided," *New York Times*, May 23, 1944.

"A Legal Strike," *New York Times*, May 25, 1944.

"'Wildcat' Strikes," *New York Times*, May 26, 1944.

"Subsidy Policy," *New York Times*, May 27, 1944.

"The Vice-Presidency," *New York Times*, May 28, 1944.

"Contempt for 'Politicians'," *New York Times*, May 28, 1944.

"Britain's Post-War Plans," *New York Times*, May 29, 1944.

"For Stable Exchanges," *New York Times*, June 1, 1944.

"Reassurance on Steel," *New York Times*, June 2, 1944.

"Ends and Means," *New York Times*, June 4, 1944.

"What England Owes," *New York Times*, June 6, 1944.

"War on Two Fronts," *New York Times*, June 7, 1944.

"An Unsettling Decision," *New York Times*, June 8, 1944.

"Controlling WLB," *New York Times*, June 9, 1944.

"The Grand Offensive," *New York Times*, June 10, 1944.

"A 'Super-Duper' Committee," *New York Times*, June 11, 1944.

"Laski's Brief for Communism" (on Harold J. Laski's *Faith, Reason, and Civilization*), *New York Times Book Review*, June 11, 1944.

"Congress has a Job to Do," *New York Times*, June 14, 1944.

"Compulsory Inflation," *New York Times*, June 15, 1944.

"What About Cartels?" *New York Times*, June 18, 944.

"Removing Wage Controls," *New York Times*, June 19, 1944.

"While Congress Quits," *New York Times*, June 20, 1944.

"But Will It Stabilize?" *New York Times*, June 21, 1944.

"Congress in Recess," *New York Times*, June 24, 1944.

"For World Inflation?" *New York Times*, June 24, 1944.

"The Conventions," *New York Times*, June 25, 1944.

"How Will It Stabilize?" *New York Times*, June 26, 1944.

"Our Monetary Delegation," *New York Times*, June 27, 1944.

"The Republican Platform" (from "All this is disappointing . . ."), *New York Times*, June 28, 1944.

"Platform Contradictions," *New York Times*, June 28, 1944.

"The Monetary Conference," *New York Times*, July 1, 1944.

"How Not to Reconvert," *New York Times*, July 2, 1944.

"Results at Bretton Woods," *New York Times*, July 18, 1944.

"An International Bank?" *New York Times*, July 19, 1944.

"Mr. Gore as a Test Case," *New York Times*, July 20, 1944.

"Mr. Roosevelt's Running Mate," *New York Times*, July 22, 1944.

"A 'Fresh Start' in Economics," *Saturday Review of Literature*, July 22, 1944.

"The Monetary Fund," *New York Times*, July 24, 1944.

"Untaxing Corporations," *New York Times*, July 25, 1944.

"To Study Cartels," *New York Times*, July 25, 1944.

"To Make Trade Free," *New York Times*, July 27, 1944.

"Manpower Shortage," *New York Times*, July 28, 1944.

"A Reckless Argument," *New York Times*, July 31, 1944.

"The Duty Before Congress," *New York Times*, August 1, 1944.

"Floundering on Reconversion," *New York Times*, August 2, 1944.

"Primary Results," *New York Times*, August 3, 1944.

"$50,000,000,000 Deficit," *New York Times*, August 4, 1944.

"Jobless Pay," *New York Times*, August 5, 1944.

"Effects of a War Strike," *New York Times*, August 6, 1944.

"Control for Control's Sake," *New York Times*, August 8, 1944.

"Behind the 'Tire Lag'," *New York Times*, August 9, 1944.

"Agreement on Oil," *New York Times*, August 10, 1944.

"The New Stab in the Back," *New York Times*, August 13, 1944.

"The Transition to Peace," *New York Times*, August 14, 1944.

"Restricting Production," *New York Times*, August 15, 1944.

"The Strikes Go On," *New York Times*, August 16, 1944.

"Wage Incentive Plan," *New York Times*, August 17, 1944.

"How PAC Raises Funds," *New York Times*, August 18, 1944.

"To Make Democracy Strong," *New York Times*, August 20, 1944.

"War and Post-War Spending," *New York Times*, August 21, 1944.

"To Clarify the Oil Pact," *New York Times*, August 22, 1944.

"Wages and Inflation," *New York Times*, August 25, 1944.

"A Political Suit?" *New York Times*, August 25, 1944.

"Failure of Team Work," *New York Times*, August 26, 1944.

"What Reconversion Policy?" *New York Times*, August 27, 1944.

"Amending a Constitution," *New York Times*, August 27, 1944.

"More on the Railroad Suit," *New York Times*, August 30, 1944.

"Cotton: A Study in 'Planning'," *New York Times*, August 31, 1944.

"The Crumbling Axis," *New York Times*, September 4, 1944.

"The Senate's Treaty Power," *New York Times*, September 5, 1944.

"Taxes for Employment," *New York Times*, September 7, 1944.

"Twilight of the New Order," *New York Times*, September 10, 1944.

"Planning for Peace," *New York Times*, September 11, 1944.

"The Line Against Inflation," *New York Times*, September 12, 1944.

"A Free World Press," *New York Times*, September 13, 1944.

"Changing the Yardstick?" *New York Times*, September 16, 1944.

"Constitution Day," *New York Times*, September 17, 1944.

"Mr. Aldrich's Monetary Plan," *New York Times*, September 19, 1944.

"Mr. Dewey's Labor Speech," *New York Times*, September 20, 1944.

"Reconversion Progress," *New York Times*, September 22, 1944.

"An Economist's View of 'Planning'" (on F. A. Hayek's *The Road to Serfdom*), *New York Times Book Review*, September 24, 1944.

"German Reparations," *New York Times*, September 25, 1944.

"Wages at a New Peak," *New York Times*, September 23, 1944.

"Collectivism in Cotton," *New York Times*, September 26, 1944.

"Social Security: Two Sides," *New York Times*, September 27, 1944.

"To Hold the Line," *New York Times*, September 29, 1944.

"International Money Plans," *New York Times*, October 1, 1944.

"Bureaucracy Defined" (on Ludwig von Mises's *Bureaucracy*), *New York Times Book Review*, October 1, 1944.

"The Senate and the Peace," *New York Times*, October 2, 1944.

"Coffee Jitters," *New York Times*, October 2, 1944.

"Administrative Puzzles," *New York Times*, October 3, 1944.

"Mr. Dewey on Taxes," *New York Times*, October 5, 1944.

"Those Strike Statistics," *New York Times*, October 6, 1944.

"Pretty Please, Mr. Petrillo!" *New York Times*, October 7, 1944.

"No Change in Little Steel?" *New York Times*, October 10, 1944.

"Mr. Petrillo Says No," *New York Times*, October 12, 1944.

"Inflation Loses a Battle," *New York Times*, October 13, 1944.

"National Income Guesses," *New York Times*, October 14, 1944.

"Cooper Union," *New York Times*, October 14, 1944.

"No Law to Stop Petrillo?" *New York Times*, October 17, 1944.

"Export Subsidy Results," *New York Times*, October 22, 1944.

"Needless Trade Fears," *New York Times*, October 23, 1944.

"Europe's Monetary Maze," *New York Times*, October 27, 1944.

"Cost of Living," *New York Times*, October 28, 1944.

"Government and Jobs," *New York Times*, October 29, 1944.

"Delegation by Congress Favored" (letter signed by "Henry Stuart Clark"), *New York Times*, November 11, 1944.

"Federal Agencies," *New York Times*, November 12, 1944.

"Matter for Consultation" (letter signed by "Henry Stuart Clark"), *New York Times*, November 11, 1944.

"Mr. Petrillo's Victory," *New York Times*, November 13, 1944.

"Measuring Living Costs," *New York Times*, November 20, 1944.

"Modernizing Congress," *New York Times*, November 22, 1944.

"The Importance of Imports," *New York Times*, November 23, 1944.

"Inevitable Socialism," *New York Times*, November 26, 1944.

"Inflationary Pay Rise," *New York Times*, November 27, 1944.

"Credit Inflation," *New York Times*, November 28, 1944.

"The Approval of Treaties," *New York Times*, November 29, 1944.

"Curbing Mr. Petrillo," *New York Times*, November 30, 1944.

"Solving the Rubber Problem," *New York Times*, December 2, 1944.

"For World Recovery," *New York Times*, December 3, 1944.

"The Big Bills," *New York Times*, December 3, 1944.

"Europe's Political Crisis," *New York Times*, December 4, 1944.

"The Social Security Tax," *New York Times*, December 5, 1944.

"No Debt Cancellation," *New York Times*, December 6, 1944.

"Hothouse Foreign Trade?" *New York Times*, December 6, 1944.

"Toward an 'Open Sky'," *New York Times*, December 7, 1944.

"A Job Well Done," *New York Times*, December 8, 1944.

"Whom the Secretary Serves," *New York Times*, December 12, 1944.

"Overlapping Labor Boards," *New York Times*, December 14, 1944.

"America's Responsibility," *New York Times*, December 17, 1944.

"The Tax Freeze," *New York Times*, December 18, 1944.

"Deficit Spending Fallacies," *New York Times*, December 20, 1944.

"Senator Nye's Parting Shot," *New York Times*, December 21, 1944.

"'Modernizing' Congress," *New York Times*, December 22, 1944.

"A 'Job Budget'," *New York Times*, December 23, 1944.

"Another Wage Increase?" *New York Times*, December 26, 1944.

"State Cooperation," *New York Times*, December 27, 1944.

"Britain's Plan for Planning," *New York Times*, December 28, 1944.

"Mirage of a Tax Cut," *New York Times*, December 31, 1944.

1945

"The Coming Economic World Pattern: Free Trade or State Domination?" *The American Scholar Forum*, January 1945.

"Mr. Vinson's Strange Logic," *New York Times*, January 1, 1945.

"The New Congress," *New York Times*, January 4, 1945.

"The Governor's Message," *New York Times*, January 5, 1945.

"The 'Job Budget'," *New York Times*, January 6, 1945.

"Post-War Economic Program," *New York Times*, January 8, 1945.

"A Fine Bond Record," *New York Times*, January 9, 1945.

"The Budget Message," *New York Times*, January 10, 1945.

"No Magical Taxes," *New York Times*, January 11, 1945.

"A Revised Oil Agreement," *New York Times*, January 12, 1945.

"Sanctioned Strike Oil," *New York Times*, January 13, 1945.

"Curing A Labor Shortage," *New York Times*, January 16, 1945.

"Gustav Cassel's Warning," *New York Times*, January 17, 1945.

"No 'Incentive' Taxes," *New York Times*, January 17, 1945.

"Strengthening Congress," *New York Times*, January 15, 1945.

"Musical Featherbed," *New York Times*, January 22, 1945.

"Jesse Jones," *New York Times*, January 24, 1945.

"Agreements and the Freedom of Trade," *The Commercial and Financial Chronicle*, January 25, 1945.

"Railroad Retirement Laws," *New York Times*, January 25, 1945.

"Mr. Jones' Two Jobs," *New York Times*, January 26, 1945.

"Republican Leadership," *New York Times*, January 28, 1945.

"The Ward Decision," *New York Times*, January 28, 1945.

"The State Budget," *New York Times*, February 1, 1945.

"Mr. Petrillo and NLRB," *New York Times*, February 1, 1945.

"The Vandenberg Proposal," *New York Times*, February 5, 1945.

"Bankers on Bretton Woods," *New York Times*, February 5, 1945.

"The Fund and the Bank," *New York Times*, February 7, 1945.

"Mr. Petrillo vs. Congress," *New York Times*, February 8, 1945.

"The Problem of Cartels," *New York Times*, February 9, 1945.

"Freedom of Exchange," *New York Times*, February 10, 1945.

"Supply Creates Demand," *New York Times*, February 11, 1945.

"The Spirit of Lincoln," *New York Times*, February 12, 1945.

"Bretton Woods Proposals," *New York Times*, February 13, 1945.

"To Curb Make-Work," *New York Times*, February 14, 1945.

"More on Bretton Woods," *New York Times*, February 15, 1945.

"Wages and Prices Again," *New York Times*, February 16, 1945.

"The Bretton Woods Bill," *New York Times*, February 17, 1945.

"Social Insurance," *New York Times*, February 20, 1945.

"Post-War Foreign Trade," *New York Times*, February 22, 1945.

"Hold the Wage-Price Line," *New York Times*, February 24, 1945.

"Spending or Economy?" *New York Times*, February 26, 1945.

"The Ives Bill," *New York Times*, February 27, 1945.

"Trouble Seen in State Bill" (letter signed by "Henry Stuart Clark"), *New York Times*, February 27, 1945.

"Legalized Wartime Strikes," *New York Times*, February 28, 1945.

"Red Lights for Inflation," *New York Times*, March 2, 1945.

"Mr. Lewis is Not Shy," *New York Times*, March 3, 1945.

"Money Plan Obscurities," *New York Times*, March 15, 1945.

"Gold vs. Nationalism," *New York Times*, March 17, 1945.

"The 1919 Prophecies of Maynard Keynes," *New York Times Book Review*, March 11, 1945.

"Economic Stabilization" (from "The immediate . . ."), *New York Times*, March 19, 1945.

"Enterprise and Housing," *New York Times*, March 20, 1945.

"Merit Rating," *New York Times*, March 21, 1945.

"Job Insurance," *New York Times*, March 22, 1945.

"Annual Wages," *New York Times*, March 22, 1945.

"The CED on Bretton Woods," *New York Times*, March 25, 1945.

"Punishing the Thermometer," *New York Times*, March 27, 1945.

"The President on Tariffs," *New York Times*, MArch 28, 1945.

"Industrial Peace," *New York Times*, March 29, 1945.

"Alice in the Coal Fields," *New York Times*, March 30, 1945.

"On Converting to Peace," *New York Times*, April 2, 1945.

"Mr. Byrnes and Mr. Vinson," *New York Times*, April 3, 1945.

"Overworked Officials," *New York Times*, April 4, 1945.

"A World Trade Conference," *New York Times*, April 6, 1945.

"Silver Boys in Bretton Woods," *New York Times*, April 7, 1945.

"Price Control: War and Peace," *New York Times*, April 9, 1945.

"Leon Fraser," *New York Times*, April 10, 1945.

"Carl Becker," *New York Times*, April 12, 1945.

"President and Congress," *New York Times*, April 17, 1945.

"New Loan Administrator," *New York Times*, April 18, 1945.

"A Telephone Strike?" *New York Times*, April 18, 1945.

"Removing Wartime Controls," *New York Times*, April 29, 1945.

"After Victory in Europe," *New York Times*, April 29, 1945.

"Unionizing Foremen," *New York Times*, April 29, 1945.

"The End of Mussolini," *New York Times*, April 30, 1945.

"Objections to the Proposed International Monetary Fund," *Congressional Digest*, May 1945.

"Implications of State Guarantee of Employment," Academy of Political Science, *Proceedings*, May 1945.

"Another Coal Strike," *New York Times*, May 2, 1945.

"The Treaty-Making Power," *New York Times*, May 3, 1945.

"Revising the Budget," *New York Times*, May 4, 1945.

"Effects of Taxation," *New York Times*, May 5, 1945.

"Mr. La Guardia's Withdrawal," *New York Times*, May 7, 1945.

"Released French Leaders," *New York Times*, May 7, 1945.

"The Strategy was Sound," *New York Times*, May 8, 1945.

"Industry After VE Day," *New York Times*, May 9, 1945.

"The Chase Bank Acquitted," *New York Times*, May 9, 1945.

"To Reduce Trade Curbs," *New York Times*, May 10, 1945.

"What We Face Now," *New York Times*, May 11, 1945.

"Draft of Peace Terms Urged" (letter signed by "Henry Stuart Clark"), *New York Times*, May 11, 1945.

"The Seventh War Loan," *New York Times*, May 14, 1945.

"Congress Boosts its Own Pay," *New York Times*, May 15, 1945.

"Congress Faces a Great Issue," *New York Times*, May 17, 1945.

"On Reducing Taxes," *New York Times*, May 17, 1945.

"The 'Anti-Strike' Act," *New York Times*, May 18, 1945.

"Reward for Striking," *New York Times*, May 21, 1945.

"Plant Seizure," *New York Times*, May 22, 1945.

"An Irresponsible Act," *New York Times*, May 24, 1945.

"Strange Tariff Arguments," *New York Times*, May 25, 1945.

"Expanding Social Security," *New York Times*, May 26, 1945.

"Post-War Relief," *New York Times*, May 29, 1945.

"Congressional Pay Rise," *New York Times*, May 30, 1945.

"The Fear of Deflation," *New York Times*, May 30, 1945.

"Bretton Woods Agreements," *New York Times*, June 4, 1945.

"The 'Full Employment' Bill," *New York Times*, June 5, 1945.

"The Need to Act," *New York Times*, June 6, 1945.

"The Danger is Inflation," *New York Times*, June 8, 1945.

"An Irresponsible Increase," *New York Times*, June 9, 1945.

"A Meaningless Extension," *New York Times*, June 9, 1945.

"Trade and Peace," *New York Times*, June 11, 1945.

"Making Bretton Woods Work," *New York Times*, June 11, 1945.

"Controlling the Budget," *New York Times*, June 12, 1945.

"The House Pay Increase," *New York Times*, June 15, 1945.

"Share of Poverty," *New York Times*, June 18, 1945.

"Extending Price Control," *New York Times*, June 18, 1945.

"Full Employment," *New York Times*, June 18, 1945.

"The Weakness of Managed Money," *New York Times*, June 18, 1945.

"Two Strikes and One Cause," *New York Times*, June 19, 1945.

"A Victory for World Trade," *New York Times*, June 20, 1945.

"Tapering of Price Controls," *New York Times*, June 21, 1945.

"Revising the Labor Laws," *New York Times*, June 23, 1945.

"Using America's Bargaining Power," *New York Times*, June 25, 1945.

"More Spending Plans?" *New York Times*, June 28, 1945.

"A 'Free' Society," *New York Times*, July 1, 1945.

"Salvation Through Cheap Money?" *New York Times*, July 2, 1945.

"Alice in Bureauland," *New York Times*, July 2, 1945.

"Mr. Byrnes as Secretary," *New York Times*, July 2, 1945.

"Public Works as Catch-All," *New York Times*, July 3, 1945.

"Justice Roberts Retires," *New York Times*, July 7, 1945.

"Mr. Vinson's 'Compensatory' Spending," *New York Times*, July 9, 1945.

"A Bad Argument for Foreign Loans," *New York Times*, July 16, 1945.

"The Dangers of Price Control," *New York Times*, July 23, 1945.

"Wage Line and Price Line," *New York Times*, July 27, 1945.

"The Railway Union Demands," *New York Times*, July 26, 1945.

"Effect of Britain's Election on U.S. Thinking Analyzed," *New York Times* July 30, 1945.

"For Quicker Reconversion," *New York Times*, July 31, 1945.

"Taking Over the Bank," *New York Times*, August 3, 1945.

"The Murray Bill," *New York Times*, August 5, 1945.

"Mr. Morris' Candidacy," *New York Times*, August 6, 1945.

"Gold Standard Held an Enemy of Unsound Economic Practices," *New York Times*, August 6, 1945.

"Heard Round the World," *New York Times*, August 7, 1945.

"America and Attlee's Britain," *New York Times*, August 8, 1945.

"Mr. Hoover for the Senate," *New York Times*, August 8, 1945.

"The President's Report," *New York Times*, August 19, 1945.

"The Decision on Japan," *New York Times*, August 11, 1945.

"Danger to National Economy Seen in Continued Controls on Industry," *New York Times*, August 13, 1945.

"To Absorb the Shock," *New York Times*, August 15, 1945.

"Reconversion: A Good Start," *New York Times*, August 16, 1945.

"The Shock of Transition," *New York Times*, August 17, 1945.

"Modified Policies On Business Urged," *New York Times*, August 20, 1945.

"Decontrol: WPB vs. OPA," *New York Times*, August 22, 1945.

"Facing Forward," *New York Times*, August 22, 1945.

"Free Enterprise Now," *New York Times*, August 23, 1945.

"Fight or Court Inflation?" *New York Times*, August 24, 1945.

"Thomas F. Woodlock," *New York Times*, August 27, 1945.

"Economics and Finance" (on *The Bogey of Economic Maturity* by George Terborgh), *New York Times*, August 27, 1945.

"What's in the Murray Bill," *New York Times*, August 29, 1945.

"Should Government Guarantee Full Employment?" *Independent Woman*, September 1945.

" 'Fighting Inflation' by Price Control," *New York Times*, September 3, 1945.

"Unemployment Compensation," *New York Times*, September 4, 1945.

"Jobless Pay or Relief?" *New York Times*, September 5, 1945.

"The Task Before Congress," *New York Times*, September 6, 1945.

"Unemployment Pay," *New York Times*, September 10, 1945.

"Unfairness to Retailers," *New York Times*, September 10, 1945.

"The British Problem," *New York Times*, September 12, 1945.

"Wages and Prices in Wonderland," *New York Times*, September 10, 1945.

"The Labor Crisis," *New York Times*, September 17, 1945.

"Notes on Aid to Britain," *New York Times*, September 17, 1945.

"A New Tax Program," *New York Times*, September 20, 1945.

"Releasing Price Controls," *Commercial and Financial Chronicle*, September 27, 1945.

"Repeal the 'Anti-Strike' Act," *New York Times*, September 22, 1945.

"Sixty Million Jobs" (with William Spencer and Henry Wallace), *The University of Chicago Roundtable*, September 23, 1945.

"Enough to Buy Back the Product," *New York Times*, September 24, 1945.

"Repeal the 'Anti-Strike' Act," *New York Times*, September 26, 1945.

"Would Increased Wages Mean Increased Prices?" (with R. R. Nathan and Fred Clark), *Wake Up America*, September 30, 1945.

"The Murray Bill Now," *New York Times*, October 1, 1945.

"The Government as Economic Forecaster," *New York Times*, October 1, 1945.

"The Wrong Way to End Strikes," *New York Times*, October 3, 1945.

"Stop, Look, and Listen," *New York Times*, October 5, 1945.

"Government Controls on Trial," *New York Times*, October 8, 1945.

"Solving the Insoluble," *New York Times*, October 10, 1945.

"Mr. Truman's Duty," *New York Times*, October 12, 1945.

"More Ways to Promote Inflation," *New York Times*, October 15, 1945.

"Cooper Union," *New York Times*, October 17, 1945.

"Taxes in a Democracy," *New York Times*, October 17, 1945.

"Mr. Lewis Bearing Gifts," *New York Times*, October 19, 1945.

"A 'Wage-Price Policy'?" *New York Times*, October 24, 1945.

"A Vain Search for a Wage Price Formula," *New York Times*, October 22, 1945.

"The Fetish of Full Employment," *New York Times*, October 29, 1945.

"Freedom or Controls?" *New York Times*, October 30, 1945.

"The New Wage-Price Plan," *New York Times*, October 31, 1945.

"Wages, Prices, and Controls," *New York Times*, November 4, 1945.

"Fighting and Forcing Inflation," *New York Times*, November 5, 1945.

"Limiting Aims on Labor," *New York Times*, November 7, 1945.

"For a Full Employment Study," *New York Times*, November 9, 1945.

"The British Loan and World Trade," *New York Times*, November 12, 1945.

"Reply to Mr. Chase" (letters), *New York Times*, November 14, 1945.

"Europe's Dreaded Winter," *New York Times*, November 14, 1945.

"Germany in the World Economy," *New York Times*, November 19, 1945.

"Results of PR," *New York Times*, November 21, 1945.

"The G.M. Strike," *New York Times*, November 22, 1945.

"The Labor Crisis and Price Control," *New York Times*, December 3, 1945.

"A Controlled Economy?" *New York Times*, December 3, 1945.

"The UAW Demands," *New York Times*, December 5, 1945.

"Moving Back to Wartime Controls," *New York Times*, December 10, 1945.

"The 'Fact-Finding' Bill," *New York Times*, December 12, 1945.

"The Hobbs Bill," *New York Times*, December 11, 1945.

"Finding the Facts," *New York Times*, December 16, 1945.

"Edwin W. Kemmerer," *New York Times*, December 17, 1945.

"Free Enterprise or Government Planning?" *New York Times*, December 17, 1945.

"The Remedy for Inflation," *New York Times*, December 21, 1945.

"Some Consequences of 'Ability to Pay'," *New York Times, December 24*, 1945.

"Free Enterprise or Government Planning?" *The Nation*, December 24, 1945.

"Petrillo 'Back to Normal'," *New York Times*, December 26, 1945.

"Mr. Truman and Congress," *New York Times*, December 30, 1945.

"The Function of Profits," *New York Times*, December 31, 1945.

1946

"The Fetish of Full Employment," *Dylogram*, January 1946.

"Mr. Truman's Labor Policy," *New York Times*, January 4, 1946.

"Inflation and the Forthcoming Budget," *New York Times*, January 7, 1946.

"Strike Dilemma," *New York Times*, January 9, 1946.

"Congress and the President," *New York Times*, January 12, 1946.

"Prices, Wages, Profits, and Politics," *New York Times*, January 14, 1946.

"Labor Legislation," *New York Times*, January 16, 1946.

"Labor Law: Which Path?" *New York Times*, January 18, 1946.

"Symptom Control vs. Inflation Control," *New York Times*, January 21, 1946.

"Ability-to-Pay Problem," *New York Times*, January 21, 1946.

"The Budget," *New York Times*, January 22, 1946.

"Inflationary Pressure No. 1," *New York Times*, January 23, 1946.

"The Labor Crisis," *New York Times*, January 27, 1946.

"The Government Builds Up Inflation," *New York Times*, January 28, 1946.

"New Labor Legislation," *New York Times*, January 31, 1946.

"Mr. Dewey's Budget," *New York Times*, February 1, 1946.

"State Public Works," *New York Times*, February 2, 1946.

"Government-Financed Strikes," *New York Times*, February 4, 1946.

"Political Problem of the British Loan," *New York Times*, February 4, 1946.

"Wages and Inflation," *New York Times*, February 5, 1946.

"The New Labor Bill," *New York Times*, February 8, 1946.

"The Choice Before Labor," *New York Times*, February 10, 1946.

"Low Interest Rates Help Inflation," *New York Times*, February 11, 1946.

"The City Crisis," *New York Times*, February 13, 1946.

"We Do Have a Wage-Price Law," *New York Times*, February 14, 1946.

"The New Wage-Price Policy," *New York Times*, February 16, 1946.

"Consequences of the Strike Settlements," *New York Times*, February 18, 1946.

"An Anti-Inflation Program," *New York Times*, February 19, 1946.

"Mr. Bowles' Remedies," *New York Times*, February 20, 1946.

"Inflationary Tug of War," *New York Times*, February 21, 1946.

"Mr. Bowles and Mr. Ford," *New York Times*, February 21, 1946.

"Production is Not Enough," *New York Times*, February 25, 1946.

"A Good Appointment," *New York Times*, February 27, 1956.

"Mr. Eccles and Inflation," *New York Times*, February 27, 1946.

"Forcing Up Living Costs," *New York Times*, February 28, 1946.

"Until Supply Catches Up With Demand," *New York Times*,March 4, 1946.

"Motives and Prices," *New York Times*, March 7, 1946.

"Inflation is World-Wide," *New York Times*, March 11, 1946.

"Wage and Price Control," *New York Times*, March 12, 1946.

"Whose 'Victory'," *New York Times*, March 14, 1946.

"More 'Planning'," *New York Times*, March 16, 1946.

"Some Consequences of Foreign Loans," *New York Times*, March 18, 1946.

"A Good Appointment," *New York Times*, March 19, 1946.

"To Save Food," *New York Times*, March 19, 1946.

"Control by 'Statistics'," *New York Times*, March 20, 1946.

"The Senate Labor Bill," *New York Times*, March 22, 1946.

"To Stop Starvation," *New York Times*, March 23, 1946.

"The Road to Peace," *New York Times*, March 23, 1946.

"Canadian Example," *New York Times*, March 24, 1946.

"Free Market vs. Black Market," *New York Times*, March 25, 1946.

"President and Party," *New York Times*, March 26, 1946.

"Minimum Wages," *New York Times*, March 27, 1946.

"Curbing Petrillo Only," *New York Times*, March 28, 1946.

"My Inflation vs. Yours," *New York Times*, March 29, 1946.

"Wheatless Days,"*New York Times*, March 29, 1946.

"Political Statistics?" *New York Times*, March 30, 1946.

"The Twilight of the Free Market?" *New York Times*, April 1, 1946.

"Why We Have a Coal Strike," *New York Times*, April 2, 1946.

"Another Inflation Victory," *New York Times*, April 4, 1946.

"Congress and Price Control," *New York Times*, April 6, 1946.

"To Get Out the Wheat," *New York Times*, April 8, 1946.

"Mr. Petrillo Moves Ahead," *New York Times*, April 11, 1946.

"That Magic Date: July 1, 1947," *New York Times*, April 8, 1946.

"Wage Facts and Theories," *New York Times*, April 13, 1946.

"Price Control Prolongs Inflation," *New York Times*, April 15, 1946.

"For Price Fact-Finding," *New York Times*, April 16, 1946.

"Wages and Prices," *Commercial and Financial Chronicle*, April 18, 1946.

"Congress and Price Control," *New York Times*, April 18, 1946.

"Lord Keynes," *New York Times*, April 23, 1946.

"Congress Moves Toward Decontrol," *New York Times*, April 22, 1946.

"Debt Limit, Spending Limit," *New York Times*, April 26, 1946.

"A Step Against Inflation," *New York Times*, April 26, 1946.

"A Policy-Made Famine," *New York Times*, April 29, 1946.

"Coal," *New York Times*, April 30, 1946.

"Wages and Prices," Academy of Political Science, *Proceedings*, May 1946.

"Petrillo as Symptom," *New York Times*, May 2, 1946.

"Strawberry Prices," *New York Times*, May 4, 1946.

"1946 Is Not 1919," *New York Times*, May 6, 1946.

"This National Disaster," *New York Times*, May 6, 1946.

"The Remedy of Seizure," *New York Times*, May 7, 1946.

"Congress and the Strike," *New York Times*, May 8, 1946.

"Washington Paralysis," *New York Times*, May 9, 1946.

"Are Strikes Good?" *New York Times*, May 10, 1946.

"Cost-of-Production Price-Fixing," *New York Times*, May 13, 1946.

"Why Lewis Needn't Bargain," *New York Times*, May 13, 1946.

"Revising Our Labor Laws," *New York Times*, May 14, 1946.

"Subsidizing Strikes," *New York Times*, May 15, 1946.

"Belated Curiosity," *New York Times*, May 16, 1946.

"A Bankrupt Labor Policy," *New York Times*, May 17, 1946.

"Political Statistics," *New York Times*, May 18, 1946.

"Seizing the Railroads," *New York Times*, May 18, 1946.

"The Government Breeds Its Own Crises," *New York Times*, May 20, 1946.

"Prelude to Surrender?" *New York Times*, May 20, 1946.

"An Emergency Labor Law," *New York Times*, May 21, 1946.

"The Strike Crisis," *New York Times*, May 23, 1946.

"The Strike Begins," *New York Times*, May 24, 1946.

"Mr. Truman and the Strike," *New York Times*, May 25, 1946.

"The Issues in the Strike," *New York Times*, May 25, 1946.

"Domestic Controls vs. Free Foreign Trade," *New York Times*, May 27, 1946.

"Mr. Truman and Labor," *New York Times*, May 28, 1946.

"A Strike-Fomenting Bill?" *New York Times*, May 29, 1946.

"The Coal Settlement," *New York Times*, May 30, 1946.

"How to Have Depression With Inflation," *New York Times*, June 3, 1946.

"No Help From Mr. Murray," *New York Times*, June 4, 1946.

"Defiance of Government," *New York Times*, June 5, 1946.

"Mr. Truman and the Case Bill," *New York Times*, June 6, 1946.

"Eugene Meyer," *New York Times*, June 6, 1946.

"Two Appointments," *New York Times*, June 7, 1946.

"The National Bureau," *New York Times*, June 7, 1946.

"The Case Bill," *New York Times*, June 10, 1946.

"The Sham War Against Inflation," *New York Times*, June 10, 1946.

"For Signing the Case Bill," *New York Times*, June 11, 1946.

"OPA and Rent Control," *New York Times*, June 11, 1946.

"The President's Veto," *New York Times*, June 12, 1946.

"After the Veto," *New York Times*, June 12, 1946.

"The Double Standard," *New York Times*, June 14, 1946.

"Do Unions Really Raise Wages," *Vital Speeches*, June 15, 1946.

"The Future of OPA," *New York Times*, June 15, 1946.

"The Prospect is Still Inflation," *New York Times*, June 17, 1946.

"Toward Price Decontrol," *New York Times*, June 18, 1946.

"Tapering Off Price Control," *New York Times*, June 21, 1946.

"Price Decontrol Problems," *New York Times*, June 24, 1946.

"More Powers to 'Fight Inflation'," *New York Times*, June 24, 1946.

"Why the Hobbs Bill?" *New York Times*, June 25, 1946.

"The New OPA," *New York Times*, June 26, 1946.

"Mr. Snyder's Fine Start," *New York Times*, June 27, 1946.

"What Should Congress Do?" *New York Times*, July 1, 1946.

"Between Price Control and a Fog," *New York Times*, July 1, 1946.

"In Economic No-Man's Land," *New York Times*, July 2, 1946.

"To End Uncertainty," *New York Times*, July 3, 1946.

"The Price Holiday," *New York Times*, July 5 1946.

"Notes on the Price Extension Veto," *New York Times*, July 8, 1946.

"Rent and Price Control," *New York Times*, July 9, 1946.

"Notes on the Price Extension Veto," *New York Times*, July 8, 1946.

"For Selective Controls," *New York Times*, July 12, 1946.

"Decentralized Rent Control," *New York Times*, July 13, 1946.

"Price Control in the House," *New York Times*, July 15, 1946.

"Our Irresponsible Budget," *New York Times*, July 15, 1946.

"Selective Price Control," *New York Times*, July 17, 1946.

"Tariffs Fade Into the Background," *New York Times*, July 22, 1946.

"Give the House a Chance," *New York Times*, July 16, 1946.

"The Fetish of Low Interest Rates," *New York Times*, July 29, 1946.

"The Broken Window Fallacy," *Reader's Digest*, August 1946.

"Workers Can't Eat Dollars," *Nation's Business*, August, 1946.

"Labor Seventy-seven Years Ago and Now," *New York Times*, August 5, 1946.

"Economy This Year," *New York Times*, August 6, 1946.

"Budget Responsibility," *New York Times*, August 7, 1946.

"Mr. Molotov and Mr. Seldes," *New York Times*, August 9, 1946.

"American and World Price Control," *New York Times*, August 12, 1946.

"Wagner Act Changes," *New York Times*, August 13, 1946.

"Price Decontrol Standards," *New York Times*, August 15, 1946.

"Mr. Coudert or Mr. Baldwin?" *New York Times*, August 16, 1946.

"The Ideals of Adolph Ochs," *New York Times*, August 18, 1946.

"Some Consequences of Bad Price Law," *New York Times*, August 19, 1946.

"The Primaries," *New York Times*, August 20, 1946.

"Meat Ceilings Again," *New York Times*, August 21, 1946.

"Short Supply," *New York Times*, August 22, 1946.

"Pockets and Bureaucrats," *New York Times*, August 23, 1946.

"The Decontrol Board Recontrols," *New York Times*, August 26, 1946.

"Lots of Government," *New York Times*, August 27, 1946.

"The Break in Stocks," *New York Times*, September 5, 1946.

"A New Mystery of Price Control," *New York Times*, September 2, 1946.

"Lessons of the Stock Market Break," *New York Times*, September 9, 1946.

"The Shipping Strike," *New York Times*, September 13, 1946.

"Aftermath of the Market Decline," *New York Times*, September 16, 1946.

"Must We Have Boom and Bust?" (debate with Isador Lubin), *Wake Up America*, September 22, 1946.

"How 'Stabilization' Unstables," *Newsweek*, September 30, 1946.

"New Ironies of Price Control," *Newsweek*, October 7, 1946.

"Twelve Weeks of Meat," *New York Times*, October 12, 1946.

"Inflation, Deflation, Confusion," *Newsweek*, October 14, 1946.

"Price-fixing Brings Bottlenecks," *Newsweek*, October 21, 1946.

"Meat and the Speed on Decontrol," *Newsweek*, October 28, 1946.

"Coal, Wages, Politics," *New York Times*, November 3, 1946.

"Squeezing the Price Balloon," *Newsweek*, November 4, 1946.

"Price Decontrol," *New York Times*, November 5, 1946.

"Free Press and Advertising," *New York Times*, November 6, 1946.

"If the President Resigns," *New York Times*, November 10, 1946.

"Leonard Ayres on Business Cycles," *Newsweek*, November 11, 1946.

"The Consequences of Decontrol," *Newsweek*, November 18, 1946.

"Repeal Anti-employer Legislation," *Newsweek*, November 26, 1946.

"How to Taper Off Rent Control," *Newsweek*, December 2, 1946.

"Should the Wagner Labor Relations Act Be Revised?" (with George Denny, William Jackson, et al.), *Town Meeting*, December 5, 1946.

"What's Wrong With Our Labor Policy," *Newsweek*, December 9, 1946.

"Inviolate Rights—For One Side," *Newsweek*, December 16, 1946.

"Twenty Labor Act Revisions," *Newsweek*, December 20, 1946.

"Collective Bargaining," *New York Times*, December 26, 1946.

"The New CIO Wage Drive," *Newsweek*, December 30, 1946.

1947

"The 'Purchasing Power' Theory," *Newsweek*, January 6, 1947.

"The High Cost of Judicial Legislation," *Newsweek*, January 13, 1947.

"How to Reduce the Budget," *Newsweek*, January 20, 1947.

" 'Stabilizing' the Economy," *Newsweek*, February 27, 1947.

"The Fruits of Foreign Lending," *Newsweek*, February 3, 1947.

"They are the Workers' Corporations," *Newsweek*, February 10, 1947.

"Boom in Mexico," *Newsweek*, February 17, 1947.

"Mexico's Oil and Export Problem," *Newsweek*, February 24, 1947.

"Chinese Handwriting on the Wall," *Newsweek*, March 3, 1947.

"How England Got that Way," *Newsweek*, March 10, 1947.

"'Planning' vs. the Price System," *Newsweek*, March 17, 1947.

"Foremen Under Judicial Legislation," *Newsweek*, March 24, 1947.

"Six Principles of Foreign Aid," *Newsweek*, March 31, 1947.

"High Taxes vs. Incentive and Revenue," *Newsweek*, April 7, 1947.

"Our Fiscal Irresponsibility," *Newsweek*, April 14, 1947.

"Switzerland as a World Mirror," *Newsweek*, April 28, 1947.

"France on a Quiet Volcano," *Newsweek*, May 5, 1947.

"Belgium: Experiment in Freedom," *Newsweek*, May 12, 1947.

"Austerity in Holland," *Newsweek*, May 19, 1947.

"The Middle Way Swings Left," *Newsweek*, May 26, 1947.

"England vs. the Price System," *Newsweek*, June 2, 1947.

"Why Europe is in a Mess," *Newsweek*, June 9, 1947.

"Why Living Costs Have Risen," *Newsweek*, June 16, 1947.

"Subsidizing Planned Chaos," *Newsweek*, June 23, 1947.

"The New Labor Law," *Newsweek*, June 30, 1947.

"Mr. Truman Invites Strikes," *Newsweek*, July 7, 1947.

"Consequences of Rent Control," *Newsweek*, July 14, 1947.

"The World's Santa Claus," *Newsweek*, July 21, 1947.

"Telling Prices What to Do," *Newsweek*, July 28, 1947.

"The Midyear Economic Report," *Newsweek*, August 4, 1947.

"A Pro-labor Law," *Newsweek*, August 11, 1947.

"Where Are We Headed Economically?" (with Robert Nathan, et al.), *The American Forum of the Air*, August 5, 1947.

"The Myth of a Dollar Famine," *Newsweek*, August 18, 1947.

"The Bankruptcy of 'Planning'," *Newsweek*, August 25, 1947.

"A Modern Corporation Reports," *Newsweek*, September 1, 1947.

"What Should the United States' Position Be?" (with Redvers Opie, Gordon Hudson, et al.), *The American Forum of the Air*, September 2, 1947.

"The Fund vs. World Recovery," *Newsweek*, September 8, 1947.

"Why Not Also Capital Day," *Newsweek*, September 15, 1947.

"Lenin Was Right," *Newsweek*, September 22, 1947.

"The Profiteer Hunt is On," *Newsweek*, September 29, 1947.

"How Much Does Europe Need," *Newsweek*, October 6, 1947.

"Europe's Four-year Plan," *Newsweek*, October 13, 1947.

"What Should We Do for Europe Now?" (with George Denny, Dean Acheson, et al.), *Town Meeting*, October 14, 1947.

"The Drive Against 'Gambling'," *Newsweek*, October 20, 1947.

"Are Profits Too High?" *Newsweek*, October 27, 1947.

"The Dilemma of the Marshall Plan," *Newsweek*, November 2, 1947.

"Who Told Us What?" *Newsweek*, November 10, 1947.

"Export Demand Lifts Prices," *Newsweek*, November 17, 1947.

"Must We Subsidize Socialism?" *Newsweek*, November 24, 1947.

"Back to Police-State Controls," *Newsweek*, December 1, 1947.

"Economic Outlook," *Commercial and Financial Chronicle*, December 4, 1947.

"Cheap Money Means Inflation," *Newsweek*, December 8, 1947.

"Can We Buy Off Communism," *Newsweek*, December 15, 1947.

"Our Inflationary Bond Shortage," *Newsweek*, December 22, 1947.

"Inflation has Two Faces," *Newsweek*, December 29, 1947.

1948

"Will Dollars Save the World?" Excerpts in *Reader's Digest*, January and February 1948.

"The Uncalculated Risk," *Newsweek*, January 5, 1948.

"A Century of Communism," *Newsweek*, January 12, 1948.

"Should the President's European Recovery Plan Be Adopted?" (with Robert Patterson, George Denny, et al.), *Town Meeting*, January 13, 1948.

"Blueprint for Disruption," *Newsweek*, January 19, 1948.

"We Cannot Buy Off the Russian Nightmare," *Newsweek*, January 26, 1948.

"Who's Protected by Tariffs?" Excerpt from *Economics In One Lesson* in *Reader's Digest*, February, 1948.

"How to Get Rid of Rent Control," *Newsweek*, February 2, 1947.

"Finance at the Crossroads," *Newsweek*, February 9, 1948.

"The Realities of Foreign Aid," *The Commercial and Financial Chronicle*, February 12, 1948.

"Significance of the Break in Prices," *Newsweek*, February 16, 1948.

"Inconsistencies of European Aid," Newsweek, February 23, 1948.

"Who Advises the Advisers," *Newsweek*, March 1, 1948.

"Communism and the Marshall Plan," *Newsweek*, March 8, 1948.

"For a Customs Union," *Newsweek*, March 15, 1948.

"The Cost of 'Soaking the Rich'," *Newsweek*, March 22, 1948.

"Steel as a Scapegoat," *Newsweek*, March 29, 1948.

"Fallacies of the Third Round," *Newsweek*, April 5, 1948.

"To Improve the Taft-Hartley Law," *Newsweek*, April 12, 1948.

"Britain's Collectivism vs. ERP," *Newsweek*, April 19, 1948.

"An Anti-inflation Program," *Newsweek*, April 26, 1948.

"How Not to Cure Inflation," *Newsweek*, May 3, 1948.

"The Fallacy of Exchange Control," *Newsweek*, May 10, 1948.

"Rewarding Railway Strikers," *Newsweek*, May 17, 1948.

"Price Fixing into Famine," *Newsweek*, May 24, 1948.

"The Incubus of Exchange Control," *Newsweek*, May 31, 1948.

"Who is a Dark Horse?" *Plain Talk*, June 1948.

"The GM Wage Pattern," *Newsweek*, June 7, 1948.

"Who Started the Third Round?" *Newsweek*, June 14, 1948.

"How to Fight Communism," *Newsweek*, June 21, 1948.

"Ordeal by Planning," *Newsweek*, June 28, 1948.

"Republican Platform Economics," *Newsweek*, July 5, 1948.

"Dangers of Dollar Diplomacy," *Newsweek*, July 12, 1948.

"Collectivism on Relief," *Newsweek*, July 19, 1948.

"Democratic Platform Economics," *Newsweek*, July 26, 1948.

"The Phony War Against Inflation," *Newsweek*, August 2, 1948.

"Will Inflation Stop Inflation?" *Newsweek*, August 9, 1948.

"Dollar Shortage Forever," *Newsweek*, August 16, 1948.

"Hypocrisy About Inflation," *Newsweek*, August 23, 1948.

"A Bear By the Tail," *Newsweek*, August 30, 1948.

"Repressed Inflation," *Newsweek*, September 6, 1948.

"Does Stalin Want War?" *Newsweek*, September 13, 1948.

"The Ethics of Capitalism," *Newsweek*, September 20, 1948.

"The Fetish of Bond Parity," *Newsweek*, September 27, 1948.

"Bond Parity Without Inflation," *Newsweek*, October 4, 1948.

"Suppressing Free Markets," *Newsweek*, October 11, 1948.

"Cheap Money Causes Inflation," *Newsweek*, October 18, 1948.

"Cryptic Economics," *Newsweek*, October 25, 1948.

"Texas Grows and Votes," *Newsweek*, November 1, 1948.

"How Free Will Our Economy Be?" *Newsweek*, November 8, 1948.

"Where Was The Opposition?" *Newsweek*, November 15, 1948.

"Pitfalls of Forecasting," *Newsweek*, November 22, 1948.

"Meat and the Price System," *Newsweek*, November 29, 1948.

"Exchange Control in Peru," *Newsweek*, December 6, 1948.

"Exchange Control vs. Peru," *Newsweek*, December 13, 1948.

"The Myth of Dollar Shortage," *Newsweek*, December 20, 1948.

"Are Profits Too High?" *Newsweek*, December 27, 1948.

1949

"We Impose Collectivism," *Newsweek*, January 3, 1949.

"Rent Control in France," *Newsweek*, January 10, 1949.

"Paradise on a Platter," *Newsweek*, January 17, 1949.

"Balance Whose Budget?" *Newsweek*, January 24, 1949.

"Our Discompensated Economy," *Newsweek*, January 31, 1949.

"Planned Unemployment," *Newsweek*, February 7, 1949.

"Inflation: Enemy of Free Enterprise," *The Commercial and Financial Chronicle*, February 10, 1949.

"'Planning'—Ah! Magic Word," *Newsweek*, February 14, 1949.

"Me Too—But Not as Much," *Newsweek*, February 21, 1949.

"What Are We Trying to Do?" *Newsweek*, February 28, 1949.

"The Case For Private Loans," *Newsweek*, March 7, 1949.

"Mr. Stalin's Marionettes," *New York Times*, March 12, 1949.

"Rent Control vs. Housing," *Newsweek*, March 14, 1949.

"4,000 Years of Price Controls," *Newsweek*, March 21, 1949.

"How Can We Legislate for the General Welfare?" (with Robert Taft, George V. Denny, et al.), *Town Meeting*, March 25, 1949.

"Sense Instead of Dollars," *Newsweek*, March 28, 1949.

"Military vs. Economic Aid," *Newsweek*, April 4, 1949.

"Whose Bold New Program?" *Newsweek*, April 11, 1949.

"Bankruptcy of the Welfare State," *Newsweek*, April 18, 1949.

"The Welfare State Runs Wild," *Newsweek*, April 25, 1949.

"Legally Certified Monopolists," *Newsweek*, May 2, 1949.

"Salvation Through Squandering," *Newsweek*, May 9, 1949.

"The Right to Strike," *Newsweek*, May 16, 1949.

"Our Irresponsible Budget," *Newsweek*, May 23, 1949.

"Arms and the Money," *Newsweek*, May 30, 1949.

"World Statism in Wheat," *Newsweek*, June 6, 1948.

"What Are We Paying For," *Newsweek*, June 13, 1949.

"The Ideological War," *Newsweek*, June 20, 1949.

"Private Enterprise Regained," *Newsweek*, June 27, 1949.

"The Pilgrims Tried Communism," *The Freeman*, June 27, 1949.

"Self-Perpetuating Pump Priming," *Newsweek*, July 4, 1949.

"The Folly of Point Four: I," *Newsweek*, July 11, 1949.

"The Folly of Point Four: II," *Newsweek*, July 18, 1949.

"More Inflation to the Rescue," *Newsweek*, July 25, 1949.

"Forcing a Fourth Round," *Newsweek*, August 1, 1949.

"The Economics of Arms Aid," *Newsweek*, August 8, 1949.

"Wrong Diagnosis, Wrong Remedy," *Newsweek*, August 15, 1949.

"Legislating Unemployment," *Newsweek*, August 22, 1949.

"When Government Fixes Wages," *Newsweek*, August 29, 1949.

"Abolish Exchange Control," *Newsweek*, September 5, 1949.

"Should the Steel Wage Recommendation Be Accepted?" (with Robert Nathan, Jules Backman, et al.), The University of Chicago Roundtable, September 11, 1949.

"Collapse of a Trick Solution," *Newsweek*, September 12, 1949.

"The Case for Capitalism," *Newsweek*, September 19, 1949.

"Camouflaged Fourth Round," *Newsweek*, September 26, 1949.

"The World Monetary Earthquake," *Newsweek*, October 3, 1949.

"Fourth Round in a False Face," *Newsweek*, October 10, 1949.

"Illusions of 'Social Security'," *Newsweek*, October 17, 1949.

"Four-Year House Term Proposed For Better Government," *New York Times*, October 23, 1949.

"Power of Industrywide Unions," *Newsweek*, October 26, 1949.

"Devaluation Instead of Freedom," *Newsweek*, October 31, 1949.

"Collectivism Marches On," *Newsweek*, November 7, 1949.

"Union Monopoly vs. Capitalism," *Newsweek*, November 14, 1949.

"What 'Monetary Management' Means," *Newsweek*, November 21, 1949.

"Gold Goes With Freedom," *Newsweek*, November 28, 1949.

"Instead of Integration," *Newsweek*, December 5, 1949.

"In Praise of Paper," *Newsweek*, December 12, 1949.

"The Compensatory Budget," *Newsweek*, December 19, 1949.

"Voices for Freedom," *Newsweek*, December 26, 1949.

1950

"The Man They All Forgot," *Newsweek*, January 2, 1950. Also *Congressional Digest*, August 1950.

"If Foreign Exchanges Were Free," *Newsweek*, January 9, 1950.

"The Future of Foreign Aid," *Newsweek*, January 16, 1950.

"The Forgotten Taxpayer," *Newsweek*, January 23, 1950.

"Free Trade or State Domination," *Newsweek*, January 30, 1950.

"Welfare State Spending 'on Trial'," *Commercial and Financial Chronicle*, February 2, 1950.

"Our Irresponsible Budget," *Newsweek*, February 6, 1950.

"Take Out the Goat," *Newsweek*, February 13, 1950.

"Fifty Billion for Tribute," *Newsweek*, February 20, 1950.

"Future of the Marshall Plan," *Newsweek*, February 27, 1950.

"The Needles Crisis In Coal," *Newsweek*, March 6, 1950.

"The American Giveaway Mania," *Newsweek*, March 13, 1950.

"Where Do We Go From Here," *Newsweek*, March 20, 1950.

"ERP vs. Recovery," *The Commercial and Financial Chronicle*, March 23, 1950.

That European Payments Union," *Newsweek*, March 27, 1950.

"Rent Control Forever?" *Newsweek*, April 3, 1950.

"How We Subsidize Collectivism," *Newsweek*, April 10, 1950.

"Global Spending Forever?" *Newsweek*, April 17, 1950.

"How to Buy More Unemployment," *Newsweek*, April 24, 1950.

"For a Responsible Budget," *Newsweek*, May 1, 1949.

"How to Tell a Totalitarian," *Newsweek*, May 8, 1949.

"Self-Perpetuating Rent Control," *Newsweek*, May 15, 1950.

"The Giveaway Mania Grows," *Newsweek*, May 22, 1950.

"The Fair Deal Family at Home," *Newsweek*, May 29, 1950.

"Toward State-Managed Cartel?" *Newsweek*, June 5, 1950.

"Man-Eating by Tigers is Silly, But They Will Go On Doing It!" *Saturday Evening Post*, June 10, 1950.

"Salvation Through Spending," *Newsweek*, June 12, 1950.

"Drought Fighting in a Flood," *Newsweek*, June 19, 1950.

"Who Are the Isolationists?" *Newsweek*, June 26, 1950.

"Free Trade or Coercion," *Newsweek*, July 3, 1950.

"Planning for a 'War Economy'," *Newsweek*, July 10, 1950.

"A Bad Tax Bill," *Newsweek*, July 17, 1950.

"The Inflation in Housing," *Newsweek*, July 24, 1950.

"Program For the Crisis," *Newsweek*, July 31, 1950.

"War Measures—Or Hysteria," *Newsweek*, August 7, 1950.

"Do We Need More Wartime Controls Now?" (with Hubert H. Humphrey and Orville Hitchcock), *Town Meeting*, August 8, 1950.

"The Fraud of Price Control," *Newsweek*, August 14, 1950.

"Transform ECA," *Newsweek*, August 21, 1950.

"Some Notes on War Taxes," *Newsweek*, August 28, 1950.

"Sham Fight Against Inflation," *Newsweek*, September 4, 1950.

"Dilemmas of Price Control," *Newsweek*, September 11, 1950.

"Shadow-Boxing With Inflation," *Newsweek*, September 18, 1950.

"When Prices Go Into Politics," *Newsweek*, September 25, 1950.

"The Need For Credit Control," *Newsweek*, October 2, 1950.

"The Fortnight" (on Truman, Dewey, Taft, inflation), *The Freeman*, October 2, 1950.

"Communism Imitates Capitalism," *Newsweek*, October 9, 1950.

"Canada Takes the Lead," *Newsweek*, October 16, 1950.

"The Fortnight" (on The Fed, exchange control, the U.N.), *The Freeman*, October 16, 1950.

"ERP Reverses Its Aims," *Newsweek*, October 23, 1950.

"Credit Control at the Source," *Newsweek*, October 30, 1950.

"The Fortnight" (on search and seizure), *The Freeman*, October 30, 1950.

"The Great American Giveaway," *Newsweek*, November 6, 1950.

"'Bankruptcy' is Here," *Newsweek*, November 13, 1950.

"On Taxing 'Excess' Profits," *Newsweek*, November 20, 1950.

"'Full Employment' as Inflation," *Newsweek*, November 27, 1950.

"Gray is for Giveaway," *Newsweek*, December 4, 1950.

"This is the Peace We Bought," *Newsweek*, December 11, 1950.

"The Fortnight" (on Korean War, Mac-Arthur, rent control), *The Freeman*, December 11, 1950.

"More Inflation Ahead," *Newsweek*, December 18, 1950.

"Total Muddleization," *Newsweek*, December 25, 1950.

"The Fortnight" (on the real enemy in Washington, price control, etc.), *The Freeman*, December 25, 1950.

"Our Political Paralysis," *The Freeman*, December 25, 1950.

1951

"The Price Control Strait Jacket," *Newsweek*, January 1, 1951.

"How to Stop Inflation," *Newsweek*, January 8, 1951.

"The Fortnight" (on Truman, the budget, etc.), *The Freeman*, January 8, 1951.

"Inflation Has One Cure," *Newsweek*, January 15, 1951.

"Mr. Truman's Wrong Remedies," *Newsweek*, January 22, 1951.

"The Fortnight" (on war, executive power), *The Freeman*, January 22, 1951.

"Our Irresponsible Budget," *Newsweek*, January 29, 1951.

"Fighting Fire With Gasoline," *Newsweek*, February 5, 1951.

"Price Control Means Politics," *Newsweek*, February 12, 1951.

"The Fortnight" (on inflation, interest rates, Soviet statistics), *The Freeman*, February 12, 1951.

"How to Curb One-Man Rule," *The Freeman*, February 12, 1951.

"Price-fixing vs. Freedom," *The Freeman*, February 12, 1951.

"Inflation Plus Usurpation," *Newsweek*, February 19, 1951.

"Abolish the RFC," *Newsweek*, February 26, 1951.

"The Fortnight" (on budget, the Fed), *The Freeman*, February 26, 1951.

"How to Cause A Famine," *Newsweek*, March 5, 1951.

"Inflation is Government-Made," *Newsweek*, March 12, 1951.

"The Fortnight" (on price control, the Soviets and the media), *The Freeman*, March 12, 1951

"Congress in Eclipse," *The Freeman*, March 12, 1951.

"Giving Grain to India," *The Freeman*, March 12, 1951.

"The CED on Price Controls," *Newsweek*, March 19, 1951.

"Point Four is Growing Up," *Newsweek*, March 26, 1951.

"The Fortnight" (on Truman, corruption, pressure groups), *The Freeman*, March 26, 1951.

"The XXII Amendment," *The Freeman*, March 26, 1951.

"International Statism Rampant," *Newsweek*, April 2, 1951.

"Is Price Control Necessary," *Newsweek*, April 9, 1951.

"The Crisis in Controls, *The Freeman*, April 9, 1951.

"Controls Create Inflation," *Newsweek*, April 16, 1951.

"Priorities vs. Price Control," *Newsweek*, April 23, 1951.

"Gold Standard vs. Inflation," *Newsweek*, April 30, 1951.

"We Have Asked for Inflation," *Newsweek*, May 7, 1951.

"Why Price Control Should Expire," *Newsweek*, May 14, 1951.

"End Price Ceilings—and Parity," *Newsweek*, May 21, 1951.

"The Fortnight" (on Truman and the Korean War), *The Freeman*, May 21, 1951.

"The Future of Fair Trade," *Newsweek*, June 4, 1951.

"The Fortnight" (on MacArthur's dismissal, Mises seminar), *The Freeman*, June 4, 1951.

"Foreign Giveaway Grows," *Newsweek*, June 11, 1951.

"Price Controllers in a Panic," *Newsweek*, June 18, 1951.

"The Fortnight" (on Administration's military strategy), *The Freeman*, June 18, 1951.

"An Anti-Inflation Program," *Newsweek*, June 25, 1951.

"They Told Us Then . . . ," *Newsweek*, July 2, 1951.

"The Fortnight" (on troops in Korea, price control), *The Freeman*, July 2, 1951.

"The Cause of Currency Chaos," *Newsweek*, July 9, 1951.

"Price Fixing as a Red Herring," *Newsweek*, July 16, 1951.

"The Fortnight" (on cease-fire, price control), *The Freeman*, July 16, 1951.

"Government: Plan Thyself," *Newsweek*, July 23, 1951.

"Iran vs. Point Four," *Newsweek*, July 30, 1951.

"The Fortnight" (on Iranian oil, Mac-Arthur hearings), *The Freeman*, July 30, 1951.

"The Mises Seminar," *The Freeman*, July 30, 1951.

"The Danger of Profit Control," *Newsweek*, August 6, 1951.

"Why the New Controls Act is Bad," *Newsweek*, August 13, 1951.

"The Fortnight" (on foreign policy, Owen Lattimore), *The Freeman*, August 13, 1951.

"Off to the Races," *Newsweek*, August 20, 1951.

"Congress's Monetary Duty," *Newsweek*, August 27, 1951.

"Inflation for Beginners: Part I," *Newsweek*, September 3, 1951.

"Inflation for Beginners: Part II," *Newsweek*, September 10, 1951.

"The Fortnight" (on negotiations with the Chinese Communists), *The Freeman*, September 10, 1951.

"Inflation for Beginners: Part III," *Newsweek*, September 17, 1951.

"Inflation for Beginners: Part IV," *Newsweek*, September 24, 1951.

"Inflation for Beginners: Part V," *Newsweek*, October 1, 1951.

"The Real Problems of France," *Newsweek*, October 8, 1951.

"To a Mitigated Socialism," *Newsweek*, October 15, 1951.

"Britain's 'Third Class'," *Newsweek*, October 22, 1951.

"This is Where We Came In," *Newsweek*, October 29, 1951.

"Chaotic Spending and Taxing," *Newsweek*, November 5, 1951.

"How to Denationalize," *Newsweek*, November 12, 1951.

"Who is Mislabeling What?" *Newsweek*, November 19, 1951.

"How to Depoliticize Money," *Newsweek*, November 26, 1951.

"Days of Disillusion," *Newsweek*, December 3, 1951.

"Arms or Economic Aid," *Newsweek*, December 10, 1951.

"Guns, Butter, and Disruption," *Newsweek*, December 17, 1951.

"A Budget Out of Control," *Newsweek*, December 24, 1951.

"Canada Breaks the Ice Some," *Newsweek*, December 31, 1951.

1952

"The Limits of Taxation," *Newsweek*, January 7, 1952.

"More About Arms Aid," *Newsweek*, January 14, 1952.

"A Ceiling on Spending," *Newsweek*, January 21, 1952.

"One Message Too Many," *Newsweek*, January 28, 1952.

"When Would You Cut?" *Newsweek*, February 4, 1952.

"Delusions of 'Productivity'," *Newsweek*, February 11, 1952.

"Calling the Market Black," *Newsweek*, February 18, 1952.

"Price Control Follies of 1952," *Newsweek*, February 23, 1952.

"How Can We Combat Inflation?" (with Paul Douglas and Frank Blair), *The American Forum of the Air*, February 24, 1952.

"Footnote on 'Statism'," *Newsweek*, March 3, 1952.

"The Lull in Inflation," *Newsweek*, March 10, 1952.

"Case Against Price Control," *Newsweek*, March 17, 1952.

"Are These Handouts Necessary?" *Newsweek*, March 24, 1952.

"Inflation and 'High Costs'," *Newsweek*, March 31, 1952.

"The 'Stabilization' Hoax," *Newsweek*, April 7, 1952.

"Price Fixing Without Tears," *Newsweek*, April 14, 1952.

"It is Happening Here," *Newsweek*, April 21, 1952.

"Toward Equality of Incomes," *Newsweek*, April 28, 1952.

"Peronism and Trumanism," *Newsweek*, May 5, 1952.

"We Took a Wrong Turn," *Newsweek*, May 12, 1952.

"The Philosophy of Seizure," *Newsweek*, May 19, 1952.

"Inflationary Double-Talk," *Newsweek*, May 26, 1952.

"Stabilization or Redistribution," *Newsweek*, June 2, 1952.

"How Europe Curbs Inflation," *Newsweek*, June 9, 1952.

"Seizure is No Solution," *Newsweek*, June 16, 1952.

"Seizure Creates Strikes," *Newsweek*, June 23, 1952.

"Why Not Try Capitalism," *Newsweek*, June 30, 1952.

"Educators vs. Free Inquiry," *The Freeman*, June 30, 1952.

"The Fallacy of Point Four," *Newsweek*, July 7, 1952.

"Our Laws Create Strikes," *Newsweek*, July 14, 1952.

"GOP Platform Economics," *Newsweek*, July 21, 1952.

"Price Control by Default," *Newsweek*, July 28, 1952.

"You Have Never Had it So Good," *Newsweek*, August 4, 1952.

"In the Wake of the Strike," *Newsweek*, August 11, 1952.

"'Isolating' Steel Prices," *Newsweek*, August 18, 1952.

"Is Inflation a Blessing?" *Newsweek*, August 25, 1952.

" 'Planning' for 1975," *Newsweek*, September 1, 1952.

"The Case for Free Markets," *Newsweek*, September 8, 1952.

"Adlai in Wonderland," *Newsweek*, September 15, 1952.

"The Bribe to the Farmer," *Newsweek*, September 22, 1952.

"Is Inflation Necessary?" *The Freeman*, September 22, 1952.

"Are You Better Off?" *Newsweek*, September 29, 1952.

"And Now, The Double-Deal?" *Newsweek*, October 6, 1952.

"Foreign Trade Follies," *Newsweek*, October 13, 1952.

"Stalin as Classical Economist," *Newsweek*, October 20, 1952.

"The Dilemma of Foreign Aid," *Newsweek*, October 27, 1952.

"What Are We Deciding?" *Newsweek*, November 3, 1952.

"World Reactions to the American Election" (with H. D. Black, et al.), The University of Chicago Roundtable, November 9, 1952.

"A Letter to Harry S Truman," *Newsweek*, November 17, 1952.

"The Dream World of the MSA," *Newsweek*, November 24, 1952.

"Why Risk an Interregnum?" *Newsweek*, December 1, 1952.

"The Tools That Make Tools," *Newsweek*, December 8, 1952.

"The Cabinet Change-Over," *Newsweek*, December 15, 1952.

"The Collapse of Controls," *Newsweek*, December 22, 1952.

"The Age of Envy," *Newsweek*, December 29, 1952.

1953

"Is a Depression Coming?" *Newsweek*, January 5, 1953.

"Fallacy in the Forecasts," *Newsweek*, January 12, 1953.

"Estimates vs. Realities," *Newsweek*, January 19, 1953.

"How to Cut the Budget," *Newsweek*, January 26, 1952.

"Making Currencies Convertible," *Newsweek*, February 2, 1953.

"Convertibility vs. Control," *Newsweek*, February 9, 1953.

"The Fortnight," *The Freeman*, February 9, 1953.

"Toward A Free Economy," *Newsweek*, 16, 1953.

"Farewell to Price Controls," *Newsweek*, February 23, 1953.

"The Price of Disinflation," *Newsweek*, March 2, 1953.

"The Meaning of Savings," *Newsweek*, March 9, 1953.

"Stalin and Our Policy," *Newsweek*, March 16, 1953.

"Trade, Plus Aid," *Newsweek*, March 23, 1953.

"A Tale About Taxes," *Newsweek*, March 30, 1953. Also *Reader's Digest*, October 1953.

"No Stand-by Controls," *Newsweek*, April 6, 1953.

"Inflation Must Have a Stop," *Newsweek*, April 13, 1953.

"Would Peace Be a Disaster?" *Newsweek*, April 20, 1953.

"Inflation Without Tears," *Newsweek*, April 27, 1953.

"To Restore Budget Control," *Newsweek*, May 4, 1953.

"Repeal the Taft-Hartley Act," *Newsweek*, May 11, 1953.

"No End to Super-Spending," *Newsweek*, May 18, 1953.

"Asking for More Inflation," *Newsweek*, May 23, 1953.

"Spending Can Be Cut More," *Newsweek*, June 1, 1953.

"Unneeded Stand-by Controls," *Newsweek*, June 7, 1953.

"Why Foreign Arms Aid?" *Newsweek*, June 15, 1953.

"A Budget Out of Control," *Newsweek*, June 22, 1953.

"Can We Prevent Depressions?" *Newsweek*, June 29, 1953.

"The Return to Gold," *Newsweek*, July 6, 1953.

"Return to Inflation," *Newsweek*, July 13, 1953.

"End Foreign Aid Now," *Newsweek*, July 20, 1953.

"How We Support The World," *Newsweek*, July 27, 1953.

"How to Help Small Business," *Newsweek*, August 3, 1953.

"Competition in Extravagance," *Newsweek*, August 10, 1953.

"Raising the Debt Limit," *Newsweek*, August 17, 1953.

"Eisenhower So Far," *Newsweek*, August 24, 1953.

"Can Taft Be Replaced?" *The Freeman*, August 24, 1953.

"The Futility of Foreign Aid," *Newsweek*, August 31, 1953.

"Why Doesn't Europe Aid Itself?" *Reader's Digest*, September 1953.

"Foreign Economic Policy," *Newsweek*, September 7, 1953.

"How to Kill Capitalism," *Newsweek*, September 14, 1953.

"Economists vs. Astrologers," *Newsweek*, September 21, 1953.

"Italy's Creeping Capitalism," *Newsweek*, September 28, 1953.

"The Welfare State in France," *Newsweek*, October 5, 1953.

"Secretarial Somersault," *The Freeman*, October 5, 1953.

"Does England Need Control?" *Newsweek*, October 12, 1953.

"How America Can Help," *Newsweek*, October 19, 1953.

"More About American Help," *Newsweek*, October 26, 1953.

"In the Sweet By and By," *Newsweek*, November 2, 1953.

"Europe's Self-Made Handcuff," *Newsweek*, November 2, 1953.

"Myth of Perpetual Boom," *Newsweek*, November 9, 1953.

"Is Depreciation a Subsidy?" *Newsweek*, November 16, 1953.

"For a Responsible Budget," *Newsweek*, November 23, 1953.

"White's Mischief Lives On," *Newsweek*, November 30, 1953.

"European Isolationism," *Newsweek*, December 7, 1953.

"Resumption of Inflation," *Newsweek*, December 14, 1953.

"Our Blind Labor Laws," *Newsweek*, December 21, 1953.

"The Ethics of Picketing," *Newsweek*, December 28, 1953.

1954

"Why Return to Gold," *Newsweek*, January 4, 1954.

"Gold Means Good Faith," *Newsweek*, January 11, 1954.

"What Price for Gold," *Newsweek*, January 18, 1954.

"How to Return to Gold," *Newsweek*, January 25, 1954.

"More About the Eggheads," *The Freeman*, January 25, 1954.

"Balance It Now," *Newsweek*, February 1, 1954.

"Price Supports Stifle Trade," *Newsweek*, February 8, 1954.

"Dr. Erhard's Philosophy," *The Freeman*, February 8, 1954.

"Ike's Semi-New Deal," *Newsweek*, February 15, 1954.

"Coffee, Butter, and Politics," *Newsweek*, February 22, 1954.

"The Dollar-Gold Ratio," *Newsweek*, March 1, 1954.

"Still More Inflation?" *Newsweek*, March 8, 1954.

"Lesson of the Greenbacks," *Newsweek*, March 15, 1954.

"Wages, Unions, and Jobs," *Newsweek*, March 22, 1954.

"Shirt-Sleeve Diplomacy," *America*, March 27, 1954.

"For Whom the Tax Bell Tolls," *Newsweek*, March 29, 1954.

"Soak Rich and Hit Poor," *Newsweek*, April 5, 1954.

"Give the House a Treaty Vote," *The Freeman*, April 5, 1954.

"Trade, Not Giveaway," *Newsweek*, April 12, 1954.

"Three Budgets," *Newsweek*, April 19, 1954.

"High Taxes vs. Revenues," *Newsweek*, April 26, 1954.

"For Whom the Tax Bell Tolls: Soak Rich and Hit Poor," *Reader's Digest*, June 1954.

"The Policy is Inflation," *Newsweek*, July 5, 1954.

"Foreign Aid Forever," *Newsweek*, July 12, 1954.

"Mistakes of Inflationists," *Newsweek*, July 19, 1954.

"Convertibility Now," *Newsweek*, October 11, 1954.

"What Kind of Convertibility?" *Newsweek*, October 18, 1954.

"Why America is First," *Newsweek*, October 25, 1954.

"Interpreting the Elections," November 1, 1954.

"Keynesian Thinking," *Newsweek*, November 8, 1954.

"When Government Lends," *Newsweek*, November 15, 1954.

"Lessons of the Election," *Newsweek*, November 22, 1954.

"The Giveaway Mania Grows," *Newsweek*, November 29, 1954.

"Watchdogs for Congress," *Newsweek*, December 6, 1954.

"Labor Law and Gangsterism," *Newsweek*, December 13, 1954.

"Who Speaks for America?" *Newsweek*, December 20, 1954.

"The Right to Work," *Newsweek*, December 27, 1954.

1955

"How to Read a Forecast," *Newsweek*, January 3, 1955.

"It Can Be Balanced," *Newsweek*, January 10, 1955.

"Raising Wages By Fiat," *Newsweek*, January 17, 1955.

"The New New Deal," *Newsweek*, January 25, 1955.

"Wonderland Trade Policy," *Newsweek*, January 31, 1955.

"Deficits Without End?" *Newsweek*, February 7, 1955.

"Inflation was the Trick," *Newsweek*, February 14, 1955.

"Time for Reappraisal," *Newsweek*, February 21, 1955.

"Truth Must Be Repeated," *Newsweek*, February 28, 1955.

"The Salaries of Congress," *Newsweek*, March 5, 1955.

"Deficits are Poison," *Newsweek*, March 14, 1955.

"To Get a Responsible Budget," *Newsweek*, March 21, 1955.

"The Stock-Market Boom," *Newsweek*, March 27, 1955.

"That Capital-Gains Tax," *Newsweek*, April 4, 1955.

"Double-Taxation Blues," *Newsweek*, April 11, 1955.

"Competition in Spending," *Newsweek*, April 18, 1955.

"Who Will Guarantee Business," *Newsweek*, April 25, 1955.

"When Government Lends," *Newsweek*, May 2, 1955.

"Foreign Aid Forever?" *Newsweek*, May 9, 1955.

"States' Rights and Labor Law," *Newsweek*, May 16, 1955.

"No Need For OTC," *Newsweek*, May 23, 1955.

"Compulsory Unionism," *Newsweek*, June 30, 1955.

"Irresponsible Spending," *Newsweek*, July 18, 1955.

"Abolish Exchange Control," *Newsweek*, July 25, 1955.

"The Seamy Side of TVA," *Newsweek*, August 1, 1955.

"Unsound Wage Boasts," *Newsweek*, August 8, 1955.

"Keynesian Confusions," *Newsweek*, August 15, 1955.

"Our Two New Deal Parties," *Newsweek*, August 22, 1955.

"A Flood of Credit," *Newsweek*, August 29, 1955.

"'Beyond' Capitalism," *Newsweek*, September 5, 1955.

"Unstable Paradise," *Newsweek*, September 12, 1955.

"What is Progress?" *Newsweek*, September 19, 1955.

"Balance it Now," *Newsweek*, September 26, 1955.

"A Fallacy Exposed Again," *Newsweek*, October 3, 1955.

"What Kind of Tax Cuts?" *Newsweek*, October 10, 1955.

"Delegation of Power," *Newsweek*, October 17, 1955.

"The Farm 'Parity' Fraud," *Newsweek*, October 24, 1955.

"Farm Fiasco: A Way Out," *Newsweek*, October 31, 1955.

"A Flood of Debt," *Newsweek*, November 7, 1955.

"Stevenson's Farm Claptrap," *Newsweek*, November 14, 1955.

"Revolt Against Spending," *Newsweek*, November 21, 1955.

"The Fourth Dimension," *Newsweek*, November 28, 1955.

"What is a Liberal?" *Newsweek*, December 5, 1955.

"Cheap Money Means Inflation," *Newsweek*, December 12, 1955.

"A Two-Point Farm Program," *Newsweek*, December 19, 1955.

"Arithmetic of Federal Aid," *Newsweek*, December 26, 1955.

1956

"Why Spending Grows," *Newsweek*, January 2, 1956.

"Hazards of Forecasting," *Newsweek*, January 9, 1956,

"Foreign Aid Forever?" *Newsweek*, January 16, 1956.

"The Presidential Burden," *Newsweek*, January 23, 1956.

"A Farm-Vote Program," *Newsweek*, January 30, 1956.

"What to Do About the Farm Parity Fiasco," *Reader's Digest*, February 1956.

"The Fourth Dimension," *The Freeman*, February 1956.

"But is it Balanced?" *Newsweek*, February 6, 1956.

"Facing Both Ways," *Newsweek*, February 13, 1956.

"Mencken: A Retrospect," *Newsweek*, February 20, 1956.

"The War on Big Business," *Newsweek*, February 27, 1956.

"Selective Credit Control," *Newsweek*, March 5, 1956.

"That Gas Bill Veto," *Newsweek*, March 12, 1956.

"Ike and the Economic Outlook," *Newsweek*, March 19, 1956.

"Extending the Farm Folly," *Newsweek*, March 26, 1956.

"More About Foreign Aid," *Newsweek*, April 2, 1956.

"Foreign Arms Aid Again," *Newsweek*, April 16, 1956.

"Ruining Peter to 'Aid' Paul," *Newsweek*, April 23, 1956.

"Why Farm Aid Runs Amuck," *Newsweek*, April 30, 1956.

"Keynesianism Crippled by Facts," *Newsweek*, May 7, 1956.

"You, too, Can Forecast," *Newsweek*, May 14, 1956.

"Cheap Money and Inflation," *Newsweek*, May 21, 1956.

"Built-in Inflation," *Newsweek*, May 28, 1956.

"The Literature of Freedom," *The Freeman*, June 1956.

"Foreign Aid Mania," *Newsweek*, June 4, 1956.

"Transitory Magic," *Newsweek*, June 11, 1956.

"Political Farm Law," *Newsweek*, June 18, 1956.

"The Great Swindle," *Newsweek*, June 25, 1956.

"Cut-Rate Currencies," *Newsweek*, July 2, 1956.

"Money and Goods," *Newsweek*, July 9, 1956.

"Steel Strike Lessons," *Newsweek*, July 16, 1956.

"Communist Production," *Newsweek*, July 30, 1956.

"Communism as Producer," *Newsweek*, August 6, 1956.

"Strike Aftermath," *Newsweek*, August 13, 1956.

"False Internationalism," *Newsweek*, August 20, 1956.

"Invitation to Seizure," *Newsweek*, August 27, 1956.

"The Great Swindle," *The Freeman*, September 1956.

"Democratic Claptrap," *Newsweek*, September 3, 1956.

"GOP Double-Think," *Newsweek*, September 10, 1956.

"People's Capitalism," *Newsweek*, September 17, 1956.

"How High is 3%?" *Newsweek*, September 24, 1956.

"Foreign-aid Mania," *Reader's Digest*, October 1956, reprinted from *Newsweek*, June 4, 1956

"A Free Man's Library," *Newsweek*, October 1, 1956.

"Policies and Votes," *Newsweek*, October 8, 1956.

"Why Anti-Capitalism?" *Newsweek*, October 15, 1956.

"Lesson From England," *Newsweek*, October 22, 1956.

"Reasons for Apathy," *Newsweek*, October 29, 1956.

"Party of Inflation," *Newsweek*, November 5, 1956.

"The Economic Meaning," *Newsweek*, November 12, 1956.

"They've Had It," *Newsweek*, November 19, 1956.

"Mathematical Economics," *Newsweek*, November 26, 1956.

"Two Kinds of Inflation," *Newsweek*, December 3, 1956.

"For the Rule of Law," *Newsweek*, December 10, 1956.

"Foreign Policy," *Newsweek*, December 17, 1956.

"When Do We Stop?" *Newsweek*, December 24, 1956.

"Forecasts for 1957," *Newsweek*, December 31, 1956.

1957

"Overrule the 'Fed'?" *Newsweek*, January 7, 1957.

"Still More Foreign Aid?," *Newsweek*, January 14, 1957.

"Ike's New Program," *Newsweek*, January 21, 1957.

"Where It Can Be Cut," *Newsweek*, January 28, 1957.

"Two Kinds of Inflation," *The Freeman*, February 1957.

"Must We Ration Credit?" *Newsweek*, February 4, 1957.

"Economic Double-Think," *Newsweek*, February 11, 1957.

"Cut to $60 Billion Now," *Newsweek*, February 18,1957.

"Blaming the Public," *Newsweek*, February 25, 1957.

"No Boom Lasts Forever," *Newsweek*, March 4, 1957.

"A 'Common' Market," *Newsweek*, March 11, 1957

"Are Unions Necessary?" *Newsweek*, March 18, 1957.

"How to Cut Spending," *Newsweek*, March 25, 1957.

"Irresponsible Budget," *Newsweek*, April 1, 1957.

"Cotton Fiasco," *Newsweek*, April 8, 1957.

"The Vice-Presidency," *Newsweek*, April 15, 1957.

"No One is Responsible," *Newsweek*, April 22, 1957.

"Britain's Budget," *Newsweek*, April 29, 1957.

"If Congress Means It," *Newsweek*, May 6, 1957.

"Unions and the Law," *Newsweek*, May 13, 1957.

"Bipartisan Economy," *Newsweek*, May 20, 1957.

"Communist Crack-up," *Newsweek*, May 27, 1957.

"Perpetual Foreign Aid," *Newsweek*, June 3, 1957.

"Private Foreign Aid," *Newsweek*, June 10, 1957.

"High Taxes vs. Yield," *Newsweek*, June 17, 1957. Also "High Taxes vs. Common Sense," *Reader's Digest*, September 1957.

"Tax Reform Now," *Newsweek*, June 24, 1957.

"The Great Swindle," *Newsweek*, July 1, 1957.

"Easy Money-Inflation," *Newsweek*, July 8, 1957.

"Why 'Tight Money'," *Newsweek*, July 15, 1957.

"Cost-Push Inflation," *Newsweek*, July 22, 1957.

"Built-in Inflation," *Newsweek*, July 29, 1957.

"Contradictory Goals," *Newsweek*, August 5, 1957.

"'Administered' Inflation," *Newsweek*, August 12, 1957.

"Easy Money Has An End," *Newsweek*, August 19, 1957.

"Tragedy of the Franc," *Newsweek*, August 26, 1957.

"Collapse of a System," *Newsweek*, September 2, 1957.

"What Makes Reuther Big?" *Newsweek*, September 9, 1957.

"Set Currencies Free," *Newsweek*, September 16, 1957.

"Creeping Inflationism," *Newsweek*, September 23, 1957.

"Subsidizing Socialism," *Newsweek*, September 30, 1957.

"The Great Swindle," *The Freeman*, October 1957.

"How to Wipe Out Debt," *Newsweek*, October 7, 1957.

"Paper-Money Blizzard," *Newsweek*, October 14, 1957.

"The Economic Consequences of ICBM," October 21, 1957. Also *Reader's Digest*, December 1957.

"Swindling Admired," *Newsweek*, October 28, 1957.

"The Cost-Price Squeeze," *Newsweek*, November 4, 1957.

"Party of Inflation?" *Newsweek*, November 11, 1957.

"Message of the Sputniks," *Newsweek*, November 18, 1957.

"Wake up the Educators, *Newsweek*, November 25, 1957.

"A Shot in the Arm," *Newsweek*, December 2, 1957.

"Our Moral Disarmament," *Newsweek*, December 9, 1957.

"To Remove Uncertainty," *Newsweek*, December 16, 1957.

"Salvation by Spending?" *Newsweek*, December 23, 1957.

"Too Much Labor Law," *Newsweek*, December 30, 1957.

1958

"To Control Spending," *Newsweek*, January 6, 1958.

"Convert the Communists," *Newsweek*, January 13, 1958

"How to Destroy Jobs," *Newsweek*, January 20, 1958.

"Notes on the Budget," *Newsweek*, January 27, 1958.

"Salvation by Deficit?" *Newsweek*, February 3, 1958.

"Inflation Arithmetic," *Newsweek*, February 10, 1958.

"Wage Rates And Jobs," *Newsweek*, February 17 1958.

"Hair of the Dog," *Newsweek*, February 24, 1958.

"Wage Boosts vs. Jobs," *Newsweek*, March 3, 1958.

"Buying Unemployment," *Newsweek*, March 10, 1958.

"Adjust—or Inflate," *Newsweek*, March 17, 1958.

"Stampede to Inflation," *Newsweek*, March 24, 1958.

"Insuring Unemployment," *Newsweek*, March 31, 1958.

"Wage Rates and Jobs," *The Freeman*, April 1958.

"Priced Out of Jobs," *Newsweek*, April 7, 1958.

"Insurance or Politics?" *Newsweek*, April 14, 1958.

"Is the Dollar Doomed?" *Newsweek*, April 21, 1958.

"Deficit vs. Jobs," *Newsweek*, April 28, 1958.

"How Many Jobless?" *Newsweek*, May 5, 1958.

"'Curing' the Recession," *Newsweek*, May 12, 1958.

"To Encourage Earning," *Newsweek*, May 19, 1958.

"The Foreign-Aid Fiasco," *Newsweek*, May 26, 1958.

"Reform Our Labor Law," *Newsweek*, June 2, 1958.

"Trade, Yes; Aid, No," *Newsweek*, June 9, 1958.

"How to Increase Jobs and Payrolls," *Newsweek*, June 16, 1958.

"USA vs. USSR," *Newsweek*, June 23, 1958.

"Preventive Cold War, Part I," *Newsweek*, June 30, 1958.

"Preventive Cold War, Part II," *Newsweek*, July 7, 1958.

"Government by Favor," *Newsweek*, July 14, 1958.

"Inflation Disrepute," *Newsweek*, July 21, 1958.

"Piano and the Stool," *Newsweek*, July 28, 1958.

" 'Have-Not' Countries," *Newsweek*, August 4, 1958.

"Time-Deposit Inflation," *Newsweek*, August 11, 1958.

"More Inflation Ahead?" *Newsweek*, August 18, 1958.

"Rates of Growth," *Newsweek*, August 25, 1958.

"How to Control Credit," *Newsweek*, September 1, 1958.

"A Century of Cycles," *Newsweek*, September 8, 1958.

"20 Ways to Giveaway," *Newsweek*, September 15, 1958.

"Bipartisan Inflation," *Newsweek*, September 22, 1958.

"Inflation by Spending," *Newsweek*, September 29, 1958.

"Balanced Labor Law," *Newsweek*, October 6, 1958.

"Interest-Rate Tides," *Newsweek*, October 13, 1958.

"Why Don't We Join?" *Newsweek*, October 20, 1958.

"Ten-Year Miracle," *Newsweek*, October 27, 1958.

"That 'Common Market'," *Newsweek*, November 17, 1958.

"Why Cheap Money Fails," *Newsweek*, November 24, 1958.

"In Franco's Spain," *Newsweek*, December 1, 1958.

"Our Policy In Europe," *Newsweek*, December 8, 1958.

"Defense Will Not Win," *Newsweek*, December 15, 1958.

"Why We Lose Gold," *Newsweek*, December 22, 1958.

"How to Halt Inflation," *Newsweek*, December 29, 1958.

1959

"The GNP Fetish," *Newsweek*, January 5, 1959.

"More GNP Defects," *Newsweek*, January 12, 1958.

"Heed the Red Lights," *Newsweek*, January 19, 1958.

"Lessons of a Strike," *Newsweek*, January 26, 1959.

"Schizophrenic Budget," *Newsweek*, February 2, 1959.

"Who Makes Inflation?" *Newsweek*, February 9, 1959.

"What Russian Trade?" *Newsweek*, February 16, 1959.

"Uncurbed Union Power," *Newsweek*, February 23, 1959.

"The 'Growth' Game," *Newsweek*, March 3, 1959.

"Wrong Aims and Means," *Newsweek*, March 9, 1959.

"1985?" *Newsweek*, March 16, 1959.

"Spending and Taxing," *Newsweek*, March 23, 1959.

"More Inflation Ahead?" *Newsweek*, March 30, 1959.

"Inflation as a Policy," *Newsweek*, April 5, 1959.

"What Is Competition?" *Newsweek*, April 13, 1959.

"Why There Are Jobless," *Newsweek*, April 20, 1959.

"How to Denationalize," *Newsweek*, April 27, 1959.

"What Russian Trade," *The Freeman*, May 1959.

"Uncurbed Union Power," *Newsweek*, May 4, 1959.

"Steel Strike Ahead?" *Newsweek*, May 11, 1959.

"Giant Step Backward," *Newsweek*, May 18, 1959.

"The Gold Outflow," *Newsweek*, May 25, 1959.

"The Full-Employment Myth," *The Wall Street Journal*, May 25, 1959.

"The Politics of a Statistic," *The Wall Street Journal*, May 26, 1959.

"Communist Strategy," *Newsweek*, June 1, 1959.

"The First Step," *Newsweek*, June 8, 1959.

"The Open Conspiracy," *Newsweek*, June 15, 1959.

"The Egg in Politics," *Newsweek*, June 22, 1959.

"The Interest Ceiling," *Newsweek*, June 29, 1959.

"The Strauss Aftermath," *Newsweek*, July 6, 1959.

"Saving is the Key," *Newsweek*, July 13, 1959.

"Portrait of Russia?" *Newsweek*, July 20, 1959.

"Why a Steel Strike?" *Newsweek*, July 27, 1959.

"On Not Interfering," *Newsweek*, August 3, 1959.

"Ordering Inflation," *Newsweek*, August 10, 1959.

"Nobody Wins a Strike" *Newsweek*, August 17, 1959.

"Real Labor Reform," *Newsweek*, August 24, 1959.

"How the Spiral Spins," *Newsweek*, August 31, 1959.

"Portrait of Russia?" *The Freeman*, September 1959.

"Painting Ourselves In," *Newsweek*, September 7, 1959.

"Shortcut to Inflation," *Newsweek*, September 14, 1959.

"Oil Import Quotas," *Newsweek*, September 21, 1959.

"Managed England" *Newsweek*, September 28, 1959

"Art of Forecasting," *Newsweek*, October 5, 1959.

"Conservative Revival," *Newsweek*, October 12, 1959.

"Progress vs. 'Plans'," *Newsweek*, October 19, 1959.

"Is Bargaining Free," *Newsweek*, October 26, 1959.

"How the Spiral Spins," *The Freeman*, November 1959.

"It Hasn't Been Tried," *Newsweek*, November 2, 1959.

"The Real Reform," *Newsweek*, November 9, 1959.

"Where We Are Now," *Newsweek*, November 16, 1959.

"Revise Our Labor Laws," *Newsweek*, November 23, 1959.

"Farm Surplus Solution," *Newsweek*, November 30, 1959.

"Men, Cars, Cities," *Newsweek*, December 7, 1959.

"The Problems We Face," *Newsweek*, December 14, 1959.

"The Nonconformist," *USA*, December 18, 1959.

"Is Gold Just a Relic?" *Newsweek*, December 21, 1959.

"Wages by Edict?" *Newsweek*, December 28, 1959.

1960

"Wage-Price Go-Round," *Newsweek*, January 4, 1960.

"Halt Inflation Now," *Newsweek*, January 11, 1960.

"Inflation Wins Again," *Newsweek*, January 18, 1960

"Logic of Do-Nothing," *Newsweek*, January 25, 1960.

"Notes on the Budget," *Newsweek*, February 1, 1960.

"Who Makes Inflation?" *Newsweek*, February 8, 1960.

"Liberty and Welfare," *Newsweek*, February 15, 1960.

"The Constitution of Liberty" (F .A. Hayek), *Newsweek*, February 15, 1960.

"Great No-Debates," *Newsweek*, February 22, 1960.

"Whose Welfare State?" *Newsweek*, February 29, 1960.

"How to Curb Spending," *Newsweek*, March 7, 1960.

"Arms and the Budget," *Newsweek*, March 14, 1960.

"Sugar Can Turn Sour," *Newsweek*, March 21, 1960.

"Foreign Aid Run Riot," *Newsweek*, March 28, 1960.

"Backward Step," *Newsweek*, April 4, 1960.

"Tying Its Own Hands," *Newsweek*, April 11, 1960.

"Cheap Money Is Dear," *Newsweek*, April 18, 1960.

"Age, 'Needs,' and Votes," *Newsweek*, April 25, 1960.

"Years of Inflation," *Newsweek*, May 2, 1960.

"Subsidizing Socialism," *Newsweek*, May 9, 1960.

"Inflation vs. Morality," *Newsweek*, May 16, 1960.

"The Big Brother State," *Newsweek*, May 23, 1960.

"Fruits of Appeasement," *Newsweek*, May 30, 1960.

"Growth of What We Owe," *Newsweek*, June 6, 1960.

"Insurance Or Handout?" *Newsweek*, June 13, 1960.

"Inviting Inflation," *Newsweek*, June 20, 1960.

"Affluent Government," *Newsweek*, June 27, 1960.

"Mr. Kennedy's Old Clichés," *National Review*, July 3, 1960.

"End the Interregnum," *Newsweek*, July 4, 1960.

"Why Our Debt Grows," *Newsweek*, July 11, 1960.

"The New Collectivism," *Newsweek*, July 18, 1960.

"Evil of Import Quotas," *Newsweek*, July 25, 1960.

"Comments on Inflation," *The Freeman*, August 1960.

"The Total Welfare State," *Newsweek*, August 1, 1960.

"A Circus or a Session?" *Newsweek*, August 8, 1960.

"To End Farm Surpluses," *Newsweek*, August 15, 1960.

"The Irresponsibles," *Newsweek*, August 22, 1960.

"How to Beat Inflation," *Newsweek*, August 29, 1960.

"Is 'Deflation' Likely?" *Newsweek*, September 5, 1960.

"Sugar, Fares, Picketing," *Newsweek*, September 12, 1960.

"The ABC of Inflation," *Human Events*, September 15, 1960.

"Legal Strike Incentives," *Newsweek*, September 19, 1960.

"Vote for Me and $7,000," *Newsweek*, September 26, 1960.

"False Internationalism," *Newsweek*, October 3, 1960.

"American Abdication?" *Newsweek*, October 10, 1960.

"How to Lose an Election," *Newsweek*, October 17, 1960.

"What Are We Deciding?" *Newsweek*, October 24, 1960.

"Galloping Inflation," *Newsweek*, excerpt from *What You Should Know About Inflation*, October 24, 1960.

"The Dollar Crisis," *Newsweek*, October 31, 1960.

"How to Restore Poverty," *Newsweek*, November 7, 1960.

"Conventional Heretic," *Newsweek*, November 14, 1960.

"The Economic Meaning," *Newsweek*, November 14, 1960.

"To Maintain the Dollar," *Newsweek*, November 21, 1960.

"A Meaningful Opposition," *Newsweek*, November 28, 1960.

"Wrong Dollar Solution," *Newsweek*, December 5, 1960.

"In the Wrong Direction," *Newsweek*, December 12, 1960.

"To Encourage Growth," *Newsweek*, December 19, 1960.

"To Promote Growth," *Newsweek*, December 26, 1960.

1961

"A World Super-Bank?" *Newsweek*, January 2, 1961.

"Are We Going Left?" *Newsweek*, January 9, 1961.

"If We Demonetize Gold," *Newsweek*, January 16, 1961.

"A Needless Risk," *Newsweek*, January 23, 1961.

"A Crime to Own Gold," *Newsweek*, January 30, 1961.

"This Tax Reform Can Set America Free To Grow," *Reader's Digest*, February 1961.

"What Is to Be Done?" *Newsweek*, February 6, 1961.

"Pledges vs. Policies," *Newsweek*, February 13, 1961.

"Kennedian Economics," *Newsweek*, February 20, 1961.

"Saving the Dollar," *Newsweek*, February 27, 1961.

"Jobs by Inflation?" *Newsweek*, March 6, 1961.

"Protectionism," *Newsweek*, March 13, 1961.

"Minimum Wage," *Newsweek*, March 20, 1961.

"An International Money," *Newsweek*, March 27, 1961.

"Aid With What Strings," *Newsweek*, April 3, 1961.

"Handout or Investment," *Newsweek*, April 10, 1961.

"Budgetary Chaos," *Newsweek*, April 17, 1961.

"Inflation Without Jobs," *Newsweek*, April 24, 1961.

"Jobs by Inflation?" *The Freeman*, May 1961.

"Propaganda in Orbit," *Newsweek*, May 1, 1961.

"National Trends," *National Review*, May 6, 1961.

"That 'Cyclical' Budget," *Newsweek*, May 8, 1961.

"The First 100 Days," *Newsweek*, May 15, 1961.

"Keep the Gold Reserve," *Newsweek*, May 22, 1961.

"How to Cure Poverty," *Newsweek*, May 29, 1961.

"What Rent Control Does," *The Freeman*, June 1961.

"Gold and the Dollar," *Newsweek*, June 5, 1961.

"Reaching for the Moon," *Newsweek*, June 12, 1961.

"The Dollar Problem," *Newsweek*, June 19, 1961.

"Day of Disillusion," *Newsweek*, June 26, 1961.

"Mock Gold Standard," *Newsweek*, July 3, 1961.

"Labor Law Gone Wrong," *Newsweek*, July 10, 1961.

"Could Credit Collapse?" *Newsweek*, July 17, 1961.

"International Money," *The Wall Street Journal*, July 19, 1961.

"A 'Dual' Economy," *Newsweek*, July 24, 1961.

"Too Much Labor Law," *Newsweek*, July 31, 1961.

"Irresponsible Budget," *Newsweek*, August 7, 1961.

"Tax Cuts for Growth," *Newsweek*, August 14, 1961.

"The New Manifesto," *Newsweek*, August 21, 1961.

"Greenback Utopia," *National Review*, August 26, 1961.

"Foreign Aid Fallacies," *Newsweek*, August 28, 1961.

"Hostility to Business," *Newsweek*, September 4, 1961. Also "Criminals and Benefactors," *Reader's Digest*, December 1961.

"Education for Individualism," *The Freeman*, September 1961.

"Aid vs. Trade," *Newsweek*, September 11, 1961.

"In Defense of Gold," *Newsweek*, September 18, 1961.

"An International Order," *Newsweek*, September 25, 1961.

"Secret of Switzerland," *Newsweek*, October 2, 1961.

"Galbraith Revisited," *Newsweek*, October 9, 1961.

"False Internationalism," *Newsweek*, October 16, 1961.

"Can Statistics Predict?" *Newsweek*, October 23, 1961.

"Shadow of Price Control," *Newsweek*, October 30, 1961.

"In the Sweet By and By," *Newsweek*, November 6, 1961.

"Downgrading Ourselves," *Newsweek*, November 13, 1961.

"Socialistic 'Reforms'," *Newsweek*, November 20, 1961.

"Inflation for Growth," *Newsweek*, November 27, 1961.

"To Preserve the Dollar," *Newsweek*, December 4, 1961.

"Profits Mean Jobs," *Newsweek*, December 11, 1961. Also *Reader's Digest*, February 1962.

"Growth Means Capital," *Newsweek*, December 18, 1961.

"Remove Trade Barriers," *Newsweek*, December 25, 1961.

1962

"An International Order," *The Freeman*, January 1962.

"Common Market and Us," *Newsweek*, January 1, 1962.

"Inflation Must End," *Newsweek*, January 8, 1962.

"Are We Anti-Capitalist?" *Newsweek*, January 15, 1962.

"On Doing Nothing," *Newsweek*, January 22, 1962.

"Power to Lay Duties," *Newsweek*, January 29, 1962.

"Notes on the Budget," *Newsweek*, February 5, 1962.

"Growth by Rhetoric," *Newsweek*, February 12, 1962.

"More Planned Chaos," *Newsweek*, February 19, 1962.

"Freedom to Bargain," *Newsweek*, February 26, 1962.

"Automation Makes Jobs," *Newsweek*, March 5, 1962.

"Jobs by Inflation?" *Newsweek*, March 12, 1962.

"Rule of Law," *National Review*, March 13, 1962.

"How to Remove Barriers," *Newsweek*, March 19, 1962.

"Incentives Bring Growth," *Newsweek*, March 26, 1962.

"Are Consumers Boobs?" *Newsweek*, April 2, 1962. And *The Freeman*, June 1962.

"A Wrong Turning," *Newsweek*, April 9, 1962.

"A Duty of Congress," *Newsweek*, April 16, 1962.

"Why Stunt Our Growth," *Newsweek*, April 23, 1962.

"Blow to Confidence," *Newsweek*, April 30, 1962.

"'In the Public Interest'" May 7, 1962.

"To Restore Confidence," *Newsweek*, May 14, 1962.

"Free Prices, Free Wages," *Newsweek*, May 21, 1962.

"Wages Must Be Free," *Newsweek*, May 28, 1962.

"Toward Freer Trade," *Newsweek*, June 4, 1962.

"Richer by Less Work," *Newsweek*, June 11, 1962.

"To Rebuild Confidence," *Newsweek*, June 18, 1962.

"Keynesians at Bay," *National Review*, June 19, 1962.

"Tax Reform Now," *Newsweek*, June 25, 1962.

"Catechism on Taxes," *Newsweek*, July 2, 1962.

"Bipartisan Errors," *Newsweek*, July 9, 1962.

"Deficits Forever?" *Newsweek*, July 16, 1962.

"Controls and Corruption," *Newsweek*, July 23, 1962.

"Is Inflation the Cure?" *Newsweek*, July 30, 1962.

"The Essentials of Free Enterprise," *The New Guard*, August 1962.

"The Welfare Mess," *Newsweek*, August 6, 1962.

"Assurance vs. Acts," *Newsweek*, August 13, 1962.

"Socialism vs. Freedom," *Newsweek*, August 20, 1962.

"Where We are Going," *Newsweek*, August 27, 1962.

"A 49 Percent Top," *Newsweek*, September 3, 1962.

"Overregulation," *Newsweek*, September 10, 1962.

"The Basis of Economics," *Newsweek*, September 17, 1962.

"The Dream of Planning," *Newsweek*, September 24, 1962.

"The Welfare Mess," *The Freeman*, October 1962.

"Planning for Growth," *Newsweek*, October 1, 1962.

"Worth the Price?" *Newsweek*, October 8, 1962.

"Taxes and Growth," *Newsweek*, October 15, 1962.

"Will Europe Split?" *Newsweek*, October 22, 1962.

"Shock of Reality," *Newsweek*, October 29, 1962.

"Tax Cut vs. Rate Cut," *Newsweek*, November 19, 1962.

"Tax Cuts for Incentive," *Newsweek*, November 26, 1962.

" 'Planning' vs. the Free Market," *The Freeman*, December 1962.

"What Is a 'Loophole'?" *Newsweek*, December 3, 1962.

"The New Mythology," *Newsweek*, December 17, 1962.

"Encouraging Strikes," *Newsweek*, December 24, 1962.

"Deficits Solve Nothing," *Newsweek*, December 31, 1962.

1963

"Who Gains by Strikes?" *Newsweek*, January 7, 1963.

"A Shortsighted Tax," *Newsweek*, January 14, 1963.

"Lopsided Labor Law," *Newsweek*, January 21, 1963.

"Invitation to Inflation," *Newsweek*, January 28, 1963.

"Fallacy of Too Much Planning," *Reader's Digest*, February 1963.

"Deficits as a Policy," *Newsweek*, February 4, 1963.

"A Dictated Settlement," *Newsweek*, February 11, 1963.

"How We Choke Incentive," *Newsweek*, February 18, 1963.

"Legalized Labor Chaos," *Newsweek*, February 25, 1963.

"How to Help the Poor," *Newsweek*, March 4, 1963.

"Hellerious Economics," *Newsweek*, March 11, 1963.

"Capitalism Without Horns," *National Review*, March 12, 1963.

"The Growth Mania," *Newsweek*, March 18, 1963.

"Inflation as Cure-All," *Newsweek*, March 25, 1963.

"Less Coffee in the Cup," *Newsweek*, April 1, 1963.

"The Right to Publish," *Newsweek*, April 8, 1963.

"For True Tax Reform," *Newsweek*, April 15, 1963.

"Do Deficits Make Jobs?" *Newsweek*, April 22, 1963.

"Price Control by Warning," *Newsweek*, April 29, 1963.

"The Web of Prices," *Newsweek*, May 6, 1963.

" 'Progressive' Taxation," *Newsweek*, May 13, 1963.

"To Defend the Dollar," *Newsweek*, May 20, 1963.

"Capital-Gain Tax Reform," *Newsweek*, May 27, 1963.

"Shortsighted Taxes," *Newsweek*, June 3, 1963.

"Fear of Free Markets," *Newsweek*, June 10, 1963.

"Capital Gain vs. Income," *Newsweek*, June 17, 1963.

"Who Provides Welfare?" *Newsweek*, June 24, 1963.

"Taxes: The Long View," *Newsweek*, July 1, 1963.

"The Foreign Aid Folly," *Newsweek*, July 8, 1963.

"Keynesian Inflation," *Newsweek*, July 15, 1963.

"Doubts About the EEC," *Newsweek*, July 22, 1963.

"The Risk Takers," *Newsweek*, July 29, 1963.

"No Help to the Dollar," *Newsweek*, August 5, 1963.

"Inflation Is the Cause," *Newsweek*, August 12, 1963.

"Double Taxation," *Newsweek*, August 19, 1963.

"Let the Dollar Drift," *Newsweek*, August 26, 1963.

"Sham Tax Cut," *Newsweek*, September 2, 1963.

"Exporting Inflation," *Newsweek*, September 9, 1963.

"History of a Law," *Newsweek*, September 16, 1963.

"Balance of Payments," *Newsweek*, September 23, 1963.

"Books for Americans," *Newsweek*, September 30, 1963.

"One World or Many," *Newsweek*, October 7, 1963.

"Farm Program Fiasco," *Newsweek*, October 14, 1963.

"World Monetary Reform," *Newsweek*, October 21, 1963.

"A Shortsighted Tariff," *Newsweek*, October 28, 1963.

"Tax Cut in Wonderland," *Newsweek*, November 4, 1963.

"Undo the IMF System," *Newsweek*, November 11, 1963.

"The Jobless, and Why," *Newsweek*, November 18, 1963.

"Does Foreign Aid Aid?" *Newsweek*, November 25, 1963.

"The Vice-Presidency," *Newsweek*, December 2, 1963.

"To Reduce Uncertainty," *Newsweek*, December 9, 1963.

"Aid-or Investment?" *Newsweek*, December 16, 1963.

"Investment as Scapegoat," *Newsweek*, December 23, 1963.

"Tax Cut Regardless," *Newsweek*, December 30, 1963.

1964

"Left Statisticians at Play," *National Review*, January 14, 1964.

"Publishing Scene," *National Review*, May 5, 1964.

"World of Inflation," *The Freeman*, June 1964.

"Confusion, Not Conspiracy," *National Review*, June 1, 1964.

"Will We Ever Pay It Off?" *Newsweek*, June 8, 1964. And *Reader's Digest*, August 1964.

"Training for Jobs," *Newsweek*, July 6, 1964.

"Rigging Interest Rates," *Newsweek*, July 13, 1964.

"Dread of a Surplus," *Newsweek*, July 20, 1964.

"The Issue of Statism," *Newsweek*, July 27, 1964.

"The Curse of Machinery," *The Freeman*, August 1964.

"Words Against Words," *Newsweek*, August 3, 1964.

"That Fiscal Revolution," *Newsweek*, August 10, 1964.

"Hoover As Scapegoat," *Newsweek*, August 17, 1964.

"The Poverty Package," *Newsweek*, August 24, 1964.

"Socialism and Famine," *Newsweek*, August 31, 1964.

"Rights," *The Freeman*, September 1964.

"World Money Reform," *Newsweek*, September 7, 1964.

"Big Brother State," *Newsweek*, September 14, 1964.

"Results of Antitrust," *Newsweek*, September 21, 1964.

"How to Beat Inflation," *Newsweek*, September 28, 1964.

"Industrialitis," *The Freeman*, October 1964.

"The Consumptionists," *Newsweek*, October 5, 1964.

"The Irreversible State," *Newsweek*, October 12, 1964.

"How New Is Inflation?" *Newsweek*, October 19, 1964.

"Why He Is Losing," *Newsweek*, October 26, 1964.

"The Economic Issues," *Newsweek*, November 2, 1964.

"Reflections at 70," remarks at birthday celebration at the New York University Club, reprinted in *The Wisdom of Henry Hazlitt*, Irvington-on-Hudson, N.Y.: Foundation for Economic Education, 1993, pp. 39–48.

"Back to Mercantilism," *Newsweek*, November 16, 1964.

"Market is Color-Blind," *Newsweek*, November 23, 1964.

"Labels vs. Policies," *Newsweek*, November 30, 1964.

"The Coinage Crisis," *Newsweek*, December 7, 1964.

"The Sterling Crisis," *Newsweek*, December 14, 1964.

"Cheap Money Mania," *Newsweek*, December 21, 1964.

"The Paper-Work Jungle," *Newsweek*, December 28, 1964.

"Two Birthdays," *National Review*, December 29, 1964.

1965

"Abiding Free Speech," *Newsweek*, January 4, 1965.

"Paradise by Deficit, *Newsweek*, January 18, 1965.

"No Gold At All?" *Newsweek*, February 1, 1965.

"The Cult of Deficits," *Newsweek*, February 15, 1965.

"Bastiat for '65," *National Review*, February 23, 1965.

"Surprising Scapegoat," *Newsweek*, March 1, 1965.

"Manipulating Interest," *Newsweek*, March 15, 1965.

"Antitrust Chaos," *Newsweek*, March 29, 1965.

"Do We Need More Money?" *Newsweek*, April 12, 1965.

"Monster Government," *Newsweek*, April 26, 1965.

"The Rueff Proposal," *Newsweek*, May 10, 1965.

"Steel as Scapegoat," *Newsweek*, May 24, 1965.

"The Right to Choose," *Newsweek*, June 7, 1965.

"The New Orthodoxy," *Newsweek*, June 21, 1965.

"One-Sided Compulsion," *Newsweek*, July 5, 1965.

"Fallible Forecasting," *Newsweek*, July 19, 1965.

"Do 'We Need More Money?" *Newsweek*, August 2, 1965.

"Chaotic Antitrust," *Newsweek*, August 16, 1965.

"Put a Price on Water," *Newsweek*, August 30, 1965.

"Rule by Guideline," *Newsweek*, September 13, 1965.

"The Effort of Every Man," *Newsweek*, September 27, 1965.

"Back to Gold," *The Freeman*, October 1965.

"Inviting Strikes," *Newsweek*, October 11, 1965.

"A World Money Plan," *Newsweek*, October 25, 1965.

"Dilemma of Foreign Aid," *Newsweek*, November 8, 1965.

"Great Society's Cost," *Newsweek*, November 22, 1965.

"The Development of Economic Thought," *National Review*, November 30, 1965.

"The Effort of Everyman," *The Freeman*, December 1965.

"Garroting by Guideline," *Newsweek*, December 6, 1965.

"Fifty Billion to Play With? The Fear of Fiscal Drag," *National Review*, December 14, 1965.

"Fixing Interest Rates," *Newsweek*, December 20, 1965.

1966

"Whom does Aid Aid?" *Swarajya Annual*, 1966.

"Manipulating Money," *Newsweek*, January 3, 1966.

"LBJ's Budget Dilemma," *Newsweek*, January 17, 1966.

"The Right to Replace," *Newsweek*, January 31, 1966.

"The Fallacy of Foreign Aid," *The Freeman*, February 1966.

"Irresponsible Budget," *Newsweek*, February 14, 1966.

"Big Brother State," *Newsweek*, February 28, 1966.

"An Election Proposal," *Newsweek*, March 14, 1966.

"Slash the Spending," *Newsweek*, March 28, 1966. And *Reader's Digest*, June 1966.

"Agnosticism and Morality," *New Individualist Review*, Spring 1966.

"Minimum Wage vs. Jobs," *Newsweek*, April 11, 1966.

"Why Inflation Grows," *Newsweek*, April 25, 1966.

"Retarding Growth," *Newsweek*, May 9, 1966.

"The Attack on Profits," *Newsweek*, May 23, 1966.

"The Cost of Guideposts," *Newsweek*, June 6, 1966.

"The Free Market," *National Review*, June 14, 1966

"Income-Tax Illusions," *Newsweek*, June 20, 1966.

"Income Without Work," *The Freeman*, July 1966

"Shortsighted Remedy," *Newsweek*, July 4, 1966.

"Socialism," *Newsweek*, July 18, 1966.

"The Case for International Investment," *The Freeman*, August 1966.

"Prices Have Work to Do," *Newsweek*, August 1, 1966.

"How to Create Strikes," *Newsweek*, August 15, 1966.

"Forced Arbitration?" *Newsweek*, August 29, 1966.

"Socialism, U.S. Style," *The Freeman*, September 1966.

"Parting Words, Last Column, Future Plans," *Newsweek*, September 12, 1966.

"A Reply to Frank Knight," *Ethics:* an *International Journal of Social, Political, and Legal Philosophy*, October 1966.

"Inflation Without Growth," Los Angeles Times Syndicate, October 30, 1966.

"Harry Flood Byrd, R.I.P.," Los Angeles Times Syndicate, November 2, 1966.

"What's in the 'Public Interest'?" Los Angeles Times Syndicate, November 6, 1966.

"Blaming the Retailers," Los Angeles Times Syndicate, November 9, 1966.

"Free Market's Bad Press," Los Angeles Times Syndicate, November 13, 1966.

"What Can We Expect of the New Congress?" Los Angeles Times Syndicate, November 16, 1966.

"Stumbling Toward Wage Controls," Los Angeles Times Syndicate, November 20, 1966.

"Political Check-Off," Los Angeles Times Syndicate, November 23, 1966.

"No Tax Boost Needed," Los Angeles Times Syndicate, November 27, 1966."

"For More Frequent Elections," Los Angeles Times Syndicate, November 30, 1966.

"The Coming Labor Crisis," Los Angeles Times Syndicate, December 4, 1966.

"Gigo, Gigo," Los Angeles Times Syndicate, December 7, 1966.

"Budget Out of Control," Los Angeles Times Syndicate, December 11, 1966.

"Who Protects the Consumer?" Los Angeles Times Syndicate, December 14, 1966.

"Is Anti-Americanism Necessary?" Los Angeles Times Syndicate, December 18, 1966.

"Abolish the Labor Board," Los Angeles Times Syndicate, December 21, 1966.

"Welcome, New British Money," Los Angeles Times Syndicate, December 25, 1966.

"Galbraith Revisited," Los Angeles Times Syndicate, December 28, 1966.

1967

"The Cause of Economic Growth," Los Angeles Times Syndicate, January 1, 1967.

"A Department of Consumers," Los Angeles Times Syndicate, January 4, 1967.

"No Responsible Budget," Los Angeles Times Syndicate, January 8, 1967.

"Who Should Decide Who Gets Credit?" Los Angeles Times Syndicate, January 11, 1967.

"Freedom to Intimidate," Los Angeles Times Syndicate, January 15, 1967.

"Building Industry in Peril," Los Angeles Times Syndicate, January 18, 1967.

"No Need for a Tax Rise," Los Angeles Times Syndicate, January 22, 1967.

"A Promise to Inflate," Los Angeles Times Syndicate, January 25, 1967.

"Social Security Explosion," Los Angeles Times Syndicate, January 29, 1967.

"How Should Prices Be Determined?" The Freeman, February 1967.

"Creating Social Insecurity," Los Angeles Times Syndicate, February 1, 1967.

"Another Planned Deficit," Los Angeles Times Syndicate, February 5, 1967.

"The Program is More Inflation," Los Angeles Times Syndicate, February 8, 1967.

"Budget Out of Control," Los Angeles Times Syndicate, February 12, 1967.

"A Shortsighted Penalty," Los Angeles Times Syndicate, February 15, 1967.

"Program for World Inflation," Los Angeles Times Syndicate, February 19, 1967.

"People Want Gold," Los Angeles Times Syndicate, February 22, 1967.

"The Worst Price Scandal," Los Angeles Times Syndicate, February 26, 1967.

"Famines are Government-Made," Los Angeles Times Syndicate, March 1, 1967.

"The Mixed-up Planners," Los Angeles Times Syndicate, March 5, 1967.

"The Fruits of Irresponsibility," Los Angeles Times Syndicate, March 8, 1967.

"Side-Effects of Inflation," Los Angeles Times Syndicate, March 12, 1967.

"Living On Fictions," Los Angeles Times Syndicate, March 15, 1967.

"Restoring an Incentive," Los Angeles Times Syndicate, March 19, 1967.

"Protecting the Consumer?" Los Angeles Times Syndicate, March 22, 1967.

"Misrepresentative Government," Los Angeles Times Syndicate, March 26, 1967.

"Currency Crisis Ahead," Los Angeles Times Syndicate, March 29, 1967.

"High Taxes Don't Help," Los Angeles Times Syndicate, April 2, 1967.

"The One-Man-One-Vote Slogan," Los Angeles Times Syndicate, April 5, 1967.

"Are Deficits Necessary?" Los Angeles Times Syndicate, April 9, 1967

"Amending the Constitution," Los Angeles Times Syndicate, April 12, 1967.

"A False Remedy," Los Angeles Times Syndicate, April 16, 1967.

"The Coming Crisis in Welfare," *National Review*, April 18, 1967.

"Let's Not Trigger A Run," Los Angeles Times Syndicate, April 19, 1967.

"The Dollar is Not the U.S.," Los Angeles Times Syndicate, April 23, 1967.

"Instant Utopia," Los Angeles Times Syndicate, April 26, 1967.

"Wrong Medicine for Latin America," Los Angeles Times Syndicate, April 30, 1967.

"A Promise to Inflate," *The Freeman*, May 1967.

"Bretton Woods is Falling Down," Los Angeles Times Syndicate, May 3, 1967.

"Stop Encouraging Strikes," Los Angeles Times Syndicate, May 7, 1967.

"Leapfrog Collective Bargaining," Los Angeles Times Syndicate, May 10, 1967.

"Bankruptcy of Labor Law," Los Angeles Times Syndicate, May 14, 1967.

"How Newspapers Are Killed," Los Angeles Times Syndicate, May 17, 1967.

"A Moral Commitment," Los Angeles Times Syndicate, May 21, 1967.

"Are Deficits Necessary?" Los Angeles Times Syndicate, May 24, 1967.

"Reducing Trade Barriers," Los Angeles Times Syndicate, May 28, 1967.

"The Cult of Violence," Los Angeles Times Syndicate, May 31, 1967.

"Private Ownership: A Must," *The Freeman*, June 1967.

"Our Mounting Deficits," Los Angeles Times Syndicate, June 4, 1967.

"An Absurd Ceiling," Los Angeles Times Syndicate, June 7, 1967.

"Decentralize Government," Los Angeles Times Syndicate, June 11, 1967.

"Fifty Years of Communism," Los Angeles Times Syndicate, June 14, 1967.

"Reappraising Our Foreign Policy," Los Angeles Times Syndicate, June 18, 1967.

"Trading With the Communists," Los Angeles Times Syndicate, June 21, 1967.

"Bankruptcy of Foreign Aid," Los Angeles Times Syndicate, June 25, 1967.

"Can the U.S. Feed the World?" Los Angeles Times Syndicate, June 28, 1967.

"False Remedy," *The Freeman*, July 1967.

"Reappraising the U.N.," Los Angeles Times Syndicate, July 2, 1967.

"Two Bad Proposals," Los Angeles Times Syndicate, July 9, 1967.

"World-Wide Inflation," Los Angeles Times Syndicate, July 16, 1967.

"How to Prevent Growth," Los Angeles Times Syndicate, July 23, 1967.

"Failure of Our Labor Laws," Los Angeles Times Syndicate, July 30, 1967.

"Is Poverty the Cause?" Los Angeles Times Syndicate, August 6, 1967.

"Causes and Cure of Riots," Los Angeles Times Syndicate, August 13, 1967.

"Slash the Spending," Los Angeles Times Syndicate, August 20, 1967.

"A Budget Out of Control?" Los Angeles Times Syndicate, August 27, 1967.

"Worldwide Inflation," *The Freeman*, September 1967.

"Price Fixing by Violence," Los Angeles Times Syndicate, September 3, 1967.

"20 Years of World Inflation," Los Angeles Times Syndicate, September 10, 1967.

"How to Amputate the Budget," Los Angeles Times Syndicate, September 17, 1967.

"Galbraith's Fantasy World," Los Angeles Times Syndicate, September 24, 1967.

"Excerpts from Address," *Congressional Digest*, October 1967.

"Choosing a Candidate," Los Angeles Times Syndicate, October 1, 1967.

"Where Is Europe Heading?" Los Angeles Times Syndicate, October 8, 1967.

"Rewarding Lawlessness," Los Angeles Times Syndicate, October 15, 1967.

"Budgetary Buck-Passing," Los Angeles Times Syndicate, October 22, 1967.

"Fifty Years of Communism," Los Angeles Times Syndicate, October 29, 1967.

"Inflation Chases Its Own Tail," Los Angeles Times Syndicate, November 5, 1967.

"Fifty Years of Communist Myths," Los Angeles Times Syndicate, November 12, 1967.

"Yale's Afraid of Arithmetic," Los Angeles Times Syndicate, November 19, 1967.

"Going Both Ways at Once," Los Angeles Times Syndicate, November 26, 1967.

"Collapse of a System," Los Angeles Times Syndicate, November 21, 1967.

"The Run on Gold," Los Angeles Times Syndicate, December 3, 1967.

"What Next For the Dollar?" Los Angeles Times Syndicate, December 10, 1967.

"The Fault is at the Top," Los Angeles Times Syndicate, December 17, 1967.

"Why the Dollar Won't Be Saved," Los Angeles Times Syndicate, December 24, 1967.

"Government as Prosperity-Makers," Los Angeles Times Syndicate, December 31, 1967.

1968

"Protecting Yourself Against Inflation," Los Angeles Times Syndicate, January 7, 1968.

"Tourists and Investors as Scapegoats," Los Angeles Times Syndicate, January 14, 1968.

"Killing the Goose," Los Angeles Times Syndicate, January 21, 1968.

"Removing the Last Restraint," Los Angeles Times Syndicate, January 28, 1968.

"What a Gold Reserve Is For," Los Angeles Times Syndicate, February 3, 1968.

"The Most Irresponsible Budget," Los Angeles Times Syndicate, February 11, 1968.

"We Owe It All To Him," Los Angeles Times Syndicate, February 18, 1968.

"The Right to Replace," Los Angeles Times Syndicate, February 25, 1968.

"The Task Confronting Libertarians," *The Freeman*, March 1968.

"The Primary Capers," Los Angeles Times Syndicate, March 3, 1968.

"Are Dollars Better Than Gold?" Los Angeles Times Syndicate, March 10, 1968.

"The Dollar Crisis: A Way Out," Los Angeles Times Syndicate, March 17, 1968.

"A Shortsighted Stopgap," Los Angeles Times Syndicate, March 18, 1968.

"End of the IMF System," Los Angeles Times Syndicate, March 24, 1968.

"Not More Taxes But Less Spending," Los Angeles Times Syndicate, March 31, 1968.

"Tourists and Investors as Scapegoats," *The Freeman*, April 1968.

"Against a Tax Increase," Los Angeles Times Syndicate, April 7, 1968.

"The Function of Profits," Los Angeles Times Syndicate, April 14, 1968.

"Paper Gold," Los Angeles Times Syndicate, April 21, 1968.

"The Irresponsibles," Los Angeles Times Syndicate, April 28, 1968.

"Return to Gold," Los Angeles Times Syndicate, May 5, 1968.

"Confiscation and Class Hated," Los Angeles Times Syndicate, May 12, 1968.

"Tax Increase, Yes. Less Spending?" Los Angeles Times Syndicate, May 19, 1968.

"Government Makes Inflation," Los Angeles Times Syndicate, May 26, 1968.

"Rule By Riot," Los Angeles Times Syndicate, June 2, 1968.

"Paying People for Not Working," Los Angeles Times Syndicate, June 9, 1968.

"Does Soak-the-Rich Help the Poor?" Los Angeles Times Syndicate, June 16, 1968.

"Election Reforms," Los Angeles Times Syndicate, June 23, 1968.

"How to Get Open Conventions," Los Angeles Times Syndicate, June 30, 1968.

"Confiscation and Class Hatred," *The Freeman*, July 1968.

"The Taxpayers Lose Again," Los Angeles Times Syndicate, July 7, 1968.

"Fallacies of the Negative Income Tax," Los Angeles Times Syndicate, July 14, 1968.

"Can We Guarantee Jobs," Los Angeles Times Syndicate, July 21, 1968.

"Reform the Supreme Court," Los Angeles Times Syndicate, July 28, 1968.

"Blaming Business For Inflation," Los Angeles Times Syndicate, August 4, 1968.

"To Reflect the People's Will," Los Angeles Times Syndicate, August 11, 1968.

"Why a Vice-President?" Los Angeles Times Syndicate, August 25, 1968.

"How Could They Do This To Me?" Los Angeles Times Syndicate, September 1, 1968.

"The Supreme Court Is Illegal," Los Angeles Times Syndicate, September 8, 1968.

"Inflation Is Worldwide," Los Angeles Times Syndicate, September 15, 1968.

"Books For Conservatives," Los Angeles Times Syndicate, September 22, 1968.

"Involuntary Welfare State," Los Angeles Times Syndicate, September 29, 1968.

"Dangerous Changeover Period," Los Angeles Times Syndicate, October 6, 1968.

"Galloping Welfare State," Los Angeles Times Syndicate, October 13, 1968.

"Our Obsolete Electoral College," Los Angeles Times Syndicate, October 20, 1968.

"Hubert Humphrey's Nonsolutions," Los Angeles Times Syndicate, October 27, 1968.

"Instead of Famine—Thanksgiving," *The Freeman*, November 1968.

"Stop Strikes by Public Employees," Los Angeles Times Syndicate, November 3, 1968.

"How We Discourage Investment," Los Angeles Times Syndicate, November 10, 1968.

"Need for Election Reforms," Los Angeles Times Syndicate, November 17, 1968.

"Is Keynes Defunct?" Los Angeles Times Syndicate, November 24, 1968.

"A Substitute For The Electoral College," Los Angeles Times Syndicate, December 1, 1968.

"World Currency Disorder," Los Angeles Times Syndicate, December 8, 1968.

"The IMF and the 'New Economics'," Los Angeles Times Syndicate, December 15, 1968.

"Inflation Must Have a Stop," Los Angeles Times Syndicate, December 22, 1968.

"C. P. Snow's Needless Nightmare," Los Angeles Times Syndicate, December 29, 1968.

1969

"Strike Blackmail," Los Angeles Times Syndicate, January 5, 1969.

"Absurdity of Profit 'Guideposts'," Los Angeles Times Syndicate, January 12, 1969.

"Abolish the Interregnum," Los Angeles Times Syndicate, January 19, 1969.

"Runaway Cost of Relief," Los Angeles Times Syndicate, January 26, 1969.

"From Spencer's 1884 to Orwell's 1984," *The Freeman*, February 1969.

"The Budget as Political Weapon," Los Angeles Times Syndicate, February 2, 1969.

"Budget in Need of Surgery," Los Angeles Times Syndicate, February 9, 1969.

"Runaway Welfare Spending," Los Angeles Times Syndicate, February 1, 1969.

"One-Sided Capital-Gains Tax," Los Angeles Times Syndicate, February 23, 1969.

"Incentives Not to Work," Los Angeles Times Syndicate, March 2, 1969.

"Nixon On Electoral Reforms," Los Angeles Times Syndicate, March 9, 1969.

"Why Foreign Aid Impoverishes," Los Angeles Times Syndicate, March 16, 1969.

"The Coming Monetary Collapse," Los Angeles Times Syndicate, March 23, 1969.

"The Fine-Tuners Are Confused," Los Angeles Times Syndicate, March 30, 1969.

"Uruguay: Welfare State Gone Wild," *The Freeman*, April 1969.

"Amendment by the People," Los Angeles Times Syndicate, April 6, 1969.

"Reduce the Surtax," Los Angeles Times Syndicate, April 13, 1969.

"Profit is the Spur," Los Angeles Times Syndicate, April 20, 1969.

"Is More Inflation Necessary?" Los Angeles Times Syndicate, April 27, 1969.

"One-Sided Capital-Gains Tax," *The Freeman*, May 1969.

"Pretending That Paper Is Gold," Los Angeles Times Syndicate, May 4, 1969.

"Penalizing Economic Growth," Los Angeles Times Syndicate, May 11, 1969.

"The Outlook For Inflation," Los Angeles Times Syndicate, May 18, 1969.

"Reform the Supreme Court," Los Angeles Times Syndicate, May 25, 1969.

"New Protectionism," *National Review*, May 29, 1969.

"Administrative Tyranny," Los Angeles Times Syndicate, June 1, 1969.

"Good-Bye To the 'New Economics'," Los Angeles Times Syndicate, June 8, 1969.

"Stop Foreign Aid Now," Los Angeles Times Syndicate, June 15, 1969.

"Amending the Constitution," Los Angeles Times Syndicate, June 22, 1969.

"Farewell to Columning," Los Angeles Times Syndicate, June 29, 1969.

"Protected to Death," *The Freeman*, September 1969.

"Welfarism Out of Control," *National Review*, September 9, 1969.

1970

"Inflation: A Tiger by the Tail," *The Freeman*, February 1970.

"Compounding the Welfare Mess," *National Review*, February 24, 1970.

"Economics," *The Freeman*, March 1970.

"Welfarism and Its Consequences," *The Freeman*, April 1970.

"What the Market Says," *National Review*, June 30, 1970.

"The Art of Thinking," *The Freeman*, August 1970.

"Foreign Investment vs. Foreign Aid," *The Freeman*, October 1970.

"Private Property, Public Purpose," *The Freeman*, December 1970.

"Nixon's Economic Dilemma," *National Review*, December 15, 1970.

1971

"Oral History of Herbert Hoover," interview by Robert Cubbedge, Herbert Hoover Presidential Library Association, 1971.

"Nobody Wins at Leapfrog," *National Review*, January 26, 1971.

"False Remedies for Poverty," *The Freeman*, February 1971.

"The Poor Laws of England," *The Freeman*, March 1971.

"The Future of Capitalism," *Modern Age*, Summer 1971.

"Poor Relief in Ancient Rome," *The Freeman*, April 1971.

"The Problem of Poverty," *The Freeman*, June 1971.

"Dollars at a Discount," *National Review*, June 1, 1971.

"Poverty and Regulation," *The Freeman*, July 1971.

"IMF: World Inflation Factory," *The Freeman*, August 1971.

"Defining Poverty," *The Freeman*, September 1971.

"Can the U.S. Escape the Regimented Economy?" *Human Events*, September 4, 1971.

"The Distribution of Income," *The Freeman*, October 1971.

"The Story of Negro Gains," *The Freeman*, November 1971.

1972

"Why Some Are Poorer," *The Freeman*, January 1972.

"Makeshift Monetary Solution," *National Review*, January 21, 1972.

"Should We Divide the Wealth?" *The Freeman*, February 1972.

"Perils of the 'Full Employment Budget'," *Human Events*, February 5, 1972.

"Nixon's 'New Economics' Won't Cure Inflation," *Human Events*, February 12, 1972.

"On Appeasing Envy," *The Freeman*, March 1972.

"The Ballooning Welfare State," *The Freeman*, April 1972.

"Welfarism Gone Wild," *The Freeman*, May 1972.

"The Cure for Poverty," *The Freeman*, June 1972.

1973

"Pity Anyone Who Has To Work," *Human Events*, January 13, 1973.

"How to Achieve a Fair Tax Structure," *Human Events*, March 17, 1973.

"Ceilings Raise Meat Prices," *Human Events*, April 14, 1973.

"Can We Keep Free Enterprise?" *The Freeman*, June 1973.

"The Mania for Price Controls," *Human Events*, June 30, 1973.

"Lifting Wage-Price Controls Could Solve Energy Problem," *Human Events*, November 17, 1973.

"Salute to von Mises," *The Freeman*, December 1973.

1974

"The Future of Money," in *Champions of Freedom; The Ludwig von Mises Lecture Series*, Hillsdale, Mich.: Hillsdale College Press, 1974.

"The Future of the Dollar," *The Freeman*, January 1974.

"You Cannot Trust Governments With Your Money," *Human Events*, April 27, 1974. Also *The Freeman*, July 1974.

"Return to Gold," *National Review*, August 2, 1974.

"How Ford Can Restore Business Confidence," *Human Events*, September 31, 1974.

"Wrong Ways to Cure Inflation," *Human Events*, October 12, 1974.

"Ford's 'Anti-Inflation' Plan May Stoke Fire Further," *Human Events*, October 19, 1974.

"Conservatives and the U.S. Constitution," *Human Events*, November 16, 1974.

1975

"We Cannot Cure Inflation With Inflation," *Human Events*, January 25, 1975.

"The Flaws in Ford's Energy Program," *Human Events*, February 1, 1975.

"The Pros and Cons of Socialism," *The Freeman*, March 1975.

"How Inflation Breeds Recession," *The Freeman*, March 1975.

"Interview on Economic Outlook," *Gold and Silver Newsletter*, April 1975.

"In Search of An Ideal Money," *The Freeman*, November 1975.

1976

"Instead of What?" *The Freeman*, March 1976.

"Where the Monetarists Go Awry," *The Freeman*, August 1976.

"What Determines the Value of Money?" *The Freeman*, September 1976.

"Is a Return to Sanity Possible?" *Modern Age*, Winter 1976.

"Our Forty-Year Inflation," *The Freeman*, October 1976.

"The Demand for Instant Utopia," *The Freeman*, November 1976.

"Lessons of the German Inflation," *The Freeman*, December 1976.

1977

"Carter Moves Toward A Regimented Economy," *Human Events*, October 1, 1977.

"The Destructive Capital Gains Tax," *Human Events*, November 19, 1977.

1978

"Inflation vs. Morality," *The Freeman*, January 1978.

"What Spending and Deficits Do," *The Freeman*, February 1978.

"Inflation vs. Unemployment," *The Freeman*, March 1978.

"Inflation and Interest Rates," *The Freeman*, April 1978.

"Indexing: The Wrong Way Out," *The Freeman*, May 1978.

"Inflation in One Page," *The Freeman*, May 1978.

"Why Inflation Is Worldwide," *The Freeman*, June 1978.

"The Specter of 'Unused Capacity'," *The Freeman*, July 1978.

"Free Choice of Currencies," *The Freeman*, August 1978.

"One Currency For the World," *The Freeman*, September 1978.

"Inflation vs. Profits," *The Freeman*, November 1978.

"Oil Imports Didn't Cause Inflation," *Human Events*, November 4, 1978.

"Deficits and Unemployment," *The Freeman*, December 1978.

1979

"Money vs. Wealth," *American Economic Foundation* (New York), 1979.

"The Torrent of Laws," *The Freeman*, January 1979.

"The Road Not Taken," *The Freeman*, February 1979.

"Interview With Henry Hazlitt," *The Review of the News*, February 7, 1979.

"Wrongheaded Approach to the Energy Shortage," *The Freeman*, March 10, 1979.

"Line-Item Veto Could Cut Federal Spending," *Human Events*, March 24, 1979.

"Gold vs. Fractional Reserve," *The Freeman*, May 1979.

"Profits and Payrolls," *The Freeman*, August 1979.

"Carter Proposes an Anti-Energy Program," *Human Events*, September 8, 1979.

"New Fed Policy on Right Track, But it's Only Half a Loaf," *Human Events*, October 20, 1979.

"The Case for the Minimal State," *The Freeman*, November 1979.

"Is Ted Kennedy Fit To Serve?" *Human Events*, December 22, 1979.

1980

"Sphere of Government: The Nineteenth Century Theories; John Stuart Mill," *The Freeman*, January 1980.

"Sphere of Government: The Nineteenth Century Theories; Herbert Spencer," *The Freeman*, August 1980.

"Sphere of Government: The Nineteenth Century Theories; Thomas H. Huxley," *The Freeman*, October 1980.

"How to Return to Gold," *The Freeman*, September 1980.

1981

"The Outlook for Inflation, The Dollar, and Gold," *The Gold Newsletter*, October 1981.

"Interview on the Outlook of the Reagan Economy," *Silver and Gold Report*, August 1981.

1982

"Keynesian Economics in a Nutshell," *The Freeman*, November 1982.

1983

"Market Prices vs. Communist Commands," *The Freeman*, February 1983.

"Understanding 'Austrian' Economics," *The Freeman*, February 1983.

"When Water is Scarce," *The Freeman*, April 1983.

"'Planning' vs. the Free Market," *The Freeman*, May 1983.

"Two Amendments to Halt Deficit Spending," *Human Events*, June 4, 1983.

"Why Anti-Capitalism Grows," *The Freeman*, July 1983.

"How 'Obscene' Are Profits?" *The Freeman*, October 1983

"Economic Forecasting: How Good Is It?" *The Freeman*, December 1983.

1984

"The Early History of FEE," *The Freeman*, March 1984.

"An Interview With Henry Hazlitt," *The Austrian Economics Newsletter*, Spring 1984.

"Why Politics is Insoluble," *Modern Age*, Fall 1984.

"Keynes's Lifelong Confusions," *National Review*, November 16, 1984.

"Interview with Henry Hazlitt at 90," *Reason*, December 12, 1984.

1985

"The ABC of a Market Economy," *The Freeman*, February 1985.

"The Limitations of Profit-Sharing," *The Freeman*, September 1985.

1986

"The Legacy of Karl Marx," *The Freeman*, March 1986.

1987

"The Inflationary Chaos Ahead" in *The Review of Austrian Economics* Vol. 1, Lexington, Mass.: D. C. Heath, 1987.

"Speech by Henry Hazlitt," *The Free Market*, December 1987. Reprinted in *The Free Market Reader*, Burlingame, Calif.: The Ludwig von Mises Institute, 1988.